I0109684

RETHINKING eLEARNING

What Works. What Doesn't. What's Missing.

Also by Michael W. Allen

Michael Allen's Guide to e-Learning: Building Interactive, Fun, and Effective Learning Programs for Any Company (two editions)

Leaving ADDIE for SAM: An Agile Model for Developing the Best Learning Experiences

Michael Allen's e-Learning Annuals (three editions)

Michael Allen's eLearning Library

Volume 1. Creating Successful e-Learning—A Rapid System for Getting It Right First Time, Every Time

Volume 2. Designing Successful e-Learning: Forget What You Know about Instructional Design and Do Something Interesting

Volume 3. Successful e-Learning Interface: Making Learning Technology Polite, Effective, and Fun

Praise for *Rethinking eLearning*

"Michael Allen is the consummate master of designing engaging, impactful elearning. Every professional in L&D and higher education should read this book to reinvigorate their design practices and elevate their instructional strategies."

—Les Howles, Emeritus Faculty Associate, Director of Distance Education
Professional Development, University of Wisconsin Madison

"Dr. Michael Allen's profound impact lies in his singular ability to diagnose the core challenges of our industry. He masterfully proves that beliefs—not just knowledge—drive behavior, showing why a learning program must change mindsets to deliver a tangible return. For decades, his principles have been the mandatory foundation for my own advisory practice, a rare blend of academic rigor and pragmatic insight that few others can match. This book is the definitive evidence for anyone ready to transform technological promise into proven human capability."

—Dr. Markus Bernhardt, Principal, Endeavor Intelligence

"Michael Allen once again challenges us to think differently and design better. *Rethinking eLearning* is a masterclass in creating meaningful, relevant, and human-centered learning experiences—an essential guide for anyone serious about improving elearning."

—Elaine Biech, CPTD Fellow and Author, *The New Business*
of Consulting and *The Art and Science of Training*

"*Rethinking eLearning* talks through all the challenges and opportunities we face today, including artificial intelligence and experience-based learning."

—Joe Ganci, President, eLearning Joe LLC,
and Recipient, 2013 Guildmaster Award

"Every few years, a new method for delivering elearning is invented. And the first thing everyone does is forget that this learning 'art form' has been around for more than 50 years. The beauty of what Michael Allen has created is that it is based on, literally, a lifetime of knowledge, skill, experience and, yes, wisdom, that can serve as a foundation for exploring how new technologies can be used to efficiently and effectively help others to learn."

—Larry Israelite, PhD, former Vice President of
HR Development, Liberty Mutual Group

"In this book, Michael Allen gives us needed insights on what we should be aiming for right now when creating online (or e-) learning materials, resources, and more. But research shows that most online learning is behind research, technologies, and design capabilities. Most people struggle to complete online learning. We need to know what is needed and possible, and *Rethinking eLearning* is a fantastic source of better ideas."

—**Patti Shank, PhD, Author,** *Write Better Multiple-Choice Questions to Assess Learning*

"Michael Allen invites us into a refreshingly honest, deeply insightful reexamination of everything we thought we knew about elearning. With a masterful blend of examples, hard-earned wisdom, and practical design strategies, Allen challenges stale assumptions and reorients us toward what matters most: the learner. If you care about the future of learning, this book should constantly be by your side and open to the appropriate page."

—**Dr. Karl M. Kapp, Author,** *Action-First Learning* **and** *The Gamification of Learning*, **and Instruction Professor, Instructional Design and Technology, Commonwealth University**

"This book is a practical goldmine for L&D professionals at every level. You don't have to read it cover to cover; each chapter is designed to be a self-contained insight, allowing you to jump straight to the topic you need and quickly gain actionable ideas."

—**Phil Cowcill, Senior eLearning Specialist, PJ Rules**

"In an age of ever-shinier objects, it's a delight to pick up a book that reminds us of the basics: learner first. Relevance to that learner foremost. Managers don't care what people *know*, but what they can *do*. This new book helps marry the shiny with the tried and true, describing the confluence of personalized training and AI with a refreshing focus on the human. And the dozens of live elearning examples from world-class design shops bring it all home in helpful, concrete ways. Michael Allen brings another great addition to our L&D libraries."

—**Jane Bozarth, PhD, Director of Research, The Learning Guild, and Author,** *From Analysis to Evaluation*

"Dr. Allen integrates academic rigor from his background in learning science and practical experience from leading the development of learning solutions at Allen Interactions to provide this comprehensive guide to making better learning."

—**Clark Quinn, PhD, Executive Director, Quinnovation**

"There's much to celebrate here with Dr. Allen's newest offering *Rethinking eLearning*, in which he refreshes our understanding of the core foundations of learning and the design and development of digital experiences, while setting the stage for new possibilities as we move into the Age of AI. Throughout, Allen keeps the focus on ways we can elevate the learning experiences we design, sparking not just competent performance in our learners but joyful performance. A highly recommended addition to the library of both new and experienced practitioners."

**—Cammy Bean, Account Director, Kineo,
and Author,** *The Accidental Instructional Designer*

"With perspective grounded in foundational principles and informed by practical experience and emerging innovations, he offers readers both anchor and sail for navigating an increasingly complex professional landscape."

**—Ellen D. Wagner, PhD, Managing Partner,
North Coast EduVisory Solutions, LLC**

"eLearning creation is absolutely going to be changed by AI tools, but the best tools in the world can't help you if you don't know what good looks like. No one is a more passionate advocate for great elearning than Michael Allen, and this book is full of the kinds of examples you need to keep in mind when creating elearning for our modern work world."

—Julie Dirksen, Author, *Design for How People Learn*

"It's about designing learning experiences that respect learners' time, needs, and humanity . . . Michael Allen creates elearning that is relevant, empathetic, and genuinely supportive of learners."

—David Kelly, former Chairman and CEO, Learning Guild

"*Rethinking eLearning* will become the new go-to guide from a pioneer who helped shape our field. XEL (eXperience-based eLearning) joins CCAF and SAM as a new foundational approach to move beyond 'tell-and-test' toward genuinely individualized, challenge-rich experiences. Packed with learning design insights, real-world examples, and project know-how, this book leaves no excuse for boring or ineffective training. You'll find actionable insights on every page and the inspiration to raise the bar for what learning can achieve."

—Megan Torrance, CEO, TorranceLearning

"Michael Allen cuts through the noise with a modern, humane blueprint for elearning: Start by understanding how learners feel and what actually matters to them, then craft challenge-first experiences that adapt to the person—not the other way around. This book moves us beyond 'tell-and-test' to meaningful, memorable practice that transfers to the job."

—Tim Slade, Creator, The eLearning Designer's Academy

"This book is structured in a manner that makes it easy for readers to understand the key principles . . . One set geared toward those interested in creating outstanding instruction and the other set in the form of a Buyer's Checklist"

—Robert Reiser, PhD. Professor Emeritus, College of Education, Florida State University

"Michael Allen's new book—*Rethinking eLearning*—is a lot like Michael himself: brimming with wisdom, curiosity, incisive case examples, and a transcendent ability to cut to the heart of the matter. Looking at elearning anew, after five decades as an elearning leader, Michael adds to his already rich portfolio by helping us design with the latest tech, timeless wisdom from the learning sciences, and empathy for our learners."

—Will Thalheimer, PhD, MBA, Work-Learning Research LLC.

"What I absolutely loved about this book is how wonderfully bite-size it is! Dr. Allen knew exactly what we learning geeks needed! My absolute favorite section is the delightful and clever 'Allenisms'! Short, sharp, and sometimes funny. Thank you, Dr. Allen, for keeping the magic alive!"

—Dr. Pooja Jaisingh, Associate Vice President, Digital Learning, Icertis

RETHINKING eLEARNING

What Works. What Doesn't. What's Missing.

MICHAEL W. ALLEN

MATT HOLT

Matt Holt Books
An Imprint of BenBella Books, Inc.
Dallas, TX

This book is designed to provide accurate and authoritative information about instructional design. Neither the author nor the publisher is engaged in rendering legal, accounting, or other professional services by publishing this book. If any such assistance is required, the services of qualified professionals should be sought. The author and publisher will not be responsible for any liability, loss, or risk incurred as a result of the use and application of any information contained in this book.

Rethinking eLearning copyright © 2026 by Michael Allen

All rights reserved. Except in the case of brief quotations embodied in critical articles or reviews, no part of this book may be reproduced, stored, transmitted, or used in any manner whatsoever, including for training artificial intelligence (AI) technologies or for automated text and data mining, without prior written permission from the publisher.

MATT HOLT BENBELLA

Matt Holt is an imprint of BenBella Books, Inc.
8080 N. Central Expressway
Suite 1700
Dallas, TX 75206
benbellabooks.com
Send feedback to feedback@benbellabooks.com

BenBella and *Matt Holt* are federally registered trademarks.

Printed in the United States of America
10 9 8 7 6 5 4 3 2 1

Library of Congress Control Number: 2025032865
ISBN 9781637748367 (trade paperback)
ISBN 9781637748374 (electronic)

Editing by Katie Dickman
Copyediting by Michael Fedison
Proofreading by Becky Maines and Marissa Wold Uhrina
Indexing by WordCo Indexing Services, Inc.
Text design and composition by Aaron Edmiston
Cover design by Jennifer Jesse
Cover art © Adobe Stock / Orapun
Printed by Versa Press

Special discounts for bulk sales are available.
Please contact bulkorders@benbellabooks.com.

For our son, Christopher Allen,
who has earned the leadership role of president at Allen Interactions
and carries forward the spirit of the talented present and former
employees of our company, all dedicated to creating the very best
individualized, technology-assisted learning experiences.

CONTENTS

BOOK 1: CRITICAL CONSIDERATIONS

BOOK 2: HOW TO DESIGN eLEARNING

BOOK 3: HOW TO BUILD eLEARNING

FOREWORD

"The illiterate of the 21st century will not be those who cannot read
or write, but those who cannot learn, unlearn, and relearn." This
quote, found in Alvin Toffler's book *Future Shock,* written in 1970,
is so relevant to those of us in the learning and talent development
community. We might sum up the idea in a concept many of us are
familiar with, the value and need for lifelong learning.

I doubt there is a person in our field who disputes that lifelong learning
is a crucial trait to possess. Learning is important. So is questioning
what we think we know and unlearning concepts, theories, skills, and
practices that no longer serve us well. It's quite probable that many of
us no longer tie our shoes the same way we were taught when we were
toddlers.

The book you hold in your hands is the product of Michael Allen's
embrace of this very idea. Michael is among the luminaries in the
elearning space. He's written countless books, articles, papers, and
presentations on the topic. He's developed hundreds of courses and
was one of the earliest adopters and educators of elearning when
it first emerged as a viable learning modality. Some call him the
"godfather of elearning."

And yet.

After all that time and experience, Michael has gifted us with a book
that helps us rethink what we think we know about elearning, and
he does it in an authentic and vulnerable way. Michael's courage in
sharing his rethinking journey is refreshing and honest.

These opening words in Chapter 1 set the tone: *"I had reached a point of comfort. Perhaps even complacency. I was thinking after the many research and application projects my colleagues, studios, and I had done and after I'd had an opportunity to observe and think about what works and doesn't, I'd come to a reasonably complete understanding of what elearning was, could be, and should be."*

What Michael shares in the short and actionable chapters that follow help us understand the evolution of this thinking, including the incredibly important lesson he learned from an inner-city fourth grader at the Northside Achievement Zone in Minneapolis.

The fact that Michael Allen wrote this book doesn't surprise me. In fact, if anything it confirms for me that Michael is an exemplar in our field precisely because of his thirst to learn, to improve, to explore, to challenge his own assumptions, and to apply his learning to his own work while also sharing it with our field. The exuberance of the learning journey that informs this book practically jumps off the pages. You'll find yourself getting excited about the new thoughts and "revolutionary realizations" Michael shares. It's all relatable and eminently practical. His singular challenge to us: elevate the learner experience.

For those who've followed Michael's work for decades you know he always has "bonus content" included in his books. This work is no exception, and Michael models for us all how to leverage technology to add relevant value from many practitioners and suppliers. I won't spoil how this bonus content is delivered; you can read on for yourself!

Toffler's *Future Shock* is 55 years old as of this writing. In it he predicted rapid change would be a hallmark of the future. That seems like an understatement today as we look around us. Change permeates everything. Toffler was interviewed by NPR in 2010 about the book's impact and what he'd noticed since writing it. He remarked, "In the past, you made a decision and that was it. Now, you make a decision and you say, 'What happens next?' There's always a next."

And there's always a "next" in learning. As Michael states, "Is today's elearning everything it should be? Of course not." We'd do well to take his advice and welcome the changes and challenges ahead, knowing that embracing disruption can lead to new opportunities.

Thanks, Michael, for writing this book. Thanks for helping all of us rethink not only the future of elearning but also our profession in a way that is both insightful and inspiring.

—**Tony Bingham**
President & CEO
Association for Talent Development

PREFACE

Spoiler Alert: eLearning has much more potential than is often realized, not just because of the common design faults documented by so many of us (and listed in the Serious eLearning Manifesto, https://elearningmanifesto.org), but also, and quite importantly, because it overlooks the importance of (1) **establishing relevancy for learners** and (2) **being empathic** as learners move along their learning journey.

Traumatic learning experiences, such as those dished out by Charles W. Kingsfield Jr., played by John Houseman in *The Paper Chase*, can be effective, but not without negative side effects.

Opposite intimidation, boredom also cripples positive learning outcomes, although in a different way. And it's so very easy to bore learners.

Boredom
"Anyone?" "Anyone?"
"Anyone?" "Bueller?"
"Bueller?"

Intimidation
"Mr. Hart, here's a dime.
Call your mother and tell
her there is serious
doubt about you
becoming a lawyer."

It's an understatement that neither Ferris Bueller nor James Hart had optimal learning experiences. We're not out to bore, intimidate, or frustrate learners. We're here to help them learn. Short of an expert human mentor, elearning is perhaps the only means of delivering learning experiences that are optimal for each learner.

Why Rethink eLearning?

Through almost six decades of work on elearning with training and educational development teams in organizations ranging from Big 10 universities to Fortune 100 corporations and organizations of every size, my teams have produced hundreds of elearning courses. We've explored countless design ideas and made continuous improvements to the process we use.

Pretty good, I guess. We hope our millions of learners have gained useful knowledge and skills. *We've* learned a lot; that's for sure!

Satisfied? No!

The Elevation of Our Humanity

Isn't that the ultimate purpose of digital technologies, to help us humans become better, happier, more productive people? Computers free us from countless menial tasks (while they introduce complications and frustrations, as well—some user interface designers need mental therapy), which, when done well, provides us the opportunity to focus on more meaningful pursuits.

Computer memory is much more reliable than our own, although not necessarily factual. It has instant access to far more information than we could ever review in a lifetime. Intelligent systems can find the most recent discoveries and synthesize information, not just remind us of what we've forgotten from our studies. Digital systems can help us perform our tasks faster, share our insights, validate our effectiveness, and help us collect input from others easily. Many more contributions could be listed—all great. But the "elevation of humanity"? How's that working out? And does artificial intelligence reframe the whole proposition while also casting a shadowy specter?

In this book, I've kept front and center the thought that as we're building elearning we should continuously strive to be our best selves—people who genuinely care about learners. We should be people who think about the experiences we create in terms of not only their benefits as we see them but also of the benefits learners will appreciate. How will learners *feel* as they traverse the learning journey we've set out for them? Will they be able to ask for and receive help and opportunities to show what they're capable of? Will they treasure every step, or will they feel like cornered victims with no choice but to trudge through it? Will they be encouraged to explore, to preview, review, and reflect? Or just click NEXT.

Is Today's eLearning Everything It Should Be?

Of course not. Probably nothing is. But we know elearning can be so much better.

This book raises design questions to consider seriously, whether employing artificial intelligence or not. It challenges us to create learning experiences that, first of all, are what we'd really appreciate ourselves. If we wouldn't want to learn from what we're creating, why think anyone else would? If it satisfies us, we then need to test with others to see if we're close to achieving the reactions and achievements we were going for. Then we modify as necessary to affirm that we are, indeed, using the digital platform to amplify our humanity, treat others with kindness and respect, and inspire others to do the same.

These are topics we'll delve into. I'm so glad to have you with me!

Michael Allen, PhD
June 6, 2025

INTRODUCTION

Awesome Learning Experiences

Inspired by reading about my favorite and diverse heroes, including Leonardo da Vinci, Albert Einstein, Walt Disney, and Elon Musk, I've tried and continue striving to find the simplest path to creating awesome learning experiences. Taking Albert Einstein's lead to find explanations that are "as simple as possible, but not simpler," I find myself in a continuous search for the simplest means to create awesome learning experiences, but not simpler via sacrifice of quality and effectiveness.

Awesome learning experiences are motivational and individualized (to be Meaningful for each learner). They provide practice (sufficient to be Memorable) and after-learning support to Motivate superior performance. Those 3M's—Meaningful, Memorable, and Motivational—have been my primary focus. But in *Rethinking eLearning*, I see those critical components aren't quite sufficient without also establishing relevance and being empathetic.

So, after some experimentation and "rethinking," I'm seeing that awesome learning experiences are built on six foundational layers.

Awesome learning experiences are:

Relevant in the minds of learners as they progress through learning experiences as well as relevant to what subject matter experts know learners need to be successful in their jobs and/or lives.

Motivational to keep learners engaged, energized, and focused to learn and later to apply their new skills and realize the benefits.

Individualized by sensing and accommodating human differences in order to make every minute of learning experiences beneficial and responsive to learner needs, just like an excellent personal mentor would.

Empathic in realizing that our feelings and emotions are part of the human condition and strongly affect our ability to learn.

Memorable because, if they aren't, they won't guide future behavior, which makes the training pretty much useless.

Supportive to keep learners on the right path until the effective behaviors they've learned become strong habits and learners become confident in their abilities and joyful in their performance of them.

Awesome Learning Experiences Simplified

This long list of essential elements may sound daunting. Let me assure you it's not as difficult to integrate these elements as it may sound. In fact, once you get the hang of it, it may be simpler to achieve than what you're doing now. Stick with me, and I'll show you how to create awesome learning experiences with relative ease.

READER'S GUIDE

Before we dig into some breakthrough, practical, and realistic ways to make elearning significantly more effective, let's quickly look at how you might best use this book for your personal needs.

Short Chapters!

I've kept most chapters short and focused to provide a bunch of practical benefits.

- First, you can skip around easily. You don't need to read chapters in sequence. I've tried to make each one stand alone. I've let in a bit of redundancy for this purpose—hopefully not too much.

- To eliminate excessive redundancy, as almost everything is truly related to everything else, there are plenty of cross-references to help guide you to what you want to know when you want to know it.

- You may only have time to read one or two. The shorter chapters will allow you to fit your reading into the time you have instead of putting it off until you have a longer period (that may never free up).

- Reading one at a time with reflection is a great learning strategy. Better than rushing through it and then wishing you could remember what you read.

- After reading the book, the short chapters should help you quickly locate those sections you want to reference as you do your work.

I hope this works for you!

A Treasure Trove of Examples

I've learned from my 120-some conference presentations, hundreds of papers, blog articles, book chapters, and my previous nine books it's the examples that people jump to with the greatest interest. I share principles and procedures because they are important. They guide us to success in developing many variations. Keep in mind, each example is just an instance, not the full story. It's the principles that will empower you to do the same; maybe outshining us!

But I'm with you. I love examples myself. So, we've assembled a bunch! Where did they come from and where are they?

As I was working on the book, we thought how great it would be to create not only a supporting website but also a Treasure Trove of the best of the best in elearning. While the Allen Interactions studios produce amazing elearning that regularly receives accolades from learners and clients, other organizations produce awesome works as well. We thought, why limit the Trove to just our works? Let's invite some others to contribute as well.

Seeking contributions from others would help us round out the coverage of the principles espoused in *Rethinking eLearning,* as not all great works can be shared so easily if at all. It takes time to prepare them, whether via video demonstration or explanation prior to direct open access. Some content is just too complex to use as a demo. And, for a variety of reasons, not all clients are willing to let the public (and especially their competitors) view training developed for them. Good training provides a major competitive advantage.

Access to the Trove is simple. Throughout the book, you will find QR codes to take you directly to associated examples gathered at the time of publication.

Treasure Trove

EXAMPLES

Note: We will continue to add examples to the Trove as they become available. Examples added after book publication will be found via menus on the website.

Designer's Notebook

Each of the six parts of the book conclude with a "Designer's Notebook" and a "Buyer's Checklist" (see below). The Designer's Notebooks list major principles covered in the preceding part that you don't want to forget. They can be an aid when designing elearning and helpful to look back to if it's been a while since you've refreshed your skills.

Buyer's Checklists

Also, at the end of each part of the book, there is a checklist designed to help buyers of either custom-built or off-the-shelf elearning. You don't need to have all the skills an instructional designer or developer needs to create great elearning, but you need to know what to look for in making purchases. Just because elearning looks pretty or has great media doesn't mean it's going to be instructionally effective or efficient.

You need to know what the earmarks of great contemporary elearning are. You can also benefit from knowing what it takes to create great elearning and to assess your organization's readiness to be a good partner with a vendor.

Allenisms

The ever-expanding *Book of Allenisms*, complete as of the time of this writing, is included in this volume. Allenisms are notions we find to be important guides for our work. They were gathered from theory, research, and/or our own experiences.

You'll see callouts to specific Allenisms throughout the book marked with this symbol.

Welcome

So, welcome! I hope you find this book to be a valuable resource in your work and a stimulus for your own insights and innovations. There's never going to be an end to finding better ways to create greater learning experiences unless we stop trying. Here's to "rethinking elearning," staying fresh, energetic, and never complacent!

Book 1

CRITICAL CONSIDERATIONS

UPDATED FUNDAMENTALS

Part 1 chapters provide a quick introduction to some of the great contributions instructional technology could make to individuals, organizations, and even our world. I think they're all very important considerations for revamping elearning into what we all want and need.

In Part 1 we briefly discuss the set of newly augmented fundamentals for successful elearning. When incorporated properly, they have a tremendously positive effect on learning experiences and their outcomes while meeting the expectations of contemporary learners.

Fundamentals include:

- **Relevancy and Empathy**. Two overlooked but essential requirements for effective learning.

- **Training as an Investment.** Organizations continually strive to minimize training costs, often harming effectiveness in the process. But treated as an investment, training done well provides a positive return and more than pays for itself.

- **Simplified Instructional Design.** Effective professional design is much more than following intuitive notions and yet easier than slow and tedious legacy approaches.

- **Learners First.** Disrupting common content-focused practice and essential to optimal training design is thinking first about addressing not only the knowledge and skills but also the affective variances that impact learning.

- **Artificial Intelligence.** AI is changing both learning experience possibilities and elearning production in exciting and powerful ways, but there are also pitfalls for the unaware.

- **Experience-based eLearning (XEL).** We learn far more by doing things and making mistakes in responsive simulations than by inactively reading, listening, or even watching how to do them.

- **Gamification.** More than adding game mechanics and fun interactions for motivation, gamification also exercises cognitive and sometimes physical response patterns that transfer to valuable on-the-job performance.

- **Challenge First.** To convey relevancy of the training to come, actively engage learners and determine how best to assist them in their personal learning journey immediately into content delivery and provide a Context-based Challenge.

These fundamentals build on each other for a complete roadmap for success with elearning. It's important to see them creating a whole that maximizes the contribution of each. To that end, these overview chapters provide an orientation for the greater depth and detail provided later and throughout the book.

CHAPTER 1

WHAT HAVE WE BEEN MISSING?

Allen Interactions was founded after my colleagues and I founded Authorware, Inc., which captured about 85% of the authoring tools market, acquired MacroMind/Paracomp, and became Macromedia. While we were overwhelmed by the widespread adoption of our technology, which made development of highly interactive elearning much easier to create, we discovered we had also made boring content-focused elearning even easier to create. Our goal with Authorware was to be unrestrictive and facilitate creation of all approaches to elearning.

In some ways, our success set us back. We were "rewarded" for enabling exactly the kind of elearning we hoped to eradicate. I had to return to our initial mission of making elearning a delightful, attractive, effective, and personal learning experience, with affordability and practicality being the starting gates. Indeed, if awesome elearning were achievable only via esoteric means by creators with rare talent, we were on the wrong path. To correct this unfortunate outcome, in contrast to our first journey, we had to work backward. We had to first define exactly what great elearning is, then define a process for creating it, and finally develop tools almost everyone could wield successfully. We should create the kind of elearning we wanted ourselves as a model for others to replicate and improve upon.

After all the accolades, awards, feedback from appreciative learners, and an opportunity to observe and think about what works and doesn't, I felt we had taken the necessary steps and had achieved the goal. I had personally reached a point of comfort. Perhaps even complacency. From the many research and application projects my colleagues, studios, and I had done, I'd come to a reasonably complete understanding of what elearning was, could be, and should be.

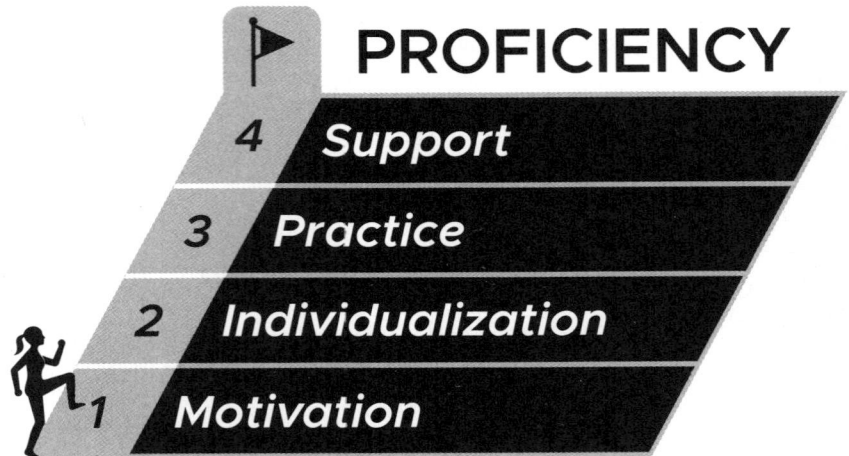

We understood that to help learners reach proficiency, they need sufficient **motivation** to focus and apply the energy essential to learning. We understood **individualization** is necessary and finally made practical in scale through elearning, which can adapt continuously to each learner's needs. We knew **practice** seats learning in long-term memory and makes our abilities more proficient. And finally, we knew **support** nourishes nascent learning during its vulnerability to forgetting.

The view seemed not only adequate but also complete. My head was in a peaceful place. For a moment.

Designing the Learner's Journey

I started to realize my folly as I was working on *Designing the Learner's Journey*—speeches, blogs, papers, and such in which I was emphasizing the importance of providing learning *experiences* as opposed to just presenting and clarifying content. I asserted, along with many others, that we learn best through firsthand experiences.

We can watch professionals perform, whether carpenters, artists, cooks, mathematicians, entertainers, or any expert, but until we try it ourselves, we'll not be learning at useful depth.

It's natural for us as instructional designers to focus on content clarity, accuracy, and comprehensiveness. But in doing so, the critical design and creation of experiences gets too little attention. This is an important understanding that many elearning designers have been slow or even reluctant to adopt. But I've expected that once most everyone realized the great gift of elearning is the ability to provide individualized learning experiences, we'd no longer have learners passively sitting through boring elearning or any other content-focused instruction. It would be just a matter of time.

I guess it still is.

Relevancy Revelation

But wait. The big aha—the big revelation (for me, anyway)—was still to come. It was eagerly jumping up and down, excitedly waving a flag and anxious to be discovered. Shouting, really. But I wasn't getting the message.

> *"The fool doth think he is wise,*
> *but the wise man knows himself to be a fool."*[1]

While reframing ID as a process of mapping out a learning journey, my exploration started revealing gaps. I saw missing elements as I tried ever harder to put myself in the learner's shoes. I realized I didn't have the comprehensive perspective on elearning I foolishly thought I had. It was quite incomplete. Thank goodness for a student from NAZ. NAZ?

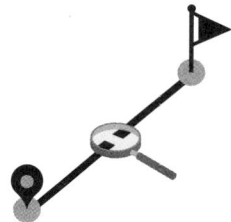

---

1   William Shakespeare (1564–1616), *As You Like It*.

My Story

Northside Achievement Zone

Northside Achievement Zone

At Allen Interactions we had the great good fortune to begin working on an exploratory project with the Northside Achievement Zone (NAZ), a nonprofit in Minneapolis that works with low-income children on the city's Northside where, as in many other communities around the country, academic scores have been declining for years. Indeed, academic scores have been declining nationally, not just since COVID when the decline was accelerated. To this day, fewer and fewer students are graduating from high school and few who do have employable skills.

With all the instructional programs we've developed at Allen Interactions—admittedly, most were for adult learners—the question was whether we had learned enough about instruction and learning to alter the downward slide in academics. We didn't want to be presumptuous, but we sure wanted to help if we could.

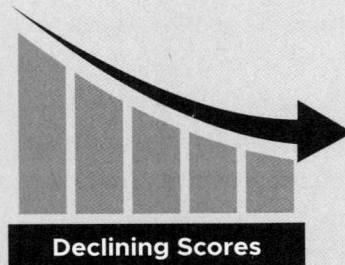

Declining Scores

We conducted focus groups and interviews, studied resource materials, and observed classroom activities looking for the dynamics of the problem. And then it spoke to us through a very bright fourth grader:

> *"Why would I want to learn that?
> That's what white kids study."*
>
> Bam! **Doesn't that make you think!** I couldn't sleep after that
> smart and energetic young Black student made this statement. He
> was being so frank and honest. And helpful beyond his realization.
> He didn't find what he was learning helpful for his safety on the
> street, playing sports, or winning popularity with his friends.

Lack of apparent relevancy indicative of a widespread problem?
How many people end up taking courses that teach things they find
so irrelevant they apply minimal effort to learn and look for ways to
escape? I've attended classes where the instructor tried to sell the
value of the course saying, "Trust me. Someday you'll be glad you
know this." This statement is essentially recognizing that the value of
the content hasn't been made apparent and might, in truth, have little
value to some learners, if any at all.

It's fairly common practice to have a CEO or another leader make a
video introduction trying to convince learners to be interested and do
their best, while most of us would be thinking, *Yeah, well, I'll be the
judge of that*. And, indeed, learners are the experts here.

In *Rethinking eLearning*, we're going to step back a bit to realize that
even with sound principles in our kit, we've been overlooking some
important barriers to achieving much greater appeal, effectiveness,
and the overall success elearning can easily deliver.

Relevancy and Empathy

Two critical building blocks need to be added to the core of our
instructional strategies to help all learners reach proficiency. Without
them, all our other efforts easily crumble:

1. Establishing personal *relevance* of the content and experience from the very beginning and also throughout our courses.

2. Sensing and responding to how learners are *feeling* as they progress through their journey.

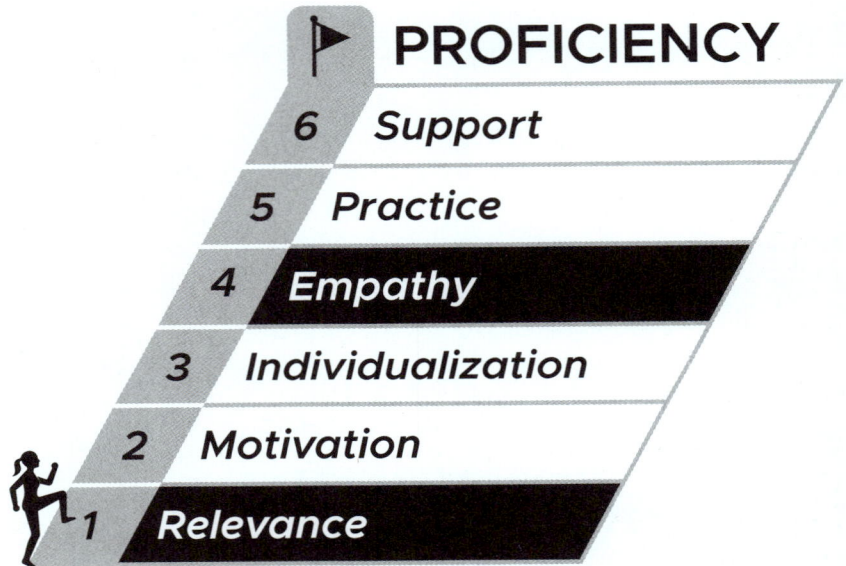

PROFICIENCY

6 Support
5 Practice
4 Empathy
3 Individualization
2 Motivation
1 Relevance

Ignoring relevancy and feelings can thwart the prospects of success for any instructional program no matter how strong the other components are. No good personal mentor would ignore them, and with the impersonal nature of digitized instruction, elearning can't afford to ignore them either.

CHAPTER 2

TRAINING AS AN INVESTMENT

CEOs have little confidence in their company's training and generally report learner engagement is mediocre.[2] Our school systems are broken despite the courageous, dedicated work by our teachers and professors. Reading, writing, math, and science skills are nowhere close to where they should be. High school graduates and even college graduates are unprepared to enter the labor market. Businesses are not finding qualified candidates.

Boring learning is failing learning.

---

2   HR.com Learning Solutions Industry Survey, May 2019.

Beyond academics and business, we're finding social discord, much of which can be traced to a lack of understanding and even awareness of other cultures, their values, and the reason for their values. The poorly educated are easy targets of misinformation and disinformation to which even the broadly knowledgeable succumb.

We have lost the protection of unbiased, thorough journalism, while power, greed, and a host of motives drive users of social media to promote nefarious agendas.

In addition to all these disasters are the challenges of rapid changes in our world and lives. Technological advancements haven't slowed but have been charging ahead, redefining needed skills at an unprecedented speed. Many of the newly defined skills require advanced expertise. We need to learn more complex skills faster just to keep up.

Opposing Pressures

We're experiencing bombardments of information overload, distractions of addictive screen time, adapting to remote learning and working, and organizational pressures to produce instructional programs fast and cheaply. As a result, we see bullet-pointed slides masquerading as teaching produced by well-meaning people with unfortunately little knowledge of learning and instruction. Everything is rushed. Everyone suffers.

Life challenges the focus needed for learning.

Time is a scarce commodity. There's pressure to skip over learning the essentials of instructional design and just get something out. But this time savings in development comes at a much greater cost of time—the learners' time. If we waste their time:

- Learners won't be able to do anything else with it (their time is gone).
- Learners won't gain anything of value.
- Their employers, organizations, and families won't benefit either.

Whose time is most important? Ours as instructional designers and developers or that of all our learners combined? Whose time accumulates to the greater number, that of the training designers and developers or that of all the learners?

Training Team   **Learners**

Asking whose time totals to a greater expense, the training team's or learners', has an obvious answer. But it's a serious question that needs objective examination, because it isn't often considered properly in budgeting. The common wisdom is: "We need to reduce the cost of our training. Let's get training programs created and delivered more quickly and less expensively. And then we'll be better off. More profitable."

Which Costs More: DIY or Professional Design?

A focus on reducing the cost of training development implies learner time in aggregate is less valuable—i.e., less costly—than the time of training designers and developers. Perhaps this thinking derives from simplistic accounting: The cost of developing a learning program is readily tracked, and so it is tracked. The cost becomes a line item. But the cost of learner time as a sum of poor performance, missed opportunities, and employee turnover is more difficult to track and is perhaps not even seen as a result of poor training. So, the costs aren't even calculated, let alone considered in the budgeting process.

Favoring reduction of training design and development costs over performance-enhancing training is irrational and poor business. It's self-defeating.

Cost = Hours x Pay + Missed Opportunities

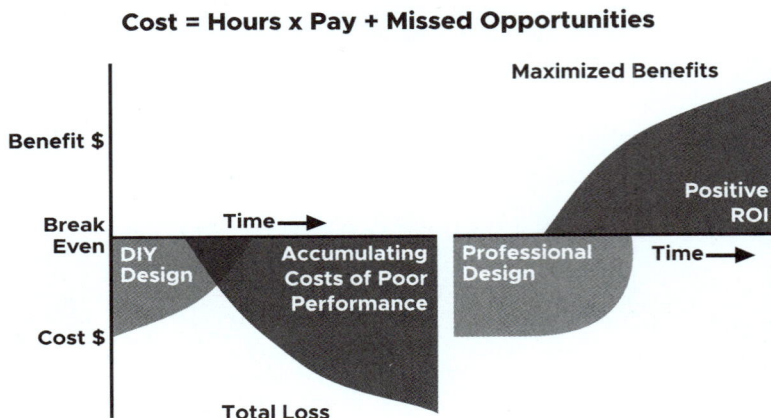

Who Can Afford Training That Doesn't Work?

If cost-cutting is the goal, one wouldn't want to take the costliest path, right? Let's clarify. The costliest path is one of:

- Cutting design and development costs
- Churning out ineffective instructional programs
- Cutting short the practice time needed to reach proficiency
- Losing work time for little if any gain
- Increasing attrition

Add up the damages. On top of learners being unproductive while they're away from the job and enduring poor training, add on potential lower margins, increased product returns or product support services, and disgruntled employees. The sum dwarfs what might otherwise have been spent creating high-impact learning experiences leading to greater efficiencies and market competitiveness.

It takes more expertise to create an inexpensive effective solution than it does to create an expensive ineffective solution.

You can't afford training that doesn't work—regardless of the cost.

Wasted learning time is costly training.

Spending More Isn't a Reliable Solution. Spending more on training design and development, however, doesn't automatically yield more effective performance outcomes. We have to be smart about it.

Instructional Design Is a Professional Undertaking. One needs knowledge and skills to do it well. It's easy to spend time, lots of costly time, developing programs that are not effective. The fact is, it takes more expertise to create an inexpensive effective solution than it does to create an expensive ineffective solution. Organizations are busy worldwide demonstrating this fact. But, again, you can't afford training that doesn't work—regardless of the cost.

My hope is that this book will set you on a path that helps you develop the knowledge and skills to achieve exceptionally valuable performance outcomes through training. And do so within practical, reasonable constraints of time and budget. It most certainly can be done.

CHAPTER 3

SIMPLIFIED INSTRUCTIONAL DESIGN

To share and learn from others, I've given many presentations on instructional design as I've forged my way through myriad challenges. I've written many papers, books, and blogs; created courses for LinkedIn Learning; and led workshops for ATD, ISPI, DevLearn, and others. But I wonder, has it helped? In some senses, it seems like selling the foundational principles of individualization and interactivity is more challenging today than it was over 50 years ago. Ironically, it's far easier to create great elearning today than it was back then, but we continue to see a preponderance of bullet-pointed presentations with a few quizzes masquerading as elearning. Puzzling.

There's no doubt in my mind that individualization and interactivity are instructional superpowers and should be the primary justification for elearning. They aren't complicated ideas, and yet they are foundational to realizing the greatest benefits elearning can provide.

In post-presentation conversations, some questions and comments have come up repeatedly. Curiously, they continue to.

- **I didn't know what I didn't know.** A frequent comment is: "I'm realizing just now I've been designing all wrong and doing so for years. I thought I was doing good as a professional. But given what I just heard, I know I'm only now about to become one."

- **Just how do you do that?** After describing principles and showing demos, I often hear: "This is interesting, but can you just *tell us* how to do instructional design? I'm new to all this."

- **That's beyond me.** "I'm just not that creative. How do you come up with these clever things?"

Well, I am always trying to help simplify principles and procedures, but it can't all be shared in an hour. Or a day. Or a week. There's a bit more to it.

My focus is always on balancing simplicity and practicality on one hand with effectiveness on the other. I'm not interested in sacrificing either for the other's sake.

Instructional design is, indeed, a professional undertaking. But you can do professional work without advanced degrees. You just need guidance and some experience because effective instructional paradigms often contradict intuition-based design and common practice. Poor legacy practices have a firm and debilitating grip. Used far too long—so long, in fact, they're accepted without scrutiny. Painful and ineffective as they may be.

How You Do It

In this book, I hope you'll learn how to create great instructional designs without spending years on a project. As much as possible, this book reveals straightforward methods for "doing it," all delivered in bite-size, hopefully painless chunks of discovery you can just scoot through and apply immediately.

You won't be surprised when I say, "It will take some practice."

CHAPTER 4

NEW FIRST PRINCIPLES

I'm excited to share an important realization—for me, it's a revolutionary realization! It's something that has been quietly but effectively holding us back from the full and perhaps most important value elearning could provide. It's preventing elearning from not only being as instructionally effective as it could be but also from creating learning experiences learners really want, need, and enjoy.

This severely inhibiting factor has been hiding in plain sight, even with plenty of relevant research focused on it.

This severely inhibiting factor has been hiding in plain sight, even with plenty of relevant research focused on it.

I've been stressing the importance of interactive learning experiences and individualization for quite some time now. I'm heartened by the feedback I've received from designers telling me these concepts have radically changed their designs very much for the better. We still have a lot of content-driven designers to convert, but I'm seeing enough movement in our profession to think the field will eventually get to the point of focusing on the essential ingredients of effective instruction, which generate Meaningful, Memorable, and Motivational learning *experiences*.

Even with experience-based learning, we've been overlooking what could be surprisingly more important than interactivity.

Enough suspense! What is it? It's the *affective influences* on learning. We all recognize we have feelings and emotions directing our attention and behavior, but we haven't taken them very seriously in instructional design. Perhaps because we have so much to deal with in developing instructional programs, we've decided our plates are full. We can't deal with more issues. We wouldn't say it out loud or even admit it to ourselves often, but even knowing enthusiastic learners learn best, we act as though affective influences aren't something we can bother with. They're outside our responsibility. Really?

Affective Influences

It's worth thinking about how our learners might be approaching what we've created for them. Are some feeling excited about the opportunity to learn from our work while others are not interested at all? Do some expect to do well while others expect to struggle? Do they worry about the possibility of an embarrassing failure? How do our learners feel about elearning in general? From previous experiences, do they expect and dread boring, screen-after-screen pages of text? Next, Next, Next, quiz. Do they worry about how much time it's going to take?

Do we routinely and continuously assess how our learners are feeling?	No.
Do we care how they are valuing their journey?	We should.
Do their attitudes matter?	Profoundly.

How we humans feel influences our behaviors, our attention, our energy. It can influence all the motivational and perception factors that determine learning outcomes for better or for worse. Just as with general motivation (something we'll talk about later), we don't have to get along with whatever motivation learners arrive with. We can heighten motivation just as we can exhaust and deflate it (which is much easier than revving it up, of course).

When Should We Consider Affective Influences?

Affective influences matter a lot, perhaps more than anything else.

After studying the research and looking at the successes of our studios in developing award-winning elearning, I'm realizing that affective influences matter a lot, *perhaps more than anything else*. Consideration of these influences should be the starting point of our design work, not something to attend to later if and when we're lucky enough to have the time.

While it's always tempting to delve immediately into content development and then design learning experiences in an attempt to bring it to life, I'm now realizing after defining success and how we will measure it, we should start with consideration of the affective influences that are likely to be stirring. They will be controlling much of learner behavior—behavior that affects our ability to help learners learn. We want affective influences assisting, not hindering.

New First Principles

There are many books, blogs, and presentations that offer a solid basis for designing great learning experiences. For comprehensiveness, I've brought forward and include herein such concepts from my previous books that remain, in my opinion, rock solid even though they are unfortunately and routinely bypassed. We're not discarding them now in this new perspective. We're just augmenting them and putting them in their appropriate places.

One would generally expect those solid, reliable, foundational concepts to be presented first in this book and then followed by newer perspectives that are more recently surfacing. But fundamental to this new thinking is doing design work in a different sequence. After defining success and how it will be measured first as always, we immediately take up affective influences and consider the variances we will probably find among our learners. Individualized learning experience design is up thereafter to define how we will adjust to affective variables, to be followed by content design.

Revised Order of Design Focus

1. Definition of success and how it will be measured
2. Affective influence assessments
3. Active individualized experiences
4. Content development

This sequence of considering affective factors before, learning experience design and content development later is "What's new!"

Hang on! It's new territory.

CHAPTER 5

ARTIFICIAL INTELLIGENCE

Recent and rapid advances in artificial intelligence offer capabilities we've dreamed of since the first days of digital instruction. Future prospects range dramatically from providing learners on-demand help and answers to their questions to creating whole training programs instantly. Our training programs can now carry on natural language conversations with learners!

Some designers express extreme alarm that their skills will become superfluous tomorrow and are thinking of abandoning the field before they are forced to seek an alternate career. Others reflect on how the long string of advances in technology expected to make training design and development quick and easy have not replaced the professional skills essential for developing learning programs that engage, intrigue, motivate, adapt, and teach effectively. In not a few cases, they've made the work more challenging.

Will AI be another valued advancement that continues to increment the potential effectiveness of digital learning experiences, but continues to require skilled designers and developers to conceive and orchestrate? Or are instructional designers to become extinct (as some claimed was already the case quite some time ago, such as with the advent of YouTube)?

My Story

In early elearning (called such various things as CAI—Computer-Assisted Instruction, CBE—Computer-Based Education, CAL—Computer-Assisted Learning, and CBT—Computer-Based Training), we had only typewriter-like computer terminals that noisily printed out text messages and questions for learners who responded by typing answers on the keyboard. Answers were often simple multiple-choice letters—A, B, C, D—to make it easy for software to recognize answers, although keywords and spelling permutations were recognized as the technology advanced.

We were imagining with great hopefulness the integration of graphics—not even imagining animation, video, portability, wireless networking, and natural language recognition. It seemed any one of these capabilities would dramatically ease design and development of great elearning.

Continuous advancement of elearning delivery platforms.

As we were treated to each magical advancement, we continued to ask for more because none of them, in themselves, made the process of creating great learning experiences fast and simple. We discovered technological advances were generally less impactful than expected, but we continued undaunted, thinking the next one would really do it!

All this is said to make the point: We have to keep our eye on the ball, especially in the presence of shiny new objects—even *very* shiny new objects. What's always most important is the quality of the learning experience, not just media or rapid access to information.[3]

Transforming with Artificial Intelligence

As thought leader Ray Jimenez pointed out in his pioneering work to harness artificial intelligence (AI) such as ChatGPT for elearning, "We ask questions and find the principles, philosophies, and values that are the drivers and reasons for the ChatGPT features. Then, find the tactical, practical, and use cases to understand the principles better and learn to find applications in our context."[4]

In this work, Ray was using "Large Language Models" (LLMs), which process natural language. Being able to broadly search the Internet for content information quickly and easily and being able to communicate with learners via natural language exchanges are just two of the incredibly useful tasks LLMs can provide for elearning.

AI Lexicon

LLM	Large Language Model
AGI	Artificial General Intelligence
ASI	Artificial Super Intelligence

As AI develops further, we will see agentic AI go beyond LLMs to enable "AI agents" to act autonomously without human oversight and collaborate as assistants to humans. At some point, although research has been pursuing it for many decades, we will likely even see

---

3   Markus Bernhardt, Michael Allen, & Steve Lee, 2025, https://trainingmag .com/navigating-the-realities-of-ai-in-learning-and-talent-development-a -guide-for-leaders/.

4   Ray Jimenez, *Transforming Learning Design with AI. ChatGPT* (Lulu.com, 2023).

Artificial General Intelligence (AGI) and, beyond that, Artificial Super Intelligence (ASI) with intelligence superior to human intelligence.

We can easily imagine AI acting at some point as a skilled personal mentor. Some claims for such an achievement are being made already, yet none I've seen own up to their claims and are ready for prime time. They will be. As these programs experiment with different approaches to assisting learners, we can expect and hope for superior instructional models to be discovered. Not just the worn-out and ineffective "tell-and-test" model yet again as we're seeing today.

Using AI to Aid Authoring and Development

AI possibilities in learning are numerous and under continuously fascinating exploration. Today, we see two primary ways of taking advantage of artificial intelligence: (1) using AI as an aid to authoring and developing elearning, and (2) using AI to interact with learners. In a terrific overview of AI as an elearning partner, Michelle Lentz notes, "Adapting AI is becoming essential for numerous reasons: enhanced efficiency . . . personalized learning . . . data-driven decisions . . . innovation in instructional design."[5]

"Adapting AI is becoming essential for numerous reasons: enhanced efficiency . . . personalized learning . . . data-driven decisions . . . innovation in instructional design."

One of the initial uses of artificial intelligence that avoids the risk of AI doing bad things when interacting with learners—such as "hallucinating," i.e., making up things when it can't find a good answer—is using it as an aid to elearning design and development. As a co-designer, it has already become common practice to use AI to:

- Generate outlines of content to consider
- Edit text, including simplifying wording and shortening passages

5   Michelle Lentz, *Partner with AI for Instructional Design* (Alexandria, VA: ATD, 2025), https://www.td.org/product/td-at-work-guide--partner-with-ai-for -instructional-design/252502.

- Create examples
- Generate graphics and illustrations
- Describe performance contexts and challenges
- List steps to perform tasks
- Identify common mistakes and misconceptions
- Add humor
- Write computer code

These are valuable and time-saving assists, to be sure. Just having AI list common misconceptions and performance mistakes people make can provide invaluable information for designing learning experiences.

Using AI to Interact Directly with Learners

There are obvious risks in using today's artificial intelligence in digital instruction, such as subjecting learners to:

- Frequently stated but incorrect information
- Fabricated information
- Information contradicting the organization's best practices
- Biased information

For the knowledgeable and skilled designer, there are controls to prevent or mitigate these AI-generated infractions. Better, contextually sensitive controls are in wide development, as are models quite different from Large Language Models that can reveal sources and even reason. Nevertheless, it's important to be aware of the risks and avoid trusting artificial intelligence blindly. Many organizations have ended up wasting a lot of time and money in their efforts to reduce both unrealistic expectations of AI. Keeping "humans in the loop" is essential now and perhaps for quite some time.

Let's practice!

Now that we have reviewed all the different techniques for prompting, let's put them into practice. This is a Prompt Fixer tool which helps you to refine your prompts. Simply enter your prompt, select Analyse, and receive feedback on how to maximize its effectiveness in obtaining a higher-quality response. Feel free to use this tool multiple times to refine your prompts!

Prompt Fixer

Explain how the universe was created.

Analyse

Prompt Fixer

The original prompt is broad and might not yield detailed responses from AI models. To improve specificity and depth, focus on particular scientific theories, philosophical perspectives, or cultural myths about the creation of the universe. This directs the AI to provide more structured and comprehensive answers..

Here is a suggested prompt that you can copy and paste directly into your AI tool:

Explain the creation of the universe according to the Big Bang theory, including key evidence supporting this scientific model.

Speak AI Fluently

Engineering AI Prompts. *"The Prompt Engineering course offers a compelling glimpse into the future of AI-enabled learning. It starts with introducing learners to the fundamentals of prompt engineering and gradually integrates AI to provide personalized, context-aware feedback through reflection questions. A standout feature is the Prompt Fixer activity, where learners receive detailed feedback and refined versions of their prompts crafted by AI. This thoughtful use of AI delivers meaningful, individualized support in real time, enhancing the learning experience without disrupting the learner's flow."* **Artha Learning**

AI Coach

EXAMPLE

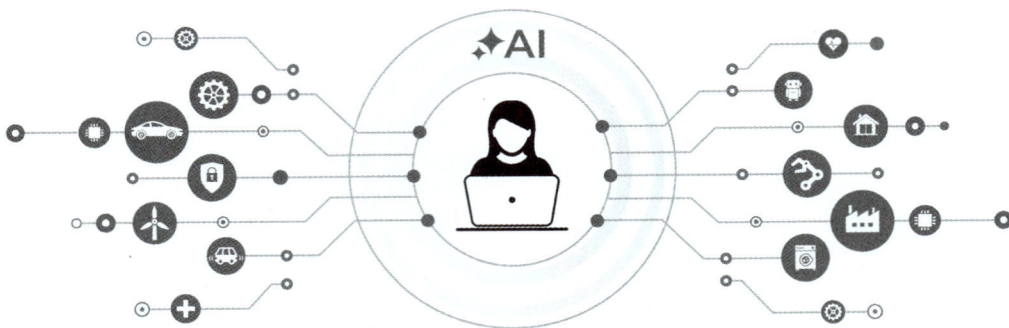

Rich, immediate access to current information offers much to elearning.

AI Fears

Facing the reality that many organizations turn to elearning just to save money, providing a higher quality learning experience might not even enter into thought. In fact, with the savings in delivery costs, even a lower quality learning experience might be fully acceptable.

Artificial intelligence is already poised to reduce costs and speed development. There are demonstrations of telling AI, "Generate an instructional program on leadership." And you'll get one. "Good enough!" is the jubilant response. "Based on what criteria?" I ask. Have you seen what you get going down this path today? Are we regressing to some bullet points, some talking avatars, and a quiz? Really?

It has seemed we were finally escaping the grasp of easy-to-create but tired, boring, and ineffective instructional paradigms. I suppose it's inevitable that the fast–easy–cheap argument will often prevail. But that's today. And it certainly doesn't always win. Requirements for quality and effectiveness usually win in the long run. See Allenism #38

Resist letting technology lead. When you can. Resist the baited hyperbole overshadowing sacrifices of important values. But also watch advances and innovate when it's in the learner's best interest to do so and helps you achieve your definition of success.

CHAPTER 6

EXPERIENCE-BASED eLEARNING (XEL)

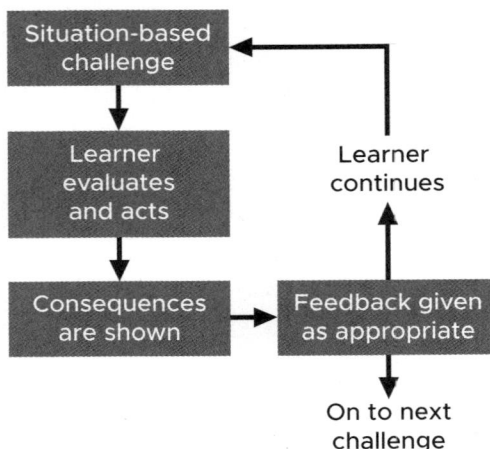

Experience-based eLearning

Situation-based challenge

↓

Learner evaluates and acts

↓

Consequences are shown

→

Feedback given as appropriate

Learner continues

↑

On to next challenge

Experience-based elearning is still a new concept for many instructional designers, although it's been a foundational principle in many studios for a long time. XEL designers focus on constructing experiences for learners to learn from rather than on predigesting information for presentation.

Learning experiences provide opportunities for learners to actively explore their abilities, witness the outcomes of their actions, and evaluate them.

Learning experiences provide opportunities for learners to actively explore their abilities, witness the outcomes of their actions, and evaluate them. Learners are engaged to think about their learning and, in the process, draw connections between conditions, actions, and consequences, which comprise the primary lesson to be learned for perhaps all performance outcomes.

Satellite Launch XEL

XEL. *"This Nova Space example asks learners to launch a satellite into orbit. Using the specially built simulation, learners experiment with making critical decisions regarding geographical launch locations to selecting an appropriate rocket and load. Feedback comes from an accurate launch simulation of what would happen using the learner's decisions."* **Allen Interactions Inc.**

Simulation-Based Experience

EXAMPLE

XEL vs. Tell-and-Test

XEL stands in stark contrast to the "tell-and-test" approach (see Allenism #14) used as a standard in classroom delivery and frequently in elearning as well, probably because it's what so many of us experienced when we were students in school. The instructor told us what we needed to know, whether by lecture, readings, videos, or other means of communication, and then tested us, usually via quizzes and tests. Grades were issued, and then, ready or not, we moved on to new content. Students who weren't keeping up generally fell further and further behind.

Tell and Test

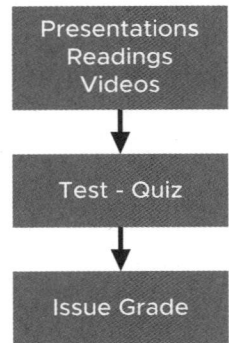

The interactive "tell" screen example shown on the next page provides access to the large lexicon of military titles. Learners could spend all the time needed to review the titles before taking a quiz, i.e., the "test." Obviously, this makes a better resource than a learning experience. (For a better approach with this type of content, see the Corrective Feedback Paradigm in Allenism #16.)

Tell-and-test has never been a good instructional model. It certainly isn't one to be replicated in elearning. In terms of individualization and interactivity, "tell-and-test" isn't even a contender. In the classroom setting where "tell-and-test" originated, individualization is very difficult. Even with concerted efforts, meeting each learner's needs happens rarely and even then only minimally. Every classroom teacher struggles with variances among learners. Just managing a group of learners who learn at different speeds or have different entry skills is very difficult, let alone dealing with the many other variances among learners.

Branches

Army
Navy
Marines
Air Force
Coast Guard

U. S. Army

- Main ground force for the U.S.
- Since June 14, 1775
- Active – 546,047
- Reserve and National Guard – 557,246
- Motto: "This We'll Defend"
- The dominant land power. The Army generally moves in to an area, secures it, and instills order and values before it leaves. It also guards U.S. installations and properties throughout the world.

Divisions

Field Army	2-5 Corps Size: 50,000+
Corps	2-5 Divisions Size: 20,000–45,000
Division	3 Brigades Size: 10,000–18,000
Brigade	3 or more Battalions Size: 3,000–5,000
Battalion	3 to 5 Companies Size: 500–800
Company	3 to 4 Platoons Size: 100–200
Platoon	3 to 4 Squads Size: 16–40
Squad	4-10 Soldiers

Ranks

Rank	Insignia
General/O10	
Lieutenant General/O9	
Major General/O8	
Brigadier General/O7	
Colonel/O6	
Lieutenant Colonel/O5	
Major/O4	
Captain/O3	
First Lieutenant/O2	
Second Lieutenant/O1	
Warrant Officers -WO1 to CWO5	
Sergeant Major/E9	
Master Sergeant/E8	
Sergeant First Class/E7	
Staff Sergeant/E6	
Sergeant/E5	
Specialist/E4	
Private to Private First Class/E1-E3	

Military Rank Training Using Tell-and-Test

Tell-and-Test. *"In this example, a large financial institution wanted to be sure ex-military candidates for hire were properly interviewed and evaluated. Knowing the ranks within each branch of service and the responsibilities of each was important for determining which candidates would have applicable experience for each job opening. And it's not that easy. For example, the rank of Navy Lieutenant is a Captain in the other branches."* **Allen Interactions Inc.**

Tell-and-Test

EXAMPLE

eLearning allows learners to work at their own pace and can assure each learner reaches mastery before moving on to advanced content. It can provide different examples, challenges, and feedback as needed, and tailor all instructional components to unlimited numbers of learners simultaneously. It's a great alternative to consider for many instructional needs. But we must remember, elearning provides such benefits only if it is designed to do so.

Find the situation where there are exactly 7 people who will buy a drink.

At $1.00 on a cloudy day, quantity of demand is 6.

1 [Raise the price by $0.50.]

2 [Lower the price by $0.50.]

3 [Wait for the sun to come out.]

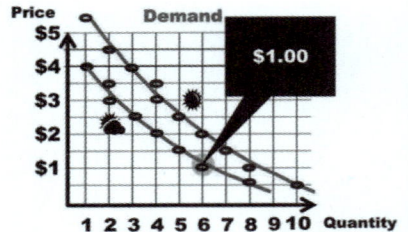

XEL via a Short Simulation

Short Simulation

EXAMPLE

Short Simulation. *"This simulation showcases intrinsic gamification by integrating learning into a decision-driven experience that mirrors real-world challenges. It uses XEL principles with an intuitive interface, meaningful choices, and immediate feedback, keeping learners focused on skill mastery. Presenting information visually emphasizes doing rather than reading. This leads to quicker, deeper learning with better job performance transfer."* **Clark Aldrich Designs**

Video Game Lessons

Video game designers methodically engineer experiences that require players' keen attention, persistence, and learning. The experiences are fun, sometimes so much so they are rightly classified as addictive. Because knowledge and skills acquisition are prerequisites to successful outcomes, video games totally contradict the notion that learning can't be fun. Of course, learning isn't fun if it isn't designed to be.

Video games demonstrate how it's possible to induce learners to willingly and excitedly put forth the time, effort, and attention needed to learn. While methods employed by entertainment game designers often teach skills unique to a particular game and may have little value elsewhere, the same methods can be powerful for teaching skills useful beyond games.

As expert game designer Manik Sahu explains:

> *Your choices, skills, and strategies shape the outcome of the game. It's a dynamic relationship between the player and the virtual environment, fostering a sense of agency and ownership over the experience.*
>
> *As you . . . immerse yourself in emotionally charged narratives, you are not merely a spectator but an active participant in the unfolding drama. This interactivity sets video games apart, drawing players into a world where they can influence events, solve problems, and conquer challenges in their unique way.*[6]

---

6   Manik Sahu, "Breaking Down the Essence of Video Games: The AROG Framework," Game Developer, July 21, 2023, https://www.gamedeveloper .com/blogs/breaking-down-the-essence-of-video-games-the-arog-framework.

Although detriments of prolonged video game playing are concerning, general benefits have been noted also in a variety of studies.[7] Voluntary overindulgence in typical distance learning and boring elearning wouldn't appear to be a risk today. Indeed, presentation-based elearning can be difficult to endure, and most people abort as quickly as possible. In contrast, and as we will cover in detail in upcoming chapters, XEL incorporates many of the structures video game designers use to keep learners thinking, practicing, and actively involved. XEL learners often practice voluntarily for the satisfaction of achieving perfect scores. That's not a bad thing.

---

7   Isabela Granic, Adam Lobel, and Rutger C. M. E. Engels, "The Benefits of Playing Video Games," *American Psychologist* 69 (1) (January 2014): 66–78, https://www.apa.org/pubs/journals/releases/amp-a0034857.pdf.

③ Orange juice.

You have breakfast, get in your car, and drive to the credit union. What do you do?

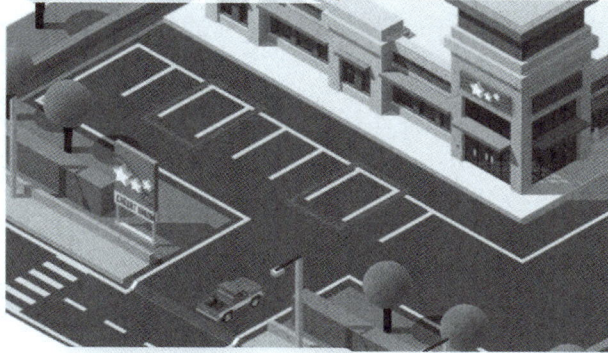

① [Park closest to the door.]

② [Park further from the door.]

③ [Drive around the parking lot.]

Preventing Hostile Robberies Through a Short Simulation

Players Occupy a Story World. *"In this short simulation about preventing hostile robbery, learners take on a role and make decisions in a simple, interactive world that looks and feels like real life. Everyday choices and high-stakes moments are mixed together, just like they are on the job. The design uses clear visuals, a consistent interface, and a short setup—'You are a [Role] and you need to [Do Something]'—to keep things focused and easy to follow. It's a fast, effective way to build real-world skills without the complexity of a full simulation."* **Clark Aldrich Designs**

Story World

EXAMPLE

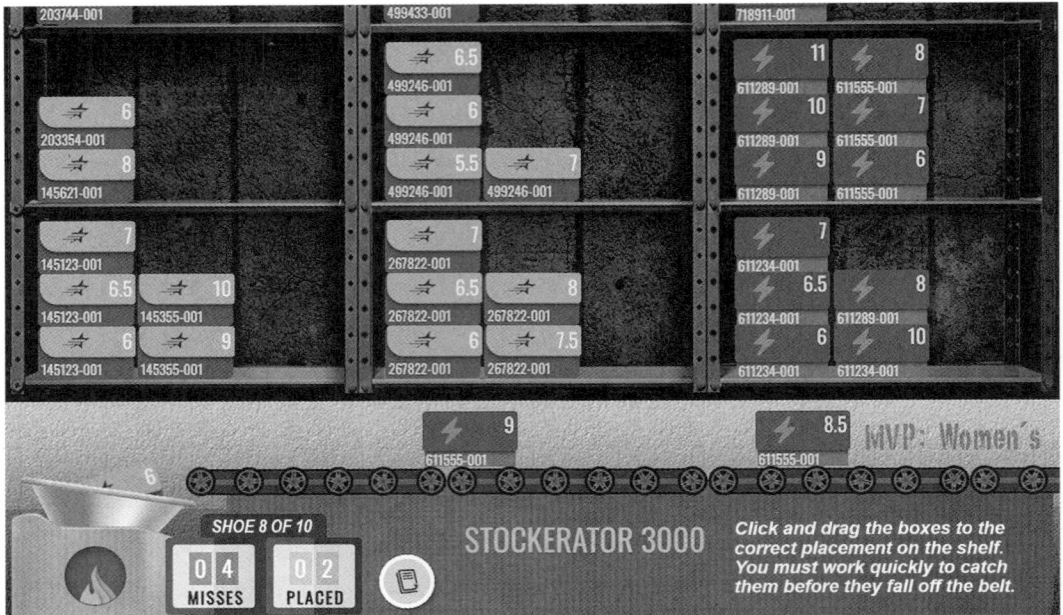

Game-Like Learning: Sorting Shoe Boxes

**Game-Like
Learning**

EXAMPLE

Sorting Shoe Boxes. *"In this example, learners must sort shoe boxes following a specific process. As they master the basics, each subsequent round becomes more challenging. This mirrors video game design with clear rules grounded in a real-world scenario. As the game progresses, additional risk is added and expectations rise. Success is demonstrated through the actual application of the process."* **Allen Interactions Inc.**

CHAPTER 7

GAMIFICATION

Why do we play games?

Knee-jerk answer: "Because games are fun, of course!"

But why are they fun, and why are they fun as we play them over and over again?

Games are fun for many reasons that differ with the particular attributes of the game. But with all games, practicing and learning to play and perform better is rewarding even if we're just competing against our personal best. While it's always fun to win, if we think we can and will do better each time around, we keep practicing. When the challenge is greater, so is the reward of doing well.

Joy

When we have reached a high point of confidence in our abilities, there's a certain joy we get just from performing our skills well and reconfirming our competency. That joy keeps us practicing and getting additional rewards as we find practice has yet again improved our skills.

The moral of this story? **We play games for the fun of *learning*!** Unless we're paid to play, it's really for the fun and joy of applying and hopefully advancing our skills.

While we're having fun, we're:

- Focusing
- Evaluating our performance
- Striving to improve
- And practicing

As Yu-kai Chou, leading gamification and behavioral designer, reports, the results of gamification can be spectacular. He lists over 90 ROI gamification examples and cases for 2024 on his website: https://yukaichou.com/gamification-examples/gamification-stats-figures/.

A few of those examples:

AstraZeneca	Gamified medicine training got 97% of their large network of agents to participate and yielded a **99% completion rate**.
Google	Gamified **travel** expense system training resulted in **close to 100% employee compliance** for travel expenses.
Deloitte	Gamified training programs took **50% less time to complete** and massively improved long-term engagement.

Focusing, evaluating our performance, striving to improve, and practicing is what learning requires and why we gamify learning.

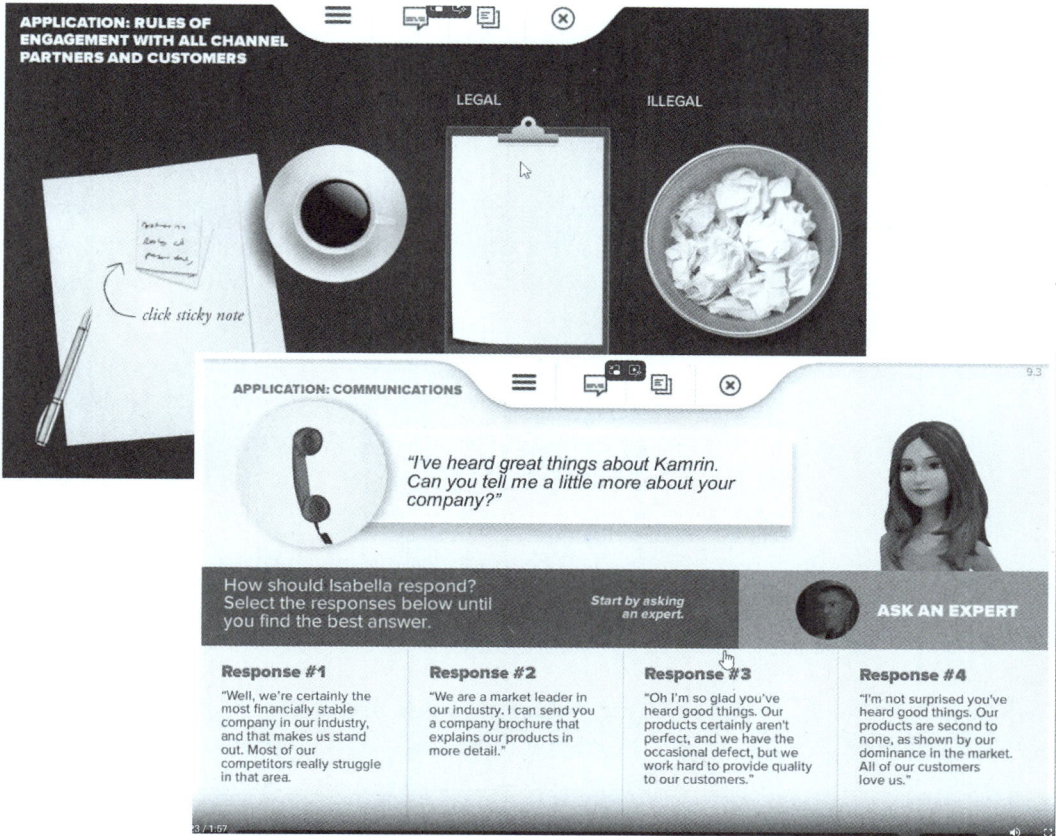

Red Flag Compliance Training Gamification

Compliance Training. *"This compliance course incorporates immersive learning techniques where learners participate in a story involving two companies collaborating on the same project. Through gamification, learners identify problems and solutions related to compliance, which helps them focus, evaluate their performance, strive to improve, and practice their skills. This approach has demonstrated measurable improvement in retention rates, translating to increased ROI."* **ELB Learning**

Gamification ROI

EXAMPLE

Motivation

People think gamification is about game "mechanics" and often define it as the application of game mechanics to elearning. While certain mechanics, such as scoring, rewards, and "level-ups," are often employed, they have to be used in ways that motivate learner engagement and activity. As Marc Rosenberg, a prominent thought leader on elearning, once said, "No one is better at stripping the fun out of a game than instructional designers."

We come back to motivation repeatedly as it's so essential to learning yet often completely left unaddressed. Countless university professors launch into rehearsed spiels thinking their fascination will be shared by their students. *Why wouldn't everyone find this fascinating?*

In short, gamification is all about motivation, not the mechanics.

Gamification is all about motivation, not the mechanics.

More often than we as instructional designers can be credited, game designers realize motivation is essential. If new players aren't engaged very quickly, they'll drop out of the game. From the very beginning, the experience needs to be related to motivations players already have—intriguing them to solve a mystery, beat a clock, or meet a challenge, all of which provide a level of instant gratification, which can wear off quickly unless successes level up to greater and more meaningful challenges.

In his book *Actionable Gamification*, Yu-kai Chou lists eight primary motivations designers can build on:[8]

- Epic meaning
- Accomplishment
- Empowerment
- Ownership

- Social influence
- Scarcity
- Unpredictability
- Avoidance

---

8   Yu-kai Chou, *Actionable Gamification: Beyond Points, Badges, and Leaderboards* (Sheridan, WY: Octalysis Media, 2015), http://ci.nii.ac.jp /ncid/BB18977357.

Less elegantly, Allenism #20 lists needs and goals that motivate people. In training, we especially focus on advancing competency and self-esteem.

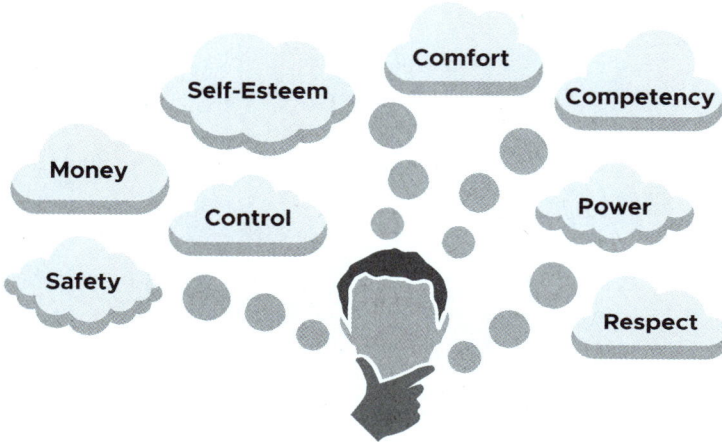

Gamification: More Than Just Game Mechanics

eLearning needs the same ability as entertainment games to engage learners quickly and sustain that engagement, all while imparting useful knowledge and skills. Today's learners expect it and are easily distracted without it.

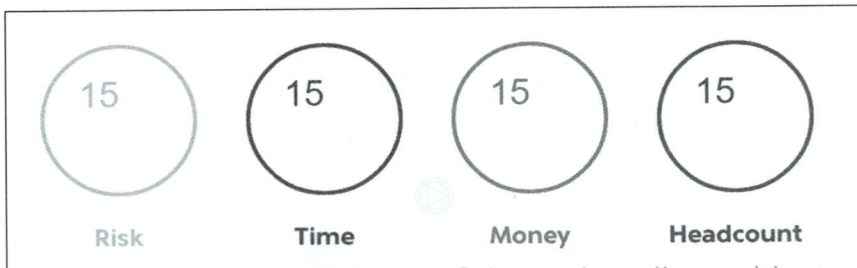

Priorities Role Play

Role Play

EXAMPLE

Priorities Role Play. *"In this simulation the learner plays the role of a chief priorities officer, emphasizing the importance of making decisions based on available resources and priorities. It highlights how focusing on key projects can solve customer pain points and drive shareholder value. It applies the principles of focusing, evaluating performance, striving to improve, and practicing by encouraging decision-makers to prioritize projects, assess their impact on value, continuously seek improvement, and apply these principles in their decision-making process."* **ELB Learning**

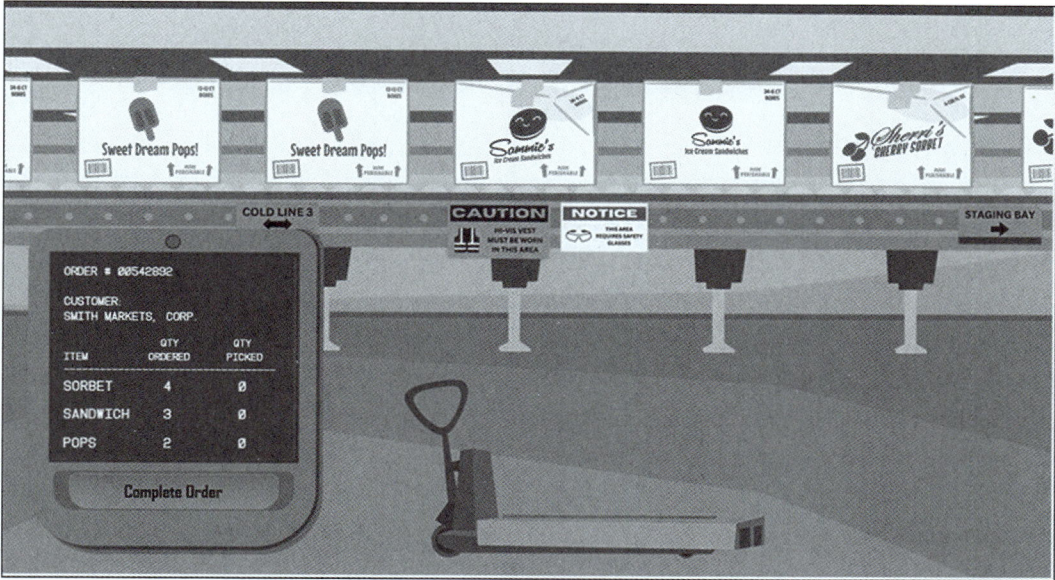

Cross Dock

Cross Dock. *"This simulation trains employees on scanning and picking materials using a newly implemented scanning system. The training includes a combination of simulated work activity with the idea of scoring based on the number of properly scanned items. If you don't scan the items properly, you will lose the game and have to start over."*
Karl M. Kapp, Commonwealth University's Institute for Interactive Technologies

Short Simulation

EXAMPLE

1 [Look at driver's license.]

2 [Look at applicant]

3 [Use photo guide.]

4 [Go back.]

Training for Confidence and Performance Joy

Realistic Application

EXAMPLE

Passport Inspection. *"Achieving performance, confidence, and joy through gamified elearning involves translating real-world steps into engaging simulations that demonstrate how concepts work, with an emphasis on where errors are more likely to occur. In this short simulation example, learners of the passport inspection process go through realistic application documents at their own pace to identify errors, gaining experience and competence. This approach encourages learners to play with concepts, make mistakes without dwelling on them, and leave the course with a strong understanding of how things behave in a real setting."* **Clark Aldrich Designs**

Practicality

It's important to understand human learning in depth as a guide to designing effective learning experiences. Once we have that understanding, we can move on to finding the most practical ways to create those learning experiences. If the methods, effort, or expenses are impractical, regardless of the value they can generate, it will be difficult to get organizations to make the needed investment. So, practicality is a high priority—right up there after effectiveness.

Remember, we're not looking for great designs that are rarely affordable, even if outstandingly effective. In Part 5 I share ways to simplify design on one hand and produce much more engaging and effective learning on the other. Among the critical topics that include gamification are:

Remember, we're not looking for great designs that are rarely affordable, even if outstandingly effective.

1. The CCAF framework of Context, Challenge, Activity, and Feedback for creating dynamic, self-adjusting, self-individualizing learning experiences

2. Techniques for motivating and engaging learners

3. The importance of delayed response judgment and the use of demonstrating the consequences of actions or decisions instead of judgment

4. The Corrective Feedback Paradigm (CFP) to optimize practice

5. The value of iterative design to produce the best possible instructional program given whatever the constraints may be

CHAPTER 8

CHALLENGE UP FRONT

Whether it was Dale Carnegie or Aristotle who said, "Tell them what you're going to tell them, tell them, and then tell them what you told them," this advice for addressing passive audiences is bad advice, indeed, for elearning (or any training). Just darting out delivering content information or listing instructional objectives is not going to energize learning experiences. So, what will?

The pervasive "tell-and test" model is exactly right, except it's completely backwards. When we want to engage learners in interactive learning experiences, we need to know their current skill level and even their feelings about this upcoming learning experience. We also need to intrigue learners from the very start. And get them active. As Karl Kapp explains and illustrates so eloquently in *Action-First Learning,* "A long preamble or a ton of prework simply bogs down the process. Engaging learners from the beginning is crucial, and encouraging some form of action at the start of a learning experience draws everyone into the content."[9]

Of course, it's important to keep learners active, not just at the start. Are there practical ways to do all this? Yes.

---

9   Karl M. Kapp, *Action-First learning: Instructional Design Techniques to Engage and Inspire* (American Society for Training and Development, 2025).

The Context, Challenge, Activity, Feedback Model (CCAF)

1. A MEANINGFUL SITUATION

2. A STIMULUS OR URGENCY TO ACT

4. CONSEQUENCES OF USER ACTIONS & GUIDANCE

3. A PHYSICAL GESTURE IN RESPONSE TO THE CHALLENGE

Throughout this book, we'll be referring to the CCAF model as it both simplifies and empowers elearning development and instructional effectiveness. Without going into depth on the model at this point (although you're certainly welcome to take a quick look at Chapter 22 for details), the CCAF model ranks as a member of the Updated Fundamentals primarily because it asserts that the initial learning experience should *not* be a content presentation nor even an introduction as is common practice. Rather, right away, a Challenge should be presented in a Context that's relevant in the eyes of learners.

True, the Challenge level needs to be carefully crafted and aimed at the most probable level of entry-level abilities. It also needs to be authentic enough to communicate the relevance of what can be learned in the program by implication: *You will be able to meet such challenges in these situations once you've completed this program.* You could say this to learners explicitly, but you don't even need that much of an introduction. Video game designers have long demonstrated the value of immediate challenges to engage, provide intrigue, and get users active. This is exactly what we want also in elearning.

If learners can readily meet the initial Challenge, we can be glad we didn't start out telling them how to do it. We would be boring them and have them questioning whether this is the right program to take. With an immediate performance success, we can congratulate their prowess and help them feel good about their abilities. We'd be off to a great start. We would then encourage them to advance and possibly demonstrate even greater skills.

If learners have trouble with the initial Challenge or any subsequent Challenge, we can give them help as they work through it—perhaps using graduated help that begins with simple tips of things to consider, eventually moving up to a full demonstration as they may request or as needed based on their continuing mistakes.

Note: With CCAF, instruction is delayed and delivered only at the moment of identified need or learner request. When delivered under these circumstances, instruction is appreciated and seen as helping the learner meet the Challenge requirements. This outcome is a win because you not only have an appreciative learner, but you now also know more about the individual learner, including what the next learning experience should address.

Research Support

If you're wondering whether you should try the Challenge First approach, thinking it's a radical shift from intuition or common practice, consider the supporting cognitive science. In the revered *Make It Stick*[10] compellation, authors Brown, Roediger III, and McDaniel note: "Trying to solve a problem before being taught the solution leads to better learning, even when errors are made in the attempt." They go on to note the value of "desirable difficulties"—or "short-term impediments" that slow learners down to permit analysis and thinking, not just reading, listening, or watching.

---

10   Peter C. Brown, Henry L. Roediger III, and Mark A. McDaniel, *Make It Stick* (Harvard University Press eBooks, 2014), https://doi.org/10.4159/9780674419377.

DESIGNER'S NOTEBOOK #1

Self-check: See if you garnered these takeaway principles and are ready to use them.

☐ The most expensive and unaffordable training is training that doesn't work.

☐ Squeezing design and development costs often results in greater operational expenses and missed business opportunities because of poorly trained workers.

☐ Awesome elearning design helps learners reach proficiency on the foundations of establishing relevance, motivating learners, individualizing the learning experience, being empathetic to learners' feelings, providing sufficient and spaced practice, and providing post-training support.

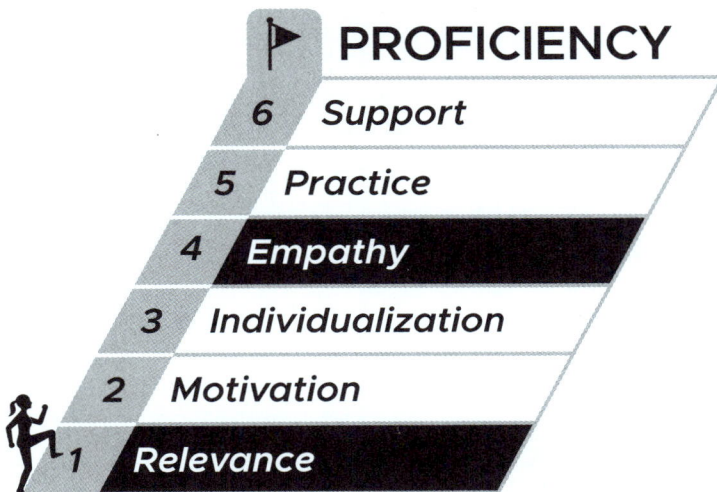

PROFICIENCY

6 Support
5 Practice
4 Empathy
3 Individualization
2 Motivation
1 Relevance

- [ ] Establishing relevancy and being empathetic have not been characteristic of elearning and are important in contemporary design.

- [ ] Training programs that ignore these factors to concentrate on the presentation of information miss unique benefits of elearning.

- [ ] There are practical methods for designing elearning that senses and adapts to learner affective states. We really must give them consideration at the start of a project rather than trying to tack them on at the end (should we happen to have time).

- [ ] Artificial intelligence has present value for assisting authors and interacting with learners, with more opportunities in the future.

- [ ] Experience-based elearning (XEL) has much greater learning value than "tell-and-test," which derives from legacy classroom instruction and its limitations of one-size-fits-all.

- [ ] Video games provide models for engaging and motivating learners to learn. Applicable to elearning, these gamification techniques are more effective than just adding "game mechanics."

- [ ] Beginning learning experiences with a Context-based Challenge communicates what can be learned from the program. It allows learners to assess its relevancy, gets learners active as soon as possible, and provides information about the learner's current skill level and needs.

BUYER'S CHECKLIST #1

To ensure a great investment in training and ROI, be sure to ask the following questions.

☐ Does the design prepare learners to succeed by enabling them to do the right things at the right times?

☐ Does the training spend most of the learner's time preparing them only to know what should be done and/or how things should be done instead of enabling them to do things correctly?

☐ Does the training provide sufficient practice under the conditions (simulated or actual) in which their effective performance will be required?

☐ Presenting information and then testing learners is a legacy approach to teaching that's about the most inefficient method there is. And it accepts the notion that some learners will do well, while others will fail to various degrees. Does this training assure that all trainees will master the skills you need them to have?

☐ The most expensive and unaffordable training is training that doesn't work. Are you getting effective training or just low-cost development and delivery?

☐ Are you providing the resources needed for a successful training to avoid greater operational expenses and missed business opportunities because of poorly trained workers?

☐ Are you seeing gamification of elearning using the motivational techniques video game designers have mastered to keep players focused and actively practicing until they reach mastery?

☐ Artificial intelligence has a history of making up facts and procedures, which requires it to be used with extreme caution in elearning. If proposed, will there be safeguards to prevent unwanted influences over the learning experiences?

☐ Does the training begin with a Context-based Challenge that communicates what learners will be able to do once they've completed the program and gets learners active immediately rather than having them wade through a lengthy introduction and manipulative encouragement?

FACING REALITIES

Sometimes we get so wrapped up in details we overlook the most obvious and important factors standing in the way of success. This is often true in training.

In Part 2, we'll quickly look at some important realities that are very much in play whether we tend to them or not:

- **If learners aren't motivated to learn**, not much learning is going to occur. Since we can't do the learning for them, it pays to enhance their motivation to learn. In fact, since a motivated learner will find a way to learn with or without our help, amplifying motivation should often be our #1 task.

- **People generally do what they believe is best.** This doesn't seem like a big revelation, but there's more to it than meets the eye. If we're training people to do things differently, but they're not convinced the new way is better than the old, performance will inevitably gravitate back to what people think is best. So, for training to be successful, we need to not only develop knowledge and skills but also convince trainees that the advantages of new behaviors outweigh the advantages of old, familiar behaviors.

- **The more effort we put into our work**, the more we appreciate our accomplishment. Our ability to assess the training we've developed becomes biased because, well, we'd look pretty foolish having put a lot of effort into something that wasn't good. We need to objectively evaluate our work. Insist on it. It's what professionals do.

CHAPTER 9

ONLY LEARNERS CAN DO IT!

Key Concept 1: Learners Must Do Their Own Learning

There's no learning the learner. You can't do the learning for them. Which makes our first goal one of ensuring learners are motivated to learn. Without motivation, no learning happens.

We can't reasonably expect all learners to arrive with great motivation or even equal levels of motivation. Some will probably be highly motivated. Others? Just because learners have enrolled in a class and shown up, whether in person or online, we can't be sure everyone has the motivation needed to benefit from a course.

Thankfully, we don't have to work with only the motivation learners have when we first greet them. This is really good news but only if we attend to motivation. It's common practice to let motivation be the learner's responsibility. *If learners don't want to learn and don't put in the needed effort, it's their fault they didn't learn.*

There's sometimes an implied or even voiced admonition: *"If you aren't ready to apply yourself in this course, you shouldn't be here."* Our success with learners is amplified when learning motivation is high and stifled when it's low. Affixing blame doesn't yield success.

As professionals in learning, addressing motivation needs to be at the top of our to-do list.

As professionals in learning, addressing motivation needs to be at the top of our to-do list.

Expecting learners to dial up their motivation, enthusiasm, and readiness to learn on their own might not be a good expectation. In any case, the risk that they won't is a risk we don't need to take.

For all of us, our motivation rises and falls many times during the day, even minute to minute as interesting things catch our eye or a class session becomes boring. And motivation is directed, not just high or low. It's multilayered as well. At any given moment, we have multiple motivations vying for our attention and directing our actions.

eLearning faces many competitors for attention and engagement.

We may be motivated to secure a good income for our family, get a painful dental cavity filled, and write a thank-you letter to a kind and generous friend all at the same time. Not all of these motivations can be front and center simultaneously, although they can easily interrupt each other. Competing motivations interfere with our ability to learn.

Learning is a process requiring energy and effort, regardless of the instructional paradigm employed. Learner brains must do the work in all cases. They must exercise and do the reps. But if the work is also fun and of obvious benefit, we become less focused on the energy and effort, sometimes even to the point of happily continuing to exhaustion.

Key Concept 2: Motivations Rule

At any given time, the strongest motivation(s) can silence other motivators. A concern about an approaching storm or a performance review easily defeats many other motivations. When learning is the strongest motivation, it allows learners to devote their full attention and energy to learning.

So, the question is, how do we heighten and focus the motivation to learn so it will silence competing motivations?

We can consider two phases of motivation and the techniques appropriate to each: Initial Engagement Motivation and Sustaining Motivation.

Engagement Motivation

Engagement Motivation

EXAMPLE

In rethinking elearning, we see great value in addressing motivation explicitly and using it as an ally, rather than just hoping low or conflicting motivations won't be a problem. As it's important to set out in the right direction for every journey, we look first at the initial Engagement Motivation to set the tone for the entire adventure.

| INTRO | EXPLORE YOUR WHY | I-STORY | YOUR STARTER KIT | BUSINESS PLAN | TOOLS FOR SUCCESS |

YOUR JOURNEY. YOUR JOY. YOUR DESTINY.

Welcome to the journey of your lifetime! You may be in business for yourself, but never by yourself. In fact, you're surrounded by women in the independent sales force who have the wisdom, experience and desire to support, inspire, and guide you. Are you ready to meet your destiny? Then simply select the video to begin.

MK University

Onboarding. *"Candidates interested in becoming a beauty consultant and setting up their own business to market May Kay Cosmetics often have reservations and even fears about their ability to perform all the required tasks well. This example demonstrates unique and very* *effective means to motivate new employees to acquire necessary skills and provide reassuring learning experiences that lead the way."* **Allen Interactions Inc.**

Basic Considerations

- Focus first on learners (not the content, technology, or bullet point styles). Think about their *goals and potential fears*. How can you assess them? How can you respond?

- What would be *relevant* to your learners? What would be the range of immediate interests? How can you find out? How can you respond?

Example

In a program we created, students are initially asked about their strengths, weaknesses, and aspirations as instructional designers through an infographic interface called the *Constellation*.[11]

The student's name appears in the middle. Movable dots or "stars" represent the student's self-assessment of skills. Students slide stars close to the center when they feel they are strong in that area and various distances away to represent lesser levels of proficiency.

We then ask learners to move the stars to create the Constellation that would represent the skill set they aspire to. This adjustment identifies the skill gaps they feel they have. Finally, learners prioritize their most concerning skill gaps, which provides a basis for selecting instructional resources and dynamically adjusting the sequence of learning activities.

---

11   Goals Constellation © 2010 Allen Interactions Inc. www.alleni.com.

Our Current eLearning

ai CONSTELLATION

We're debating whether to outsource design and development.

Outsourcing

Undecided

In-house only

Fun Interactivity
Learner Confidence
Blended Learning Modalities
Artificial Intelligence
Practice-to-Mastery
Learner Attitudes
ID Expertise
Learner Needs
Outsourcing
Return On Investment (ROI)
Learner Engagement
Cost to Deliver
Learning Outcomes
Cost to Develop
Learning Time

- EFFECTIVENESS
- COST
- ROI
- INDIVIDUALIZATION
- EXPERIENCE
- INSTRUCTIONAL DESIGN

Click Download for a PDF of your current Constellation. Click Continue to set your goals.

HELP ?   BACK ⊗   DOWNLOAD ⬇   CONTINUE ⊙

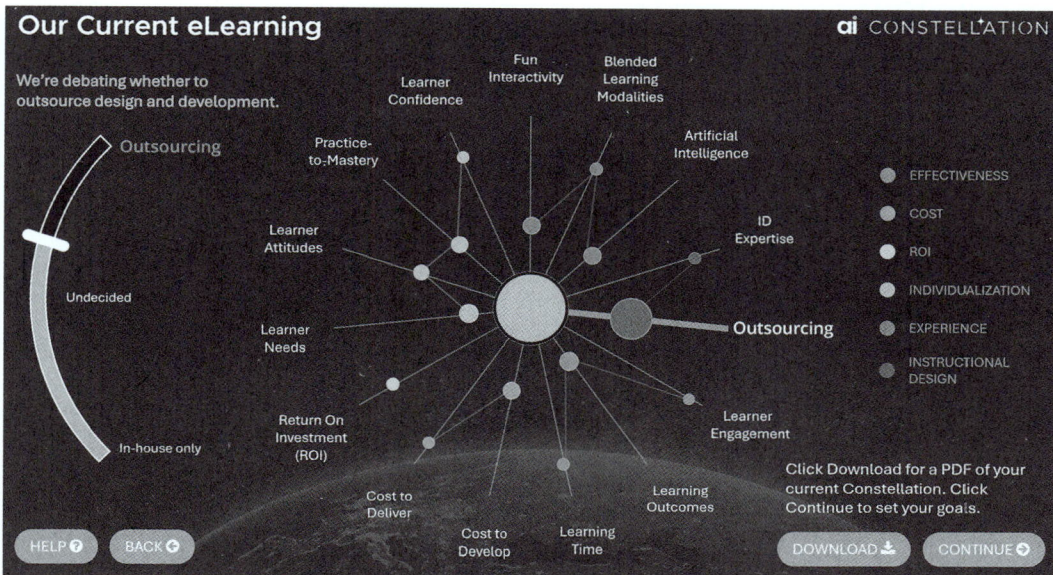

Goals Constellation.™ Source: Allen Interactions

Initially engaging learners in ways that recognize them as individuals about whom the instructional program is centered can go a long way to create engagement, focus, and motivation.

Sustaining Motivation: Fun and Value

While the initial events in a course set the tone, the first impression won't sustain motivation if what comes next is grueling or fails to deliver on the expectations set at the start. Every moment should be sustaining motivation if not lifting it ever higher.

Learning takes energy, but good designs divert learner awareness from their effort and make learning seem easy—even fun—and clearly worthwhile.

Many games sustain focus and engagement for long periods. Even physically challenging games can keep us moving until we almost

Goals Constellation

EXAMPLE

drop. And even then, we laugh at how much fun we had and wish we could keep going.

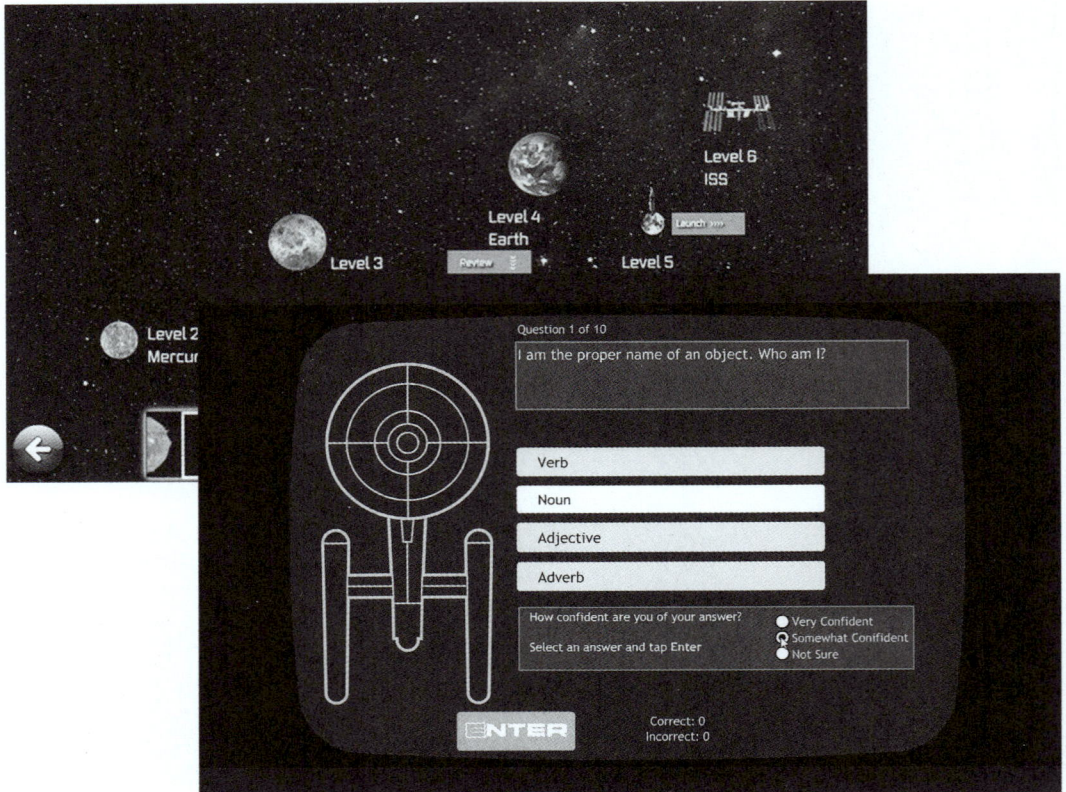

Learning Sentence Structure

Fun Context

EXAMPLE

Learning Sentence Structure. *"In this course as the learners fly through our solar system they start to identify parts of sentences. Each level provides information on the planet, moon, or technology that their rocket ship has landed on. By learning the syntax of sentences with interesting content, they improve their writing skills while earning badges and rewards. To deepen understanding, each lesson includes Confidence-Based Learning, encouraging learners to reflect on how sure they are about their answers—building not only accuracy, but self-awareness and stronger decision-making skills in sentence construction."* **Phil Cowcill**

Key Concept 3: Learning Can and Should Be Fun

In fact, most games and sports are all about learning. I know, most of us don't say, "I'm going to learn baseball, Monopoly, or poker this afternoon." We say we're "going to *play* baseball, Monopoly, or poker." But what we hope is that we'll play better each time—that we'll *learn* to win by beating the computer, our previous scores, or our competitors. And we expect to have fun while we're learning to do so. So, it's very possible to make learning itself a motivating experience. It's our job to do so.

How to Make Learning a Motivational Experience

- Make it fun. (I'm listing this first because making the experience fun shouldn't be an afterthought. Think fun from the start. Consider amusing consequences, pop-up challenges, accumulating rewards, etc.)

- Make what's to be learned relevant and its value apparent.

- Continually report progress.

- Treat learners like people you respect:

  - Give them control.
  - Ask learners how they're feeling.
  - Ask learners what they'd like to do next.

After giving attention to all of the above:

- Imagine the context of the experiences learners would find relevant. Where do you want learners to focus? What reactions do you want? Can you build intrigue into the experience to help sustain engagement?

- Create and fold in content that empowers learners; rewards their investment of time and energy; and creates Meaningful, Memorable, and Motivational learning experiences.

- Finally, think about the mistakes people make in performing the tasks you're teaching. Make it possible for your learners to make those same mistakes and experience what happens. See if they can identify their mistakes and correct them on their own before you step in with guidance.

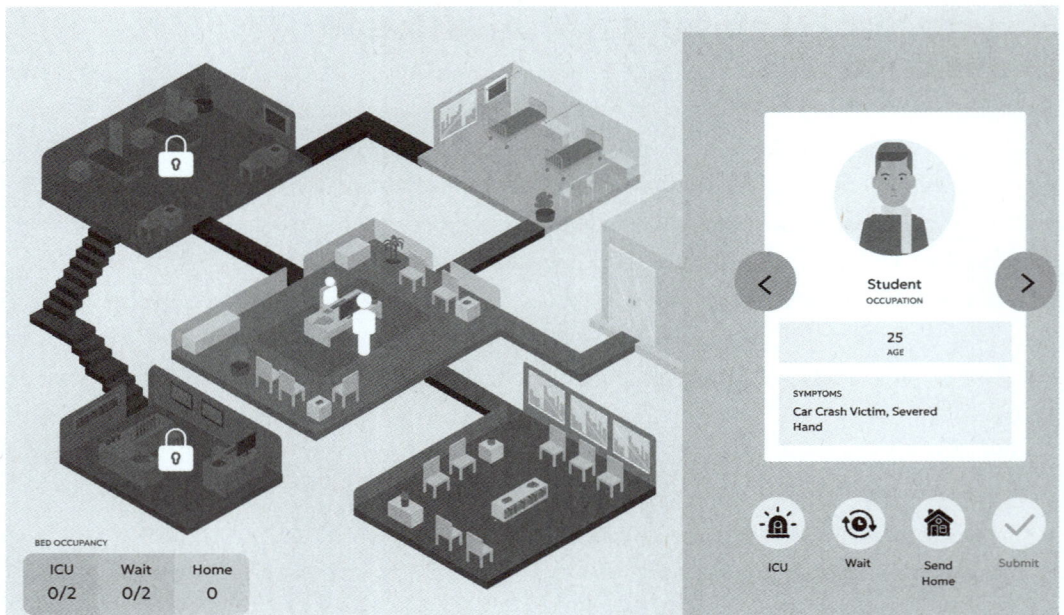

Emerging Illness Outbreak Simulation

Engaging Simulation-Based Game. *"This narrative-based sorting game places learners in the role of a healthcare triage worker responding to an emerging mystery illness. Designed around trial and error, the game encourages learners to make decisions, see the consequences, and adjust their approach in real time. Through pattern recognition, evolving clues, and mistake-driven feedback, players gradually uncover the profile of the affected population, aligning with intrinsic gamification principles to enhance engagement and learning outcomes."* **Artha Learning**

Intrinsic Engagement

EXAMPLE

7 Magic Keys to Motivation

We'll talk specifically and in detail about how to do all of this throughout the book, especially when we discuss the "7 Magic Keys" to motivational learning (see Chapter 25). When we explore them, you'll probably find at least some of them run counter to intuitive notions about what makes a good learning experience. Discovering these notions has been something of a breakthrough for me and has empowered our studios to produce exceptional learning experiences.

CHAPTER 10

BELIEFS DRIVE BEHAVIOR

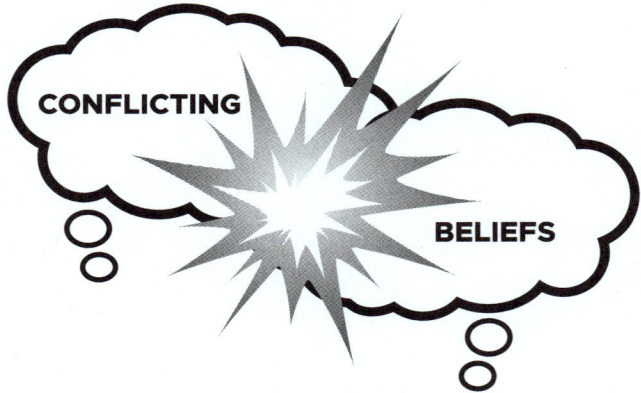

If you don't look behind the curtain, you won't find beliefs lurking there that you might never have expected your learners to be holding. And if you ignore learner beliefs, they'll sabotage all your efforts to improve behavior.

Here are some examples of what you might find:

> "I know we're supposed to give urgent attention to all our employees who feel bullied or discriminated against, but I've always found if I just wait it out, things resolve on their own. I'll probably make things worse if I get involved."

> "I've tightened auto door hinges by feel for years. I don't need to use one of those newfangled torque-adjustable pneumatic multiplier guns. That's for guys with no experience."

"My sales prospects don't have time for building a cozy relationship. They just want a competitive price, and I'm out of there."

In Julie Dirksen's insightful book on the challenges of changing behaviors, she notes, "People have a tendency to attribute other people's behavior to their innate character, whereas they explain their own actions as being due to circumstances."[12] Again, it's beliefs in control, whether they are founded on reality or not.

Training skills is hard when trainees don't see the need to learn them. Getting people to modify their performance is doubly difficult when they believe they know better. It's important to be aware of these circumstances and address them, as doing otherwise results in going through the motions without accomplishing anything.

Improving Behaviors

Training is pretty much always instituted for the purpose of changing behaviors. As Gloria Gery, the brilliant retired training industry guru, often said,

> Employers don't care about what their employees know, but they care very much about what their employees do. Employers want their people to perform as if they were experts, whether they are or not.

The operative system is this:

Current Skills → Current Beliefs → Current Behaviors → Current Outcomes

---

12   Julie Dirksen, *Talk to the Elephant: Design Learning for Behavior Change* (New Riders Publishing, 2023).

In the attempt to achieve better outcomes, training is often provided to upgrade skills. But if currently held beliefs are not addressed, outcomes often remain unchanged.

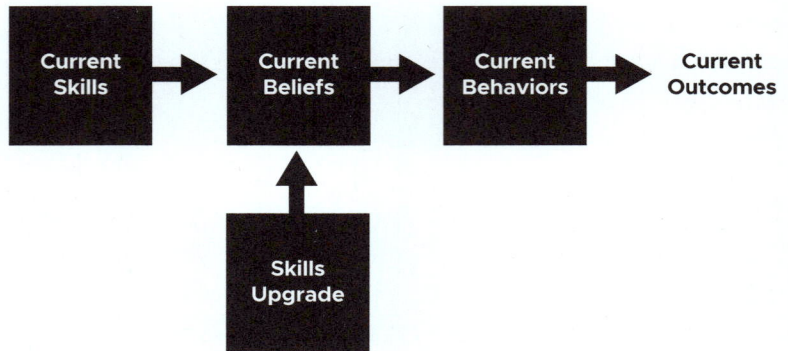

The problem isn't that training was the wrong solution. It was likely a necessary part of the solution, but only a part of the solution. And probably the wrong place to start.

Changing Beliefs

A better place to begin, given that desired performance and behavioral outcomes have been defined (see the Behavior Catalog in Chapter 16), is with addressing beliefs up front:

Changing beliefs isn't just a matter of telling someone what to believe.

My Story

I confessed to my mom one day that I was shy. Her response? "No, you're not."

Well, I'm still shy. Or at least I still feel and believe I'm shy. There's plenty of evidence in support of my beliefs (but I've gotten better not acting as shy as I feel).

It can be hard to change beliefs. But it's necessary to do so in order to establish new and sustained behavior patterns.

Two critical lessons here:

1. **You can't usually change someone's beliefs by telling them what they should believe.**
2. **It's hard to behave in ways contrary to your beliefs.**

In my personal experience, if I work extra hard at trying to believe, even for just the afternoon, that I'm not shy, I manage to get much more comfortable in social situations. I always benefit from them, so a helpful competing belief is that overcoming my shyness is beneficial and usually pleasant after all (even though I often find myself soon wanting to retire to a quiet place—old beliefs are hard to extinguish).

A third, primary, and critically important lesson for successful training is this:

3. **Our beliefs are based on our personal experiences.**

Experiences Change Behaviors

Behaviors evolve and change much more readily by additional experiences than by contradictory information. While we may question the veracity of information, we are strongly disposed to believe our experiences.

"I can't believe what just happened!" is the sign of a person recognizing a conflict between their beliefs and an experience. Creating such experiences within training programs opens the door to a change in beliefs, which, in turn, can provide the necessary support for changing behavior.

This insight is particularly good news and explains why so many training programs fail. In addition, we understand better and remember our experiences better than things we've just seen or read about, so we have a chance of solving two major problems, change and retention, with one solution!

Beliefs as a Tool

Since current beliefs can sabotage behavior change efforts, it's best to take on beliefs immediately and directly rather than hoping they won't get in the way. If problematic beliefs aren't altered, they'll rule the day, eventually, if not immediately, thwarting training efforts.

Thank you for showing me those examples! They really look amazing. Our company has just barely looked into 3D and we haven't implemented anything around it yet.

Great, that's no problem. Can we start by talking about what your current product image workflow looks like and any challenges you might be experiencing?

Right now, we have graphic designers who do photography and editing in Software A and Software B. It sounds simple and straightforward, but it can be slow and costly. With all our new products and variations, we need to produce more images faster than we currently can—despite our proficiency with the tools.

00:20 —————————————————————— 00:20

What should you say?

Tell me more. For example, have you put a budget in place to improve these bottlenecks?

Tell me more. How are those challenges impacting your organization?

Discovery Score

100%
60% (Your Goal)
0%

Q1   Q2   Q3   Q4   Q5

Thank you for showing me those examples! They really look amazing. Our company has just barely looked into 3D and we haven't implemented anything around it yet.

Great, that's no problem. Can we start by talking about what your current product image workflow looks like and any challenges you might be experiencing?

Right now, we have graphic designers who do photography and editing in Photoshop and Illustrator. It sounds simple and straightforward, but it can be slow and costly. With all our new products and variations, we need to produce more images faster than we currently can—despite our proficiency with the tools.

00:20 —————————————————————— 00:20

What should you say?

Tell me more. For example, have you put a budget in place to improve these bottlenecks?

Tell me more. How are those challenges impacting your organization?

Discovery Score

You're doing great! How are you feeling about this practice so far?

✓ I'm not sure how to address customer objections.
☐ I think I'll be fine after more practice.
☐ So far, so good.

Handling objections is challenging! Here's an example of a customer's concern and how to respond effectively.

100%
60% (Your Goal)

Q1   Q2   Q3

Handling Beliefs and Objections

Beliefs and Objections. *"This interactive conversation helps learners practice selling skills with virtual customers. Prompts for self-reflection guide learners to recognize their current beliefs. Reflection as part of the exercise opens the door for the intended change and retention. Learners can revisit key lessons as needed."* **Allen Interactions Inc.**

One means (as we'll see also when we address relevancy—another key influence on learning; see Chapter 29) is to begin with a dialogue, such as:

Belief as a Tool

EXAMPLE

"Do you believe your sales effectiveness would be improved by creating a custom strategic plan for each prospect?"

Learner's Answer	Response
☐ Yes, for sure.	That's great. Let's dive in.
☐ Probably.	We think so. Let's create one so you can judge for yourself.
☐ I really don't have time for that.	OK. Let's do a couple of things. (1) Let's look at a video of someone who thought it was too time-consuming at first but discovered her sales took a giant leap when she started doing strategic plans. (2) Let's create a plan together and time it. You might be surprised how quickly you can do it.
☐ No, I don't need it.	Sales are that good! That's good to hear. But maybe, just maybe, you could stay at that level with less effort—or even improve. Let's do an experiment just to see what might happen.

Knowing the learner's perspective gives us a chance of engaging them more effectively, but we must then respond differentially and directly, starting perhaps with acknowledgments such as those above.

Learning experiences that relate to individual learner perspectives can diminish negative beliefs and deliver extraordinary performance improvements. We'll address practical means of establishing relevance beginning in Chapter 28.

CHAPTER 11

PASSIONATE DESIGN

I'm always questioning as I design, if I had the choice, *Would I elect to learn this content in this way? Would this be my first choice? If it wouldn't, why am I creating this?* If I wouldn't like my design, why should I expect anyone to like it?

Put more positively, I'm also always questioning, even if I thought my initial designs were good, *What would I wish for if I could have any learning experience I wanted? What would I find most helpful and the best use of my time and energy? **What might be unexpected, appreciated, and even delightful?** Can I make that happen?*

Effort vs. Objectivity

The more effort we put into a product, the more we naturally think it's good. Learners are surely going to appreciate the learning experiences we created. But our effort is not a yardstick learners use to evaluate their experience. They don't care about the time and effort we invested; they care about theirs. Rightly so.

Increased effort means decreased objectivity.

How can we be sure our designs are good? It's pretty easy. Consider the following expedient, simple, and valuable evaluations, asking yourself, *Is every minute learners spend in our program going to be worthwhile?*

Remember . . .

- When learners give us their time, we have an obligation to use it for their benefit.

- If we waste learners' time, perhaps because creating something more effective appears too hard, too expensive, or too time-consuming, learners can't get a refund. Their time is gone forever. Why should they thank us for wasting their time?

- As we go through the design process, we should be mindful to question ourselves: *Is what I'm offering learners going to be the best use of their time and energy?*

- If the answer is no, stop. Come up with something different. Your time is valuable, of course. Just as with learners, once you've spent it, you can't get it back. So, we don't just want to go through a routine, filling in the blanks of a template and calling it good enough. It's important to do good design because, especially with elearning, it's possible a large number of people, quite possibly over years, will be investing their time.

Ask a Friend: What Would Be Better?

Using your likes and dislikes as a guide seems like a pretty simple and obvious criterion, yet often other factors take control, such as what an authoring system makes easy to do. Our preferences aren't infallible, but they provide a good place to start. If you don't find your design engaging, perhaps even intriguing and fun, others are pretty likely to feel the same way. But if you really like what you're doing, will others have the same reaction?

The next step is to ask a friend, spouse, or someone less involved in the design and more like your learners than yourself. Ask what might be better, not just if they like what they're seeing. Otherwise, friends are likely to say what they think you want to hear.

Again, this seems like a pretty simple and obvious thing to do. But I think it's not done enough. Getting honest and objective reactions as early as it makes smart sense to do can help make sure you're on a promising path.

Ask Learners: What's Your Frank and Honest Assessment?

The genuine experts on how learners will engage are, of course, the learners. When we discuss the Successive Approximations Model (see Part 6) as a process for designing and developing elearning, we'll discuss how and when to involve learners for maximum advantage. It's probably earlier than you would expect. And so critically important. Even trying our best to think and react as we expect learners will, it can be very surprising to discover what learners find helpful and appealing and what they don't.

A Word About Authoring Tools

Good design may put you and your authoring tools in a boxing ring. Tools often make simplistic things gratifyingly quick and easy to do, while making the best things for learners hard and complicated to create. They tend to push us into repetitive, boring, and time-wasting paradigms, such as what I've called "tell-and-test" (see Allenism #14)— presenting content via text, graphics, or video and then questioning learners to see if they got the message.

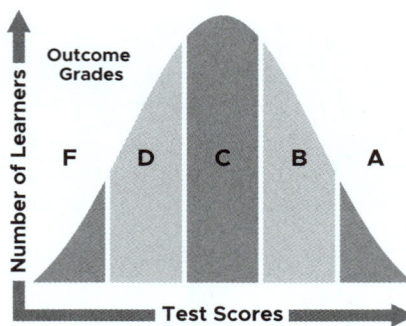

Tell-and-Test Isn't Teaching

It's clear many authoring tool developers and vendors think the market values ease of use and rapid development over quality of learning experiences. And, although I dearly hate to admit it, there's pretty strong supportive evidence. To me, this is exactly backwards.

Yes, I want speed. Yes, I want easy authoring. But of what? I want first and foremost to be able to build the learning experiences that will greatly benefit my learners. If you don't know how to build the learning experience you want for your learners, fret not. There are ways. Ways you can learn and are worthwhile learning. Find a capable authoring tool or a programmer to help you. We absolutely must find ways to overcome the sometimes-inimical influences of today's authoring tools or accept wasting the precious, irreplaceable time of learners (see the Serious eLearning Manifesto in Allenism #22).

_____

We must commit to creating the most effective learning experiences possible within our constraints. Before we compromise to producing boring learning experiences and other forms that have so little benefit, we must be sure we can't do what we need to do.

Throughout this book, I'm relaying ideas for how to design and build learning experiences that work exceedingly well and yet aren't unreasonably challenging to create. But when we can't produce what's needed, as professional trainers we absolutely must push for constraint relief. Producing ineffective programs hurts our clients, our organizations, and our own credibility.

DESIGNER'S NOTEBOOK #2

Self-check: See if you garnered these takeaway principles and are ready to use them.

☐ Since an unmotivated learner will learn little, if anything, and a highly motivated learner will find ways to learn, an important means to achieving instructional success is to boost learning motivation (rather than make do with whatever motivation learners happen to arrive with).

☐ If possible, people gravitate to behaving in accordance with their beliefs regardless of what they are told or taught to do.

☐ Experiences, not information, are the bases of beliefs. So, to change beliefs and therefore behaviors, we need to provide learning experiences and not rely on providing information.

☐ Learners don't rate and respond to instructional programs based on how much time and effort we put into creating them, but our objectivity does. So it's important to get reactions from others early enough in the process that we can make whatever alterations are called for.

☐ Most authoring tools today tend to impose structures and limitations that ease development of "tell-and-test" and complicate development of highly adaptive individualized elearning.

BUYER'S CHECKLIST #2

To ensure a great investment in training and ROI, be sure to ask the following questions.

☐ Motivation is essential to learning. While training often ignores the fact and works without assessing motivation and pumping up low motivation, there are instructional techniques such as game-based simulations, amusing consequences, and performance score cards to increase learning motivation. Are these effective techniques used or proposed?

☐ People behave in line with their personal beliefs. Managerial directions often fail if they go contrary to beliefs, which ultimately win over. Does the training address learner beliefs to help achieve behavioral change?

☐ Beliefs are formed from experiences. So, the way to change behaviors is not by giving orders (which have only temporary effects when contrary to beliefs) but by providing experiences that change beliefs. Do you see the training providing such experiences?

☐ One way to decide whether a vendor or a courseware package is right for you is to go through their courseware as a learner yourself. If you find it boring, confusing, or lacking in other ways, chances are good your employees will too. Have you taken the time to personally experience the training produced by your prospective vendors?

Part 3

eLEARNING = INDIVIDUALIZED INTERACTIVE LEARNING

The preponderance of my work over the last 55 years has focused on elearning. I'm still learning and working to fully understand and harness all the advantages it offers while being alert to the downsides. I continue to see individualized, interactive learning experiences as a primary justification of elearning because they are so effective and yet impractical, if not impossible, via other delivery platforms.

My Story

Through some introspection, I've realized I probably value individualization so highly because of some personal grade school experiences in which some students, including me, were treated by our teachers as not so smart because we were dyslexic or just slow readers. Others got the same assessment because they weren't artistic, good spellers, interested in history, or mathematically inclined. Some of my classmates came to accept a diminished view of themselves, which has been a difficult impediment to overcome.

From comments at class reunions decades later, it was clear that unfortunate assessments were ingrained in us. Some were stymied by them, while others found the wherewithal to shake them off—even feeling motivated by the challenge.

What I saw going on and experienced myself in school led me to realize that all of us can learn better, faster, and even more easily if instructional experiences are sensitive to our individual differences and provide the support we need.

Only elearning can provide individualized instruction in practical ways for any number of learners, but only if we design and build it to do so.

So, let's do so! I'd like to help you if I can.

CHAPTER 12

WHY INDIVIDUALIZED eLEARNING?

Why do we create elearning, any elearning?

Because we love computers? No.

Because we're lazy? No. (Well, sometimes.)

Because we don't like teaching? Heavens, no. Many of us love to teach.

Why, then?

Because we want optimal performance outcomes in the shortest time possible.

Because we want to reach learners wherever they may be located and whenever they have time to learn.

Because learners have individual needs.

Because it's available 24/7 as learners have time in their individual schedules.

Because developing skills requires practice (different amounts for different folks).

Because expert teachers are in short supply.

Because we want learning to be fun.

And, oh, yes:

Because we want to reduce our training costs while meeting all the needs and opportunities above.

And because so many of us are now working from home.

Let's take up these reasons one at a time.

Why eLearning?

- **Because we want optimal performance outcomes in the shortest time possible.** There are many inefficiencies in classroom-based and distance learning programs that deliver the same instructional content in the same sequence, at the same speed, and in the same way for all learners. That's necessary for almost all forms of instructional delivery other than elearning. With elearning, however, we can make sure we're not teaching skills an individual learner has already developed and that we provide the instruction and practice where it's needed. With responsive branching based not only on entry skills, but also by continually observing learner performance, elearning delivers optimal performance outcomes in the shortest time possible.

- **Because we want to reach learners wherever they may be located and whenever they have time to learn.** It costs a lot to transport learners to a school or training facility, not only in direct expenses, but also in non-learning time spent getting there and back. It can also be disruptive to operations if groups of people need to be taken off the job all at the same time as may be necessary to fill classes and optimize availability of instructors, classrooms, labs, and so on.

- In addition, some learners find they're most able to focus early or at other times in the day. Some may find short learning periods optimal and perhaps value the flexibility to work them into a busy schedule, while others prefer to really dig in for an intensive period of study. All such variations are no problem for elearning.

- **Because learners have individual needs.** I don't think it can be said too many times, given how often individual needs go unrecognized by the organization's desire for easy management of standard classes with lockstep programs keeping all learners studying the same thing at the same time and providing the certainty of when classes will conclude. These organizational conveniences are so desirable that insensitivity to individuals becomes acceptable, even expected. Only some learners will reach proficiency, while some will have wasted time because they were already proficient and still others will drop out (if allowed) because pacing was too fast or too slow or any of a number of other reasons. But with elearning, we have the adaptive means to be sure each learner receives training relevant to their needs and goals and keeps learning motivation and engagement strong so that outcome proficiency is assured.

- **Because developing skills requires practice (different amounts for different folks).** Practice is essential to building complex skills or infrequently performed skills to be sustained over time. We can cram for tests and then quite efficiently forget much of what we've learned in a remarkably short time. Deeply internalizing skills and developing new and efficient habits requires practice. The more complicated tasks are to perform, the more practice is needed. And yes, individualization again: Some of us need more practice on some skills than others. eLearning is tireless and patient. It can generate an infinite number of problem variations for learners to practice with. And it can continuously measure how much more practice is needed on specifically identified skills.

- One practical and powerful bonus of elearning, often overlooked, is that practice can be incrementally and beneficially spaced over time for each learner regardless of when they finished a course. So-called massed practice (i.e., cramming) helps learners do well on post-tests but is susceptible to rapid forgetting. But when practice is distributed over time with the time gaps between practice sessions increasing over days, weeks, months, and even years, retention can be maintained at very high levels. Eventually becoming permanent and needing no further practice.

- **Because expert teachers are in short supply.** Organizations often prefer to have apprentices learn from their most talented and successful performers. They want the best practices of their experts replicated. But they also want to keep those highly skilled people on the job, performing the tasks they perform so well. They don't want them being unbillable, as they are when they're teaching. In elearning, we can work with the best of the best to fashion programs that encapsulate the principles and processes top performers use and make sure that's what each novice learns. The top performers can then maximize their time on the job.

- **Because we want learning to be fun.** Some instructors are inspiring. Some are entertaining. Some know how to keep learners focused. Some sense when to adapt on the spot to keep learners energized. But not a lot of instructors are good at these skills, nor good at them all the time, even though they recognize the importance of engaging learners. Game designers have discovered many ways to keep players focused, engaged, improving, and having fun. eLearning, when designed well, can keep learning fun, rewarding, and impactful—making adjustments consistently to keep it that way.

- **Because we want to reduce our training costs.** Training is expensive, not so much because of how much it costs to develop but because of the time it takes learners away from their jobs.

My Story

When I asked the VP of Sales in a large company what his top three training wishes were, his first wish was that he could hire people who needed no training and could hit the road selling effectively on their first day.

"Okay. What's your second wish?"

He replied, "That I could shorten our training time significantly. It's so expensive paying people who aren't yet providing any value."

Whether training new hires or upskilling the present workforce, nonproductive time is expensive. And if that training isn't effective, the costs mount further. Individualized, interactive elearning can cut training time and costs significantly, often over 60% of traditional training methods.

- **Because so many of us are now working remotely.** Working from home is more possible now than ever, in large part because so many jobs are performed online. While there are advantages of face-to-face collaboration, it's clear a significant percentage of work will continue to be done remotely.

eLearning builds on delivery platforms already in place for many workers. It adapts to fluctuating available time and can provide just-in-time training as tasks may require.

The advantages of elearning are numerous, but as Allenism #38 says, "The most unaffordable training is training that doesn't work." Not all elearning provides all these advantages. Perhaps some elearning provides none of them. To glean these advantages requires design based on successful algorithms—the algorithms for success coming up in Part 4.

IS eLEARNING ALWAYS THE BEST OPTION?

No. Sometimes people just need information, a checklist, a video, or a cookbook.

No. Sometimes we really, really need a human mentor.

No. Sometimes we don't have enough learners to warrant developing elearning.

No. Sometimes we don't have enough time to create elearning.

No. Sometimes technology isn't available.

No. Sometimes training just isn't the best or even a workable solution.

And sometimes we really need a blended approach in which we use elearning for the things it does best complemented by additional instruction, coaching, and/or real-world practice.

Figure 13.1 provides a helpful decision tree for determining when elearning is an appropriate investment.

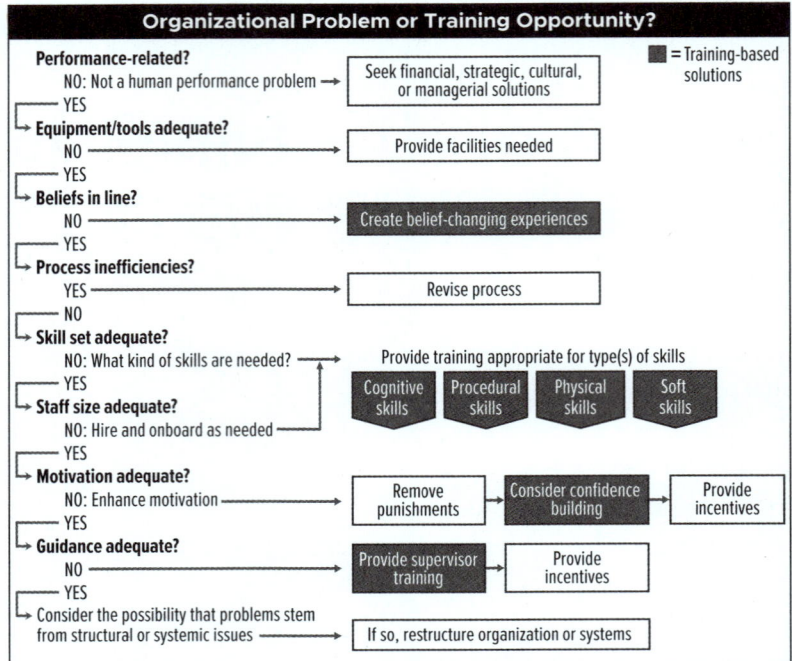

Figure 13.1. Decision Tree for Selecting Performance Solutions

Of Movies and the Stage

My Story

I once had a memorable conversation with the head of robotics at Carnegie Mellon about elearning and the clever ways it was being used in their physics department. Their platform was the PLATO system imported from the University of Illinois and Control Data Corporation. Somewhat out of the blue, he indicated his department was making some interesting advances in video distribution, and it was now possible for videos of classroom lectures to be played on TVs in lounges and in many places across campus.

He was ecstatic about this "futuristic" possibility.

Uh. Keeping my facial expression under control as best I could, I kept trying to say something other than, *"Why on earth would you want to do that?"*

In the face of his enthusiasm for video distribution of recorded lectures, I wasn't very successful in discussing with the robotics professor how interactivity is a primary way we learn. Beginning from birth we move, watch, make sounds, and begin making connections to the effects they have. While we can learn vicariously by watching and listening, learning that way is generally superficial and shallow.

But put your own finger in the flame. You remember that.

Why would you want to replicate the limitations of lecture-based learning?

There's something unique and special about passionate, articulate, and inspiring presenters. It's great to have them captured on video and have those resources available. But content presentation is only a part of effective instructional paradigms, not the whole or maybe even the most important part. There are better ways to teach.

Make Tasks Easier

Not all performance goals can or should be addressed by training. One of the most obvious questions to ask when considering a performance enhancement initiative is, *Can we make the job easier so there's less to learn? Can we / should we automate? Can we provide better tools to assist? Can we eliminate steps, forms, approvals, hoops, and barriers to provide a better level of service?*

If we can make a job easier, that might be a good solution. I say *might be* because efficiency isn't always master. Sometimes we want to make a process more personal, even getting more people involved to pursue building a stronger customer relationship. There are many circumstances when just making something easier doesn't address the primary goal as well as training does, but we shouldn't err in either direction. Being thoughtful and strategic is pretty important. Quite often, the best solution is both making a process easier and providing better training.

Use Video

With today's rapid pace and bombardment of information, patience for reading has dwindled.[13] Even patience for videos of more than a few minutes is scarce. YouTube Shorts consistently engage more viewers than long-form content, gaining 9x more interactions.[14] With the tendency of elearning designers to burden learners with exhaustive text, many look to video as the preferred instructional medium, even though it's a passive medium.

We've become a video culture heavy with digital devices, ubiquitous small screens, fueled further by pandemic-driven adaptation to remote work and videoconferencing. It would seem we would be desperate to escape screens whenever and wherever we could. But instead, we continue the rush toward more and more screen dependencies and more video.

But how good and useful is video for learning? It has its moments, as shown in the table on page 99.

---

13 Christopher Allen, "Every Word Counts," *TD Magazine* 78(5) (2024): 26–31.
14 Quinn Schwartz, "The Rise of YouTube Shorts + How to Include Them in Your Influencing Marketing Strategy," Grin, https://grin.co/blog/youtube-shorts-in-influencer-marketing/.

Performance Improvement Options

	Task Modification	Instruction	
		via Video	via eLearning
Task complexity	Simplify where possible	Good for simple tasks	Good for entire range, simple to complex
Risk	Reduce errors through clarity and safeguards	Can dramatically communicate risk and prevention techniques	Provides safe practice Simulates outcomes
Frequency	Save significant total time and errors in high-frequency tasks	Good (although slow) for on-demand help with infrequent tasks	Good for internalized proficiency; less so for very infrequent tasks
Retention		Generally poor	Good, especially with practice spaced over time
New terms and concepts		Generally poor	Introduces terms as useful tools when applicable
Varied entry skills and motivation			Individualization capabilities to maximize learning

When video is used specifically as an aid to learning, it can add energy and dramatic components to stimulate motivation and interest. It can communicate mechanical, process, or conceptual information and data better than text in most cases. But unless video is used interactively, video communication for learning tends to fall short, surprisingly so for retention and skills development.

Leadership Development: The Blame Game

Effective Video

EXAMPLE

Interactive Video. *"This scenario-driven, third-person role-play video is a fun, engaging way to apply the behavioral concepts that beliefs drive behavior and people resist changing strategies until they experience better results through alternate means. It encourages exploration and team collaboration."* **Allen Interactions Inc.**

Performance Support vs. eLearning

Sometimes internalizing information and procedures isn't necessary. If we can provide guidance in real time as tasks are being performed, it's not only sufficient but also sometimes preferable. We call this assistance "Performance Support" (sometimes EPSS for Electronic Performance Support Systems), and while it helps people navigate through tasks, it shouldn't be confused with training, which intends to enable performance without support present.

Video doesn't always work well as a Performance Support aid. Some of the common circumstances that rule out Performance Support are:

- When you don't have space or support for a digital device you can easily see and control while you work

- When there are in-process decisions to be made that require adding, omitting, or rearranging steps

- When there is a requirement for applying corrective actions very quickly

Remember, Performance Support isn't really about learning and retention; it's about getting a specific job done with minimal advance training or learning. It can be a terrific solution, especially for safe, relatively simple, and infrequently done tasks. In that sense, it's a solution similar to task modification, such as simplifying the system or using specialized tools, neither of which are about learning. But both can be appropriate and effective performance solutions.

Retention

My Story

Our company used to teach the use of software tools in a classroom setting. (It was actually the primary service of Allen Interactions when we founded the company.) We had a high-tech learning center with multiple presentation screens that could be commanded to show demonstrations and student work screens in real time. We would show students how to perform tasks, have them perform those very tasks along with the instructor, and then ask them to perform the tasks again on their own. It seemed like a great instructional process and learning opportunity. But it wasn't.

Almost immediately after students began performing tasks on their own, hands went up for help. *"How did you do that second thing?"* *"I chose the wrong option. How do I correct it?"* We had asked, of course, does everyone feel ready to do the task on your own? Yeses all around. But they didn't know they weren't ready until they tried their hand at it. Thankfully we had a live instructor to help, although usually only one, but the process was all wrong. We completely changed up our teaching methods by teaching basic principles first, demonstrating one application of them, and then giving learners a problem they hadn't seen before. We gave them only hints of what to think about when they floundered.

By reasoning out solutions and trying them, learners knew they would be able to solve this and similar problems in the future on their own.

Video and even live lectures and demonstrations are one-way communications that easily yield a false sense of learning. "Click along with me" would seem effective at the time, but learners are just practicing their follow along skills, not thinking through the logic and steps of performing a task. Even any kind of "Let me show you how" rarely provides learning that sticks, let alone enough understanding to solve problems and adapt a solution when needed.

Skills Development

Knowledge is fundamental to performance but also fundamentally different from performance ability. We can know how something should be done without having the slightest capability to do it. In most situations, training programs that only impart knowledge fail to produce what's most needed.

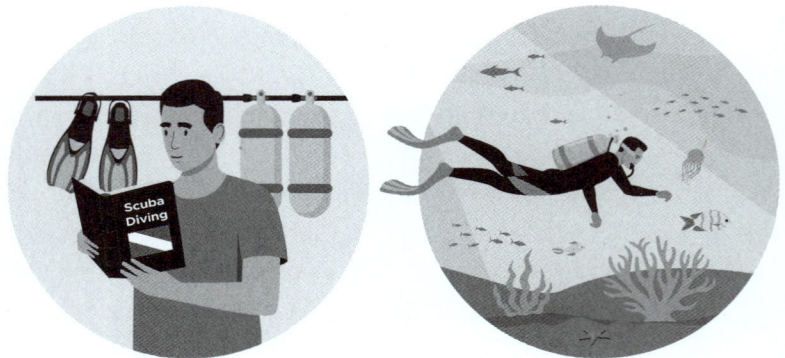

As described in our software training scenario, a presentation (live in our case, but it would have been even worse on video) typically fails to teach knowledge well. It has even less power to help learners develop skills.

Sedative Agents

Review of Systems

- General: Usually healthy, no recent fevers
- Ear/Nose/Throat: No runny nose or nasal congestion; no snoring or apnea since his T&A
- Feeding/Nutrition: No vomiting or diarrhea; Grandmother says he is a very picky eater but snacks a lot and drinks lots of juice
- Gastrointestinal System: No frequent vomiting
- Respiratory: No asthma, wheezing, cough, or pneumonia
- Sleeps lying flat
- Cardiovascular: Able to play and keep up with other children his age

NPO: Last fatty meal greater than 8 hours, last clears greater than 2 hours

Choose a sedative and analgesic combination regimen, and then select **Submit**.

Sedative Agents	Analgesic Agents
Benzodiazepines	Opioids
Barbiturates	Ketamine
Propofol	

Refer to the Medication Section of the SPS Provider Course Syllabus for more detailed information about the use and properties of these agents.

Submit

Society for Pediatric Sedation (SPS)

Learning Complex Skills. *"This course is for non-anesthesiologists who sedate children outside of the operating room. (Think dental procedure or MRI for a young child.) Each of the four modules walks through a different case study—each with an increasing level of case complexity. Learners go through the on-the-job tasks such as reviewing charts and talking to family members. Then they make decisions about what to do."*
Artisan Learning

Complexity

EXAMPLE

If Not eLearning, What?

What if elearning isn't the best delivery option? Does it mean we need different design principles?

No. The design principles that make elearning most effective make other delivery platforms more effective as well, but only as far as those platforms have the necessary capabilities. In designing elearning with our recommended approaches, learners are kept active immediately and throughout. The so-called passive learning that's supposed to happen in presentation-based delivery struggles to maintain learner engagement and doesn't provide essential practice.

Active learning can be delivered without using an elearning platform, of course. Many schoolteachers have found innovative ways both to keep learners active and to provide a good dose of individualization. In one model, learning is done by having small teams do projects. The projects require application of principles to be learned—principles that are either presented ahead of time in short presentations or discovered as teams work on projects. The teacher circulates, observes, and asks questions more often than giving instruction. Students learn from their work, from each other, and from the teacher.

Mentors and coaches typically keep learners active as well. Flipped classrooms in which learners read or watch videos as homework in lieu of sitting through in-class teacher presentations reserve classroom time for activities. But what's common among all these alternatives is that they are not scalable to large or distributed audiences. With elearning, once a course has been made active and adaptive for any one unknown learner, it's deliverable, almost cost free, to an unlimited number of learners, wherever they are and whenever they have time to learn.

Here's a twist: It can be wise in some situations to experiment with interactive, individualized instruction without digital delivery prior to implementing it via elearning. You will be able to instruct only a few learners in this role-playing manner because the student-to-instructor ratio will have to be very small. It's probably best to mentor just one student at a time with you playing the role you are designing the software to play. Even role-playing with only a few students, you may learn quite a bit about the strengths and weaknesses of your design before you begin building elearning.

DESIGNER'S NOTEBOOK #3

eLearning is often used for pragmatic reasons:

- [ ] It's available 24/7 as learners have time in their individual schedules.

- [ ] It can reach across distances, benefiting the many trainees who are working remotely.

- [ ] Delivery is inexpensive (almost free).

- [ ] Content can be updated and distributed instantly.

- [ ] Expert teachers are in short supply.

Beyond pragmatics, from a learning point of view, there is a long list of reasons elearning is the instructional platform of choice but which are realized only if elearning is used in ways that take advantage of its capabilities.

Potential instructional advantages to consider include:

- [ ] Achieving deeper learning from each learner performing tasks in a simulated environment and witnessing the consequences of their actions

- [ ] Achieving optimal outcomes in the shortest time possible through performance-sensitive responsive branching

- ☐ Improving retention through spaced practice, perhaps prompted via email/text notices

- ☐ Ramping up engagement, motivation, and fun via gamification and active learning

- ☐ Overcoming barriers of high and low self-efficacy

- ☐ Using Performance Support for live on-the-job guidance where applicable

BUYER'S CHECKLIST #3

There are solid, pragmatic reasons for using elearning. Are you situated to take advantage of these attributes?

- ☐ It's available 24/7 as learners have time in their individual schedules.

- ☐ It can reach across distances, benefiting the many trainees working remotely.

- ☐ Delivery is inexpensive (almost free).

- ☐ Content can be updated and distributed instantly.

- ☐ It is useful when expert teachers are in short supply.

But all these advantages mean little if the elearning program doesn't develop the skills needed. And it's very easy to develop elearning that doesn't achieve that primary goal.

Are you looking for programs that:

- ☐ Challenge learners to make good decisions and perform authentically simulated tasks?

- ☐ Avoid a lot of on-screen text (as people have become poor, impatient readers)?

☐ Ramp up motivation and make sure learners experience the personal relevancy of learning new skills?

☐ Use performance aids instead of learning programs when tasks are rarely performed and depend only on basic skills?

Part 4

ACHIEVING SUCCESS

"If you don't know where you are going,
you'll end up someplace else."

Robert Mager keyed into Yogi's wisdom when he introduced instructional objectives as a design tool in 1962, saying, "If you're not sure where you're going, you're liable to end up someplace else."[15] Mager suggested instructional objectives should always describe:

- For whom these objectives are applicable
- Observable behavior
- Conditions under which learners must perform that behavior
- The level of performance perfection required

Yogi Berra

15   Robert F. Mager, *Preparing Instructional Objectives* (West Yorkshire, UK: Pitman Learning, 1975).

Structured instructional objectives have been valuable to designers since then and remain a foundational approach to design. But contrary to common practice, jumping into writing instructional objectives *is not* the place to start, as we'll discuss in more detail in Book 3: "How to Build eLearning."

Mager appropriately differentiated goals from objectives. At the outset, every project needs a clearly stated goal or definition of success. In other words, what are we trying to achieve?

Defining how we will know if we've achieved the goal is something of a test for the success definition. Considering the challenges and pragmatics of how a project's success will be measured often causes a constructive reconsideration of the success definition. If you can't or wouldn't measure the impact, you won't know if you've achieved it. No one wants that. Yet that's the situation many projects end up in.

Instructional designers and clients alike often skip over two fundamental questions—*How is success defined for this training?* and *How will that success or failure be measured?*—perhaps because everyone thinks the answers are obvious and unanimous agreed. But whatever the reason, it's a big mistake not to get clear answers up front.

In Part 4, we'll look closely at methods to ensure outcome successes are achieved.

CHAPTER 14

THE PERFORMANCE IMPROVEMENT GOAL

Sometimes the primary goal gets lost while managing the many complications of developing and delivering training programs. It's not just individuals who sometimes lose sight of the goal; it can be whole organizations from top to bottom, including the training development team. Each person becomes tightly focused on their individual responsibilities and doing their work the best they know how. Designers, writers, media developers, programmers, subject matter experts, and so on all working diligently can roll out a creative, appealing program that is enthusiastically received by trainees. On time. On budget. Accurate and comprehensive.

And ineffective.

The primary goal isn't to be creative, appealing, on time, on budget, accurate, or comprehensive, although they're all important. The goal is to change performance for the better.

My Story

In a project team meeting at the University of Minnesota, I was stunned to hear a professor from another Big 10 university make this statement, word for word:

> *"We all know training programs don't change behavior. Never have. Never will."*

Allen Interactions was engaged by the university to design and develop an Internet-delivered program intended to modify intractable unhealthy habits. It was a research project funded by the National Institutes of Health and admittedly attempting to tackle a tough challenge. For objectivity, a different Big 10 university was engaged to conduct an unbiased evaluation of our study.

I liked the setup. Conscientious. Good science. Serious. Great subject matter experts. It was a terrific opportunity for us. Spoiler alert: The project turned out to be impressively successful, earning commendations from NIH. But that's not really the point I want to make here.

Startled by the professor's assertion that training programs never change behavior, I had trouble staying seated. I probably spoke a little louder than I intended in my rebuttal. I did my best to remain calm and credible. My response was a question: *"Why, then, would we ever bother with training? Or any educational program, for that matter?"*

In my view, both education and training have the same goal—enabling *and motivating* effective behavior. There's really no other reason for it, is there? It's true, many instructional programs don't do it well, but even those that just focus on knowledge acquisition assume (rightly or wrongly, mostly wrongly) that newly acquired knowledge will result in some form of performance success even if it's only becoming able to discuss a topic intelligently. It's easy to be "successful" with training by measuring the wrong things, such as the number of learners put through or the lack of complaints or technical issues. Even post-test scores can give a spurious reading (see Allenism #19).

It's risky to assume knowledge acquisition, especially that measured by multiple-choice questions, will alone produce new desired behaviors. It might or might not, so why not focus directly on the desired outcomes: enabling behaviors that lead to the defined measurable success goal?

It's easy to be "successful" with training by measuring the wrong things.

CHAPTER 15

BAD ASSUMPTIONS RUN RAMPANT

Success almost always comes from one thing—and the same thing: doing the right thing at the right time.

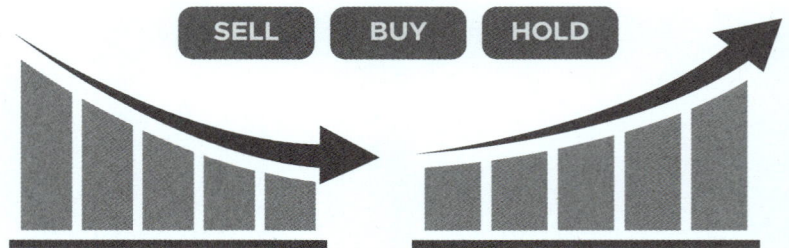

Success Is Doing the Right Thing at the Right Time

Whether it's personal success or organizational success, value is created by the things people do. And success comes only if we do the right things at the right times—not from just being able to correctly answer multiple-choice questions about how it should be done.

Assumptions are always risky. Assuming an instructional program will enhance an organization's success is a big assumption built on a lot of other assumptions. A few common but hazardous assumptions are:

- "We know what performance changes will achieve our goals."

- "Our employees aren't doing what they need to be doing because they don't know how."

- "If our employees knew *how* to perform better, they would. Our employees are always eager to change and improve."

- "Our disappointing profitability is a result of our poor onboarding."

What companies intend to achieve with instructional programs is improved business, organizational performance, and, typically, improved employee retention. They aim to reduce risk and accidents while improving the human performance that leads to functional and/or monetary success.

The linkage of expected training outcomes to organizational goals needs to be made explicit at the start of training development projects. When assumptions are stated in black and white, they often sound naive, and that's good because assumptions need to be questioned.

Questioning Assumptions

Let's challenge the example assumptions above individually:

- **"We know what performance changes will achieve our goals."** Okay, but have all the barriers to success been identified and evaluated? Such as:

  - Might there be more work than the staff or system can handle?
  - Are products and services priced competitively and also providing sufficient margin?
  - Are targets being missed because of poor products or out of date information?
  - Are customer relationships leading to repeat business or one-offs?

- **"Our employees aren't doing what they need to be doing because they don't know how."** There are many other reasons employees might not be doing what's desired. Such as, they:

  - Don't know what's desired.
  - Don't have the information needed to do it.
  - Don't have time because of higher priority demands.
  - Don't have the necessary resources or equipment.
  - Are rewarded for doing something else.

- **"If our employees knew *how* to perform better, they would. Our employees are always eager to change and improve."** Employees might know full well how to perform better or as directed, but they might:

  - Hate doing it. So, they avoid it, procrastinate, or do it in a way they prefer.
  - Be criticized by coworkers for showing off (the dreaded smarty-pants syndrome).
  - Finish faster, resulting in fewer chargeable hours and therefore see their income or apparent value to the organization reduced.
  - Lack confidence and fear the embarrassment of making mistakes.

- **"Our disappointing profitability is a result of our poor onboarding."** Profitability is a function of many things. Lack of it could be due to factors completely unrelated to employee skills:

  - Pricing too low or carrying high overhead.
  - Competitors having access to lower-cost resources.
  - Competitors having better equipment.
  - Employees in other organizations are more actively recognized for performance excellence.

Many factors determine behaviors. Some may be hidden, disguised, or simply overlooked. It's often the case that some primary influences are not obvious. In defining success for training programs, it's critical at the outset to affirm that improved performance of specifically identified behaviors would contribute to that success.

CHAPTER 16

DOING THE RIGHT THING AT THE RIGHT TIME

We'll start with a critical question: How do we define training success? It's important to be specific about the success target, because otherwise, how would we measure it?

As mentioned in Chapter 10, the brilliant and hilarious Gloria Gery pointed out, *"Employers don't care what their employees know."*

Wow! Wait! What?

"No," she said, *"employers care only if their employees are performing as if they were experts."*

It's only the performance that matters, not just the knowledge of how it should be done. Adding some multiple-choice questions after content presentations doesn't tell us if learners can do the right thing at the right time, unless we're training them only to answer multiple-choice questions. Even if all learners scored 100% on questions, would we know if our training was successful? No, not in most cases.

EPSS—Electronic Performance Support Systems

Gloria was making her statement in promotion of what she coined Electronic Performance Support Systems (EPSS), which are aids to guide performance in real time. We see EPSS at work everywhere today, such as in the online systems that bankers, gate agents, and call centers use. Even doctors use EPSS to guide them through asking essential questions, evaluating answers, retrieving and recording data, and following up with more questions as may be necessary. These performers and many others are guided by their data entry screens every step along the way, their expertise guided or even provided by the system.

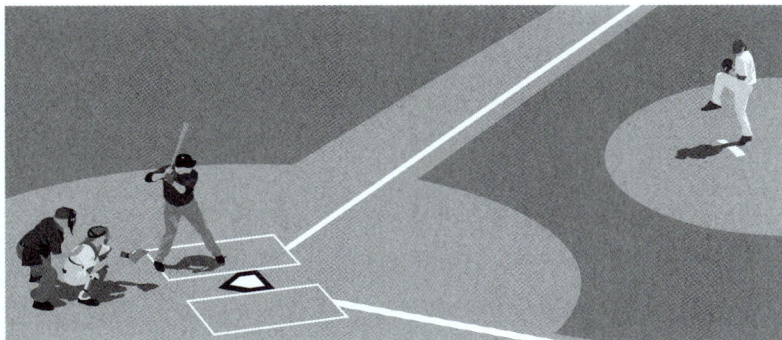

When It's Time to Perform, It's Too Late to Practice

It's not what we know that provides value; it's what we actually do. It matters little whether our guidance comes from internal knowledge or an EPSS as long as we *do the right thing at the right time.* With our digital devices handier and more mobile than ever before, EPSS solutions are increasingly practical and have the advantage of being kept up to date instantly.

Training must always fit the situation and prepare people to perform by teaching required levels of knowledge and providing opportunities to practice until they are ready to perform, with or without an EPSS as appropriate.

Internalized knowledge and skills are always with us, and they keep our eyes, ears, and hands fully available to perform tasks. You can't always take the time to look something up in a manual or online, nor even take your eyes off your task to read a checklist. An EPSS can be present and used in many situations, while in others, it would interfere with the speed and responsive performance that are critical to success. If you're high up on a power pole to reconnect live wires damaged in a storm, taking your eyes off the task to use an EPSS could threaten your life. Although even here, with advanced technology, a body or helmet camera can allow experts on the ground or artificial intelligence to analyze the situation and give the repairperson step-by-step instructions.

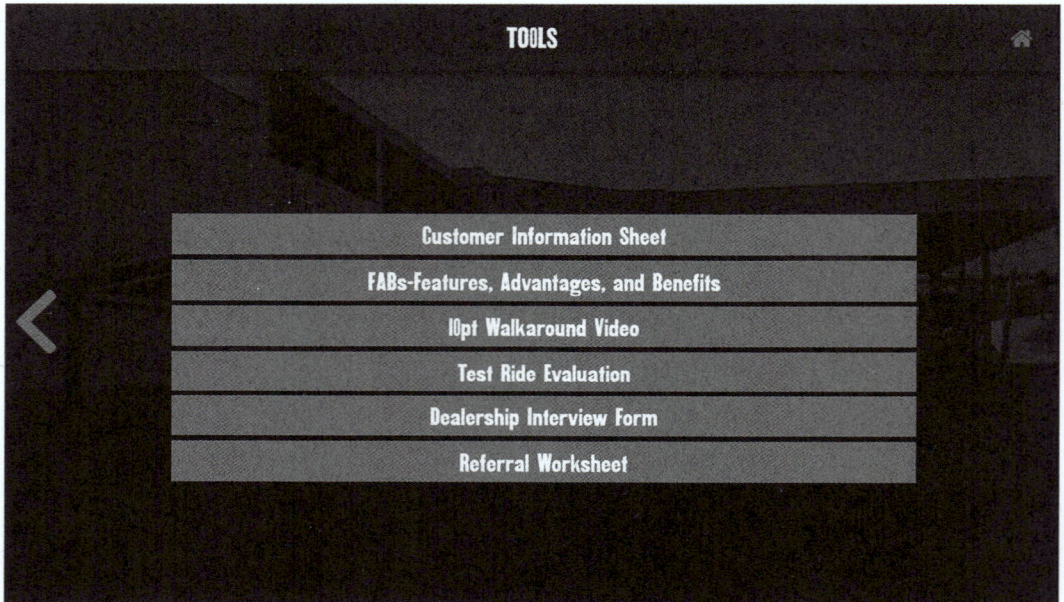

TOOLS

- Customer Information Sheet
- FABs-Features, Advantages, and Benefits
- 10pt Walkaround Video
- Test Ride Evaluation
- Dealership Interview Form
- Referral Worksheet

EPSS Supports Motorcycle Sales

EPSS

EXAMPLE

Practical Sales Support. *"This project provided learners with access to microlearning resources and other job aids to supplement their formal training. These tools enabled them to perform tasks promptly during a complex sales process."* **Allen Interactions Inc.**

Matching Instructional Experiences to Desired Outcomes

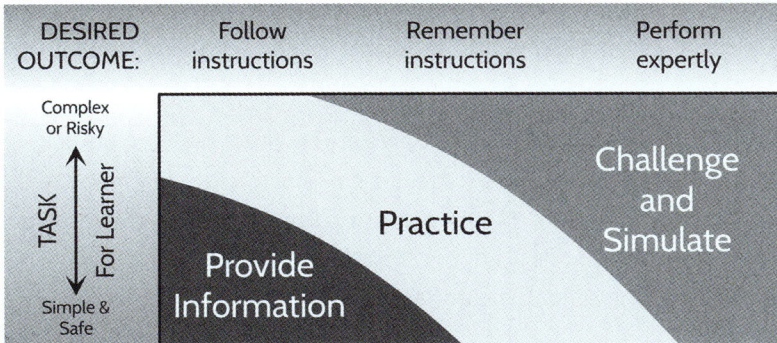

Figure 16.1. *Decision Matrix for Choosing Appropriate Instructional Strategies*

To use the decision matrix in Figure 16.1, follow these steps:

1. **Determine the type of desired outcome.** Will learners have instructions to follow as they perform their task(s)? Or must they have memorized the process(es)? Or must they perform expertly, knowing the generally applicable process(es) to a sufficient depth such that they can identify when a unique solution is needed and perform it? Pick a corresponding column.

2. **Characterize the performance task.** Consider whether it is simple and safe or complex or risky. Where does it lie on the continuum?

3. **Find the intersection of outcome and task.** With the knowledge of these parameters, you can select to simply provide information, have learners practice until they are proficient in applying memorized processes, or provide a range of simulated challenges for learners to assess and solve.

For example, if a performance task is either complex or risky and cannot be assisted with an EPSS or other guidance, learners should be given simulated challenges and practice the applicable procedures until a high level of mastery and confidence are achieved.

Timing Matters

It's important to recognize both of the critical components in the goal of being able to do the right thing *at the right time* and not just focus on being able to do the right thing.

Timing is often a critical aspect of performance, not only performing tasks as fast as may be required, but also being able to determine when it's the right time. This involves practicing the skills of assessing situations, considering the things that could be done, determining whether anything should be done, and acting in a timely, effective manner.

Defining "Right Things" and "Right Times"

A great way to be sure projects focus on the right things from the start is to create a Behavior Catalog. The Behavior Catalog is a tool for identifying specific behaviors that—if performed well and at the right times—would result in identifiable, measurable value.

Specific essential behaviors are listed with expected business outcomes (positive, negative, strategic). Being explicit about the linkage of behaviors to valued outcomes at this detailed level not only provides great guidelines for designing instruction but also can provide justification for training initiatives and the basis for an adequate budget.

Example Behavior Catalog

Business Objective	Expected ROI
Increase tire sales by ≥15%	$250k net per year increase 260 days x 54 = 14,040 sales (currently 12,110) 1,930 increase x $150 avg sale = $289,500

Behavior	Type	Assessed By	Performed By	Headcount	Frequency
Recognize tire sale opportunity	Remember and follow instructions	Service Manager	Car Intaker	400 Nationwide	.5x/day/ Intaker = 200x/day
Measure tread wear	Remember and follow instructions	Service Manager	Service Technician	520 Nationwide	200x/day
Verify stock	Remember and follow instructions	Parts Manager	Service Technician	520 Nationwide	60x/day
Offer best current price	Follow offer guide instructions	Sales Manager	Service Rep	280 Nationwide	60x/day
Close sale	Perform expertly	Sales Manager	Service Rep	280 Nationwide	54x/day

Sample questions to be answered when creating a Behavior Catalog:

- What are the critical behaviors of a process/procedure?

- How many roles and individuals perform the behavior?

- With what frequency is the behavior performed?

- Are the behaviors measured? Can they be? Are they tied to current KPIs (Key Performance Indicators)?

- Is there risk to the business, actor, or others from poor performance? If yes, what are the potential consequences?

- Can talent be hired, or must the behavior be trained?

- Does compensation or management recognition drive performance? Are there incentives?

Justifying the Training Budget

One more and perhaps the most critical reason to create a Behavior Catalog: While completing the Behavior Catalog is an invaluable exercise for instructional design, its value is no less for the business justification of a training investment.

There have probably been very few cases, if ever, that training budgets were excessive or even sufficient for all that would seem justified in the eyes of a training development team. But we hear one earnest question pop up with regular frequency: *How do you get the budgets necessary to produce the kinds of training programs your studios produce?*

While our studios definitely do produce what would be considered "high-end" training programs, we've worked hard to develop methods of stretching budgets to the max. Using the principles and processes shared in this book, we are able to produce more engaging, individualized, and effective training projects than might be expected from typical budgets. But we always go for big benefits and returns, which are rarely achieved on bargain-basement budgets.

A strong success record definitely helps secure needed budgets. When that's not in place, being prepared to talk in specifics about how a training program is going to result in significant positive contributions to an organization's performance is mandatory. The Behavior Catalog is a great tool to prepare you for those discussions.

Additional considerations in the following chapters are related to the components of success. They will also help you make the case for the budgets you need.

CHAPTER 17

DEFINING *PROJECT* SUCCESS

There are multiple success measures for any learning project. It's obvious we want learning to occur, so that's one measure and not necessarily a simple measure. Learning outcomes are clearly an important measure of success, but sometimes the reality is that other achievements are weighted as heavily or more heavily, even to the exclusion of measures of learning and skills development. It's not unusual for project success to be defined in terms of:

- Development speed
- Smooth launch, on schedule
- Survey responses indicating learners like the training
- Specific media used, such as video or augmented reality
- Cost minimization / budget containment
- Visual appeal
- Brevity
- Novelty

While we may disagree about the appropriateness of various success criteria and object to constraints imposed, when such criteria remain in place, it's important to address them. We want *both* perceived success and real success—i.e., what we trainers think of as "real" success. In other words, we want to define project success in terms of performance improvement and impact on the organization's efforts to achieve their primary goals, such as profitability, reputation for quality, customer service excellence, and reduced employee attrition.

But we won't even have the opportunity to address learning and business goals if we can't meet the organization's or client's definition of project success.

Project Management

Leaving ADDIE for SAM

It's beyond the scope of this book to detail project management. It deserves its own treatise. However, in upcoming chapters, we will cover the important topics of how our process manages to blend creativity, efficiency, process, and communication into successful elearning projects. For more detail on project management, please see my book *Leaving ADDIE for SAM*.

It's most important to stress at this point that disregarding any project success criteria, as annoying as they might be, can result in major problems and even project cancellation. If the client organization has training on the critical path to product launch, it may be totally unacceptable and very costly for training to roll out late. If training required by law must be completed within the calendar year, but the company makes 80% of their profits in the fourth quarter, launching training in November is similarly costly and unacceptable.

If the requisitioning department's head feels a multiple-choice post-test is essential, it's not smart to disregard this preference hoping for approval when the final product rolls out with an authentic interactive simulation to measure performance proficiency instead. You might, however, suggest a delayed post-test. See Allenism #19.

Three Success Imperatives: Communication, Communication, Communication

My Story

With over 200 instructional designers and developers in our PLATO elearning teams at Control Data, all schooled and led by ADDIE experts (ADDIE = Analysis, Design, Development, Implementation, and Evaluation—a design and development model widely used in the 1970s), considerable volumes of courseware were produced each year.

Some of the elearning courseware was fantastic and rivals the best of what see being produced even today. But not everyone gave raving approval to the majority of the courses. Even those who actually did the design and development were regularly disappointed.

I had been a proponent of ADDIE and even taught it in graduate schools. But seeing such project missteps and failures, I started questioning ADDIE as an effective framework. As I interviewed clients and development teams, I repeatedly heard comments such as these:

"I was so surprised to see the final course. It seemed completely different from what I imagined and expected from our discussions."

"I was excited about the ideas we had for interactivity. Why were they abandoned?"

"Very significant content elements are missing. Learners will be handicapped on the job without that knowledge."

For more on ADDIE, see Chapter 30.

I can't stress too much how important it is to identify expectations and constraints and then communicate throughout the project about how they are being addressed. When we delve into our Successive Approximations Model (SAM) in Part 6, we'll discuss in detail how communications are primary.

If you're using another model, consistent communications and a constant eye on the target criteria will be just as important, if not more so. Communicate, communicate, communicate!

CHAPTER 18

DEFINING *LEARNING* SUCCESS

Behavioral Objectives

Since 1962, when Robert Mager defined the components of instructional objectives, instructional objectives have been a mainstay of professional instructional design and continue to be powerful tools. They provide both a map of where we're trying to take our learners and the means of measuring success in terms of performance outcomes.

The ABCD (Audience, Behavior, Conditions, Degree) mnemonic and concept are powerful and perhaps deceptively simple, yet too often one or more of its essential components is ignored.

Required Elements of Behavioral Objectives

- **Audience**—If it's all about learners, who are they? We need to find out rather than assume we know and act as if everyone were alike.

  - What are their anxieties and aspirations?
  - What is their current skill level and what responsibilities do they have?
  - Does the course content match or conflict with their self-efficacy?

- What level of reading skills do they have? Are they familiar with the jargon used in the subject matter?
- Where do they see their strengths and needs?
- How do they feel about the instructional platform (instructor-led training, training camps, online social media, blended learning, elearning, etc.)?
- What do they hope to learn?

Think of learners as persons, first and foremost! Not empty shells.

- **Behavior**—What observable skills will evidence successful training?

  - Success is rarely, if ever, just about knowledge, unless knowledge is sufficient to perform effectively. Sometimes it is.
  - What behaviors can be observed and taken as evidence of successful training?
  - What measures will inform us of their entry and developing performance confidence? Even the ability to perform successfully isn't enough if learners avoid applying their skills due to lack of confidence.

- **Conditions**—Under what conditions, constraints, and with what present and absent resources must successful performance be demonstrated?

  - What tools and resources can be used?
  - What environmental distractions will be present?

- **Degree**—What level of performance perfection is required?

  - How fast must trainees perform tasks to demonstrate proficiency?
  - Do self-corrected errors demonstrate proficiency, or must there be zero errors?
  - If errors are allowed, how many? How many instances in a row, per hour, etc.?

Examples of Useful Performance Objectives

Not Useful	Useful	What's the Problem?
Student will answer 80% of post-test questions correctly.	Given 10 résumés, student will select the two most qualified applicants within one hour.	Presumably, we aren't training people to do well on post-tests; we're training them to perform tasks.
Student will understand the importance of spaced practice.	Given an instructional program that masses practice at the end of instruction, the student will lay out a schedule of incrementally spaced post-training practice.	We can't readily observe understanding. And this objective is made even less specific by "the importance of." The most useful objectives provide *observable* instances of skillfulness.
Student will appreciate the positive impact of delayed feedback.	The student will modify an elearning program that gives immediate feedback to provide opportunities for learners to appraise and self-correct their responses before receiving feedback.	"Appreciate" is another problematic word. What does it mean and how can we observe it? The better objective describes measurable application of a learned principle.

On Post-Tests

Logical and commonplace as they are, post-tests are poor measures of learning. Why?

1. We have described elsewhere the importance of learning experiences being Meaningful, Memorable, and Motivational—all three. If one is missing, training is headed for failure. While a well-constructed post-test might in the best instances provide a measure of the learner's ability to apply content concepts or procedures (Meaningfulness), it doesn't provide any indication of expected retention or interest in applying new skills (Memorable and Motivational).

2. When learners understand their success in a course will be measured via a post-test, they often prepare themselves for the test by the decades-popular method of "cramming." Which means quickly putting as much as possible into short-term memory, which in turn means it will most likely evaporate within days, if not hours, after testing.

Better Methods

A couple of methods for more accurately determining learning success are:

1. Asking learners to expect the appraisal of their learning will be accomplished via covert observations of their behavior several weeks or more later.

2. Informing learners there will be a post-test, but it won't be given for several weeks and without warning.

Module 7: Ethical Decision Making for the Professional Educator

Practice and Apply---The Ride Home

Scenario and Feedback

1. Select the "play" button and watch the video scenario.
2. In the Choices area, review the different options and select the best option you would choose if you were the teacher, Mr. Arnold.
3. In the Performance area, you will receive feedback across the PROETHICS principles on your progress.

Choices

Call the principal.

Call the police.

Give her a ride home.

Just leave.

Performance

Promoting Solution Discovery
Risk Mitigation
Objectivity and Neutrality
Ensuring Student Welfare
Transparency
Honoring Boundaries
Integrity of the Profession Promoted
Code of Ethics Maintained
Stewardship of the Law/Public Trust

0:41 / 1:22

Making Ethical Decisions

Practice to Mastery

EXAMPLE

Decision Making—Mastery. *"This scenario-driven video role-play on ethical conduct in schools was for teachers and staff. Its engaging approach of knowledge application replaced an insufficient traditional multiple-choice test. The need to assess learners' ethical understanding prompted the creation of this more dynamic testing approach."* **Allen Interactions Inc.**

Secrets (Little White Lies)

You will gain benefits from method 1 (page 133), even if you never appraise the learner's performance. It doesn't mean you'll have the precious data we want to evaluate our learning programs unless you implement other measures, nor the ability to boast about post-test scores (as meaningless as they are), but when learners know at the outset of taking a course they will be expected to retain and apply new skills, they will realize cramming will be useless. Many will opt to practice enough to retain their learning and to do well whenever their skills are evaluated.

With method 2, you will also benefit from announcing measurement will be delayed after the conclusion of the course, even if the post-test is not given. And for the same reasons. But watch out: If word gets out that no post-test is ever given, these techniques will fail big-time.

CHAPTER 19

RESOLVING CONFLICTING MANAGEMENT AND INSTRUCTIONAL GOALS

Good ID

One of the irritations I think all instructional designers have is the pressure to churn out instructional programs at breakneck speed. It's understandable, of course. Once you've realized performance improvement is needed, you want to see it right away. If your products are requiring too much warrantee service, if your customers are complaining about wait time, or if your sales team isn't closing sales, you want the situation improved pronto. So, get that training out there fast! *"I don't see why it should take long."*

Everyone else's job looks like it's easier than your own, usually because we don't know what all the challenges are and haven't faced them in context. We can see some of them, but many of them aren't readily recognized until we get into the work. Skilled instructional designers are amazingly fast at what they do, but their work calls on a lot of knowledge and experience and requires hours of focused attention, information gathering, and application of hundreds of principles, many that are counterintuitive.

While the credits at the end of a movie roll by, we realize the amazing number of people it takes to create a movie—even a bad movie. There are jobs to be done we wouldn't even think of. Quite similarly, the design and development of instructional programs involves many, many tasks. If they aren't done well, the program is going to fail to accomplish business goals and waste a lot of learner time. It's unfortunate we rarely see a list of credits in elearning.

There are many challenges to creating a successful elearning project.

Consider the following perspectives:

Perspective 1: Does it make sense to cut costs by trimming design and development costs to the bare bones when the almost certain result will be wasted learner time? What's the ratio of design and development time to learner time? How many designers and authors are there compared to the number of learners? 1:100? 1:1,000? 1:≥10,000? Do you want to save the time of 10 people in training development to waste the time of many more learners?

Perspective 2: Forget perspective 1 (even though it doesn't make sense to). Forget that the training might have minimal impact and could well waste a lot of hours. What if the performance problem persists? What if product durability problems continue? Or customer complaints? Or lost sales? Was it a good decision to cut the investment in performance-improving programs to continue battling persistent business problems?

There are many challenges to creating a successful elearning project. Many. I hasten to say that people who haven't tried to create highly successful elearning really have no idea how many challenges there are, nor do they comprehend how the challenges interact to complicate and magnify the impact of each of them.

One of the most important impediments is often the lack of a clear and fully accepted definition of success, including definitions of both *project success* as well as *learning success*, as described in the previous two chapters.

It's easy not to learn of expectations or criteria held by stakeholders early on, because people who matter most may not share their preferences, thoughts, and concerns until late in the project's development when they can see what all the conversation had been about. They may assume what others think is important is what they would also think is important and reserve comments until later (when it's become problematic). We as project leaders may do the same and find our work disrupted when we realize our values prove unshared as projects approach the goal line.

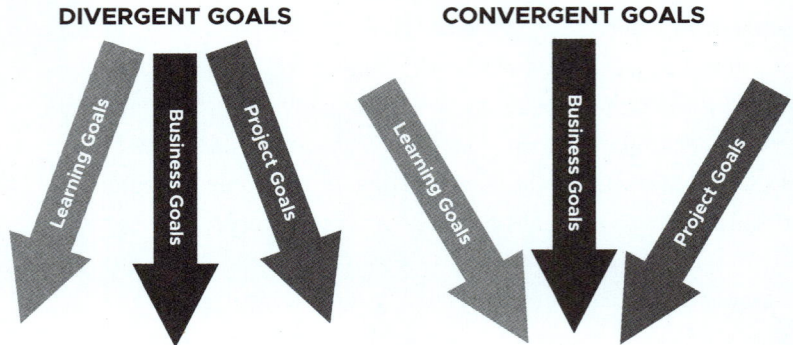

DIVERGENT GOALS   **CONVERGENT GOALS**

Learning Goals · Business Goals · Project Goals   Learning Goals · Business Goals · Project Goals

It's critical to get on the same page early and stay on the same page throughout. The definitions of success may shift (which they often do, and we should therefore expect) as new opportunities are discovered or hidden needs revealed. If this happens early in the process and everyone shifts together, this can be a very good thing. It can avoid redoing a lot of work. But if shifts occur late or if the shifts are not accepted by all critical stakeholders, the whole effort can flounder. Badly.

How to Avoid Goal Misalignment

The cost of misalignment can hardly be overstated. It's a risk we need to recognize and respond to proactively. We should never take for granted that everyone will enthusiastically embrace whatever may surface at the end of a lot of hard work. So, what precautions and preventive measures can be taken?

Here are some checklists to help:

1. Get Aligned at the Start

Call together the stakeholders and project principals. Discuss the importance of aligning learning goals *and* project goals (list them separately and acknowledge both groups of goals exist) and how they can and must support each other for overall success.

Checklist

☐ Create a Behavior Catalog (see Chapter 16)

    ☐ Write down the project goals and needed outcomes.
    ☐ Write down how each goal will be measured.
    ☐ Write down specific expected learning outcomes.

☐ Get agreement to support these goals from every individual.

☐ Get agreement on how divergences will be processed.

☐ Get sign-offs from each person and distribute the dated document with signatures to everyone. It really helps to have a record.

2. Identify the Decision-Maker

Too often, the decision-maker is assumed to be someone other than the person who truly pulls the strings. Even worse, various team members may assume a different person is the decision-maker. A common and difficult situation occurs when the budget-maker delegates project authority to someone else but silently retains control, only to swoop in at various points to contradict the project manager or set new criteria. Too many times the swooping occurs near the project's conclusion when the work is ready for review. This causes pain and havoc for everyone. Last-minute compromises may weaken design integrity and the training program's effectiveness as a whole.

Here's some very good practical advice: At the outset of a project, perhaps at the Savvy Start (see Chapter 34), ask stakeholders to declare who will be the decision-maker. People will usually agree at this early stage that having a declared decision-maker is smart. So, it can be easy to achieve. However, if delayed until differing opinions have surfaced, getting consensus on who would be the best decision-maker can be hard if not impossible.

Checklist

- [ ] Get agreement on who is truly the decision-maker.

- [ ] Make sure the persons assigning this role truly want to divest of project control and will support whatever the delegate decides.

- [ ] If there's hesitancy, then get an understanding that to make good decisions, project involvement, including discussions of alternatives and timely reviews of work-in-progress, is paramount to project success.

- [ ] Clearly document who is truly the decision-maker. Half in and half out creates a major liability, which no one should want and with which few projects survive.

3. Plan for In-Process Changes

Midstream changes can be smart and a good thing. No one should expect a project to sail through from start to finish with no new ideas, additions, and substitutions. In fact, as we talk about the design process in later chapters, we will encourage changes and anticipation of them. But you're in trouble if you haven't planned for any diversions from the design no matter how great it looked early on.

There's a reason for this: While sketches and prototypes are essential to an instructional design, they still leave room for varied expectations of how the final implementation of the design will come together. And further, as the final product begins to emerge, it will spawn new opportunities that were difficult to see earlier.

Checklist

- ☐ Make everyone aware that an iterative design and development process allows taking advantage of ideas that come along, but the cost in time and expense rises the later changes are made.

- ☐ Similarly, make everyone aware that the iterations planned to occur early in the project *welcome and encourage* exploration of alternative ideas. Expressing them as soon as possible is much more constructive and valuable than raising them later.

- ☐ Ask everyone to agree that no project ever reaches perfection. Ever. There will always be thoughts about how the work could be improved. Always. Perfection is never attainable, no matter how many iterations and improvements are made. Late-arriving ideas for design improvement (again, as there always will be) doesn't mean the current design won't be very effective.

- ☐ Try your best to get everyone to understand (early on, well before someone is strenuously promoting a late-occurring modification) that rolling out a Beta version and observing its success in real use will generate other, and often better, ideas than theoretical projections.

- ☐ The first rollout shouldn't be considered the last rollout. Try to get a plan endorsed (again, early on) for field testing the first version while time and money remain to make responsive modifications.

4. Communicate When Critical Alignment Check-Ins Will Occur

It takes project management experience and the support of many people to keep an elearning project on schedule. Just generating a workable and acceptable schedule is a challenge few people do well. Those who do it well have the horror stories of projects going way off the rails to guide them.

The most frequent problems are (1) getting timely and sufficient input from subject matter experts (SMEs) as they're usually the busiest people around and (2) getting timely and thorough reviews because good reviews take time and focus and sometimes because people want to retain the right to demand modifications indefinitely. Because SMEs and other reviewers are in high demand with busy schedules, they often agree in advance to be available for project needs and then later find those needs occur at a time when they have conflicting obligations.

You need timely, thorough reviews. Late reviews hold up the schedule and complicate commitments of future availability of other team members. Superficial reviews are perhaps worse as they lend false confidence, which later requires rework when problems are identified.

Checklist

- ☐ Seek the help of an experienced elearning producer / project manager (if you aren't one) to plan the project and schedule and monitor progress throughout.

- ☐ Review specific dates when SME input and reviews need to take place, asking people to put these times on their calendars and safeguard these times to the best of their ability, notifying you as far in advance as possible when adjustments have to be made.

☐ Use techniques to give the project resiliency with respect to availability of SMEs and reviewers, such as having contingency plans for doing some work concurrently instead of sequentially in order to make up time.

5. Get a Signed Understanding That Out-of-Scope Changes Have Cost and Schedule Impact

Checklist

☐ Ask clients to understand and agree that delays caused by lack of key resources cannot usually be overcome on a 1:1 basis. That is, if a critical resource person or persons are late one day, the final deliverable may have to be delayed by more than one day. And the cost to the project may well be more than one day's work.

☐ Identify the person to whom notice of project interruption should be sent and who will give approval to Change of Scope costs.

6. Create Safety Nets

Experienced producers or project managers keep two powerful weapons in their pocket:

☐ A safety net to be discussed with clients includes funds and time to be used reluctantly and only on special conditions, such as unavoidable delays or content modifications required by unexpected events.

☐ A safety net *not discussed* with clients for similar purposes.

Having dual safety nets gives you the best chance to complete your project on time, within budget, and at target quality. The first, or "public," safety net gives clients comfort at the outset and isn't usually hard to sell. Everyone knows that business life throws unexpected challenges along the way, and realistic plans for dealing with them is smart. But clients can easily become wedded to a newly identified "must-have" and are ready to use safety net resources immediately to pursue them, even while the probability of further unexpected challenges still looms high.

You can wisely resist doing so, but if clients are adamant, as they may well be, you can use the first safety net giving advice that no more midcourse corrections may be possible. Then, if unforeseen delays occur, you still have the second safety net to save the day.

DESIGNER'S NOTEBOOK #4

Self-check: See if you garnered these takeaway principles and are ready to use them.

☐ The purpose of training and education is to enable people to do things, not only to know things.

☐ It's unnecessarily risky to assume deeper knowledge will result in better performance; instructional programs need to confirm learners can translate knowledge into performance.

☐ Barriers to desired performance need to be identified before jumping into creating training programs as necessary skills may already be in place and not the problem.

☐ Success almost always comes from one source: doing the right thing at the right time.

☐ An Electronic Performance Support System (EPSS) may be sufficient for people to perform successfully if (1) it is practical to reference aids during performance and (2) tasks don't require undeveloped skills.

☐ If expertise is required, training programs need to give learners practice working problems they have not seen before and have not been specifically trained to resolve.

☐ A Behavior Catalog is a helpful tool to determine what skills are needed to achieve desired business/organizational outcomes, such as ROI, and what training budget is acceptable.

☐ Project success and learning success have different measures and should not be confused so that key performance goals are not achieved.

☐ Timely and consistent communication among team members, management, and clients is essential to successful training development projects.

☐ Learning objectives are important guides to keep design properly focused.

☐ Post-tests encourage cramming, which undercuts retention and accurate measures of learning. If they are to be used as measures of instructional success, they should be delayed, perhaps several weeks after the conclusion of training.

☐ Better than a post-test, observing learner performance and effective application of new skills provides a more valid assessment of a training program.

☐ While requiring more professional experience and a larger budget, expert instructional design saves overall training costs while poor instructional design (presumably less expensive) raises the cost when poor performance of trainees is taken into account.

BUYER'S CHECKLIST #4

To ensure a great investment in training and ROI, be sure to ask the following questions.

☐ Are you making sure each training development project starts with a definition of success and an agreement of how success will be measured?

☐ The criteria for project success and learning success are different but often confused. For example, a project that is delivered on time and budget and puts through 3,000 employees may look good but could be an extravagant waste of time and money. Are you set to measure both project success and learning success?

☐ Are you keeping yourself aware of assumptions and questioning them, such as supervisors or others saying they know what employees want and appreciate? They rarely do. Questioning assumptions takes time and effort, but the risk in not doing so is something you'll likely pay dearly for.

☐ Communication is critically important during custom training development. Do you have a Communications Plan that clearly specifies who will communicate with whom, when, and about what? For each type of communiqué, do you have commitments from both the vendor and the procuring organization to respond within a specified amount of time by a qualified person?

☐ Post-tests aren't accurate assessments of learning but only of short-term memory. Assessments in which on-the-job performance observations are made are much more meaningful. They also motivate learners to retain their learning until at least the time of observation (which also makes it more likely the learning will stick longer than that). Are you arranging to have delayed, covert assessments of post-training performance?

☐ Are you budgeting a safety net reserve for either problems that arise or discovered opportunities that it would be unfortunate not to pursue?

Book 2

HOW TO DESIGN
eLEARNING

Part 5

DESIGNING HIGH-IMPACT INSTRUCTIONAL PROGRAMS

Aiming Higher

Much of the ground we've covered up to this point has been rethinking the whole of what we're up to from some different and important perspectives. Now, at this point, where we get into the nitty-gritty of design, it's fitting to wonder what we would do differently if we aspired to create much better learning experiences. Could it be we're stuck in a rut? Would we know if we were?

I've had conversations with smart designers who are impressively certain there is a correct way to design, implying every other way is just wrong. I'm struck by their confidence and realize how comforting it must be. But whenever I read or hear something expressed with such certainty, I get *un*comfortable. Uncertain. Concerned and ready to find the exception that might reveal important overlooked possibilities.

I mean, the world was flat . . . until we discovered it wasn't. Until then, people had great certainty it was flat and the sun revolved around the earth. Our world would end on a certain date. And then it didn't. Dietary cholesterol was clogging your arteries. COVID vaccinations prevented contracting the disease. You know what I'm saying. It's *always* possible we've got it wrong or there's a better way. Even Einstein revised his principles as he investigated further. As new data arrived.

Let's all keep asking questions and improving.

Awesome Yet Practical Instructional Design

Here in Part 5, we'll take up the following instructional design topics:

Knowing your learners. How can we deliver the best learning experiences for each person if we only know their names?

Ask and observe. Mentorship provides a good model for continually assessing what would be exactly the right way to help each learner.

Interactivity. Active learning results in deeper, more sustained learning. But what is and isn't a learning interaction?

Context, Challenge, Activity, and Feedback. These elements together provide a strong and yet versatile framework for assessment, engagement, and developing skills in a very practical, individualized, and game-like way.

Individualization concepts. Designing an instructional program in traditional ways and then trying to tack on individualization later doesn't work. We have to start with the intent to individualize and build forward on it to adapt content and respond to affective influences.

Practical content individualization. Thankfully, there are some ways to simplify the expected effort and complexity needed to adapt content to individuals. It's probably more practical than you think and worth doing even if it does take some extra effort.

Practical adaptation to affective states. If we want to really up our game and act like a caring mentor who is sensitive to how learners are feeling—bored, anxious, confused, frustrated, etc.—there are many ways we can respond to these affective states. But can we make this practical as well? We'll look into that important concern.

CHAPTER 20

HEALTHY SKEPTICISM

Trained as a researcher in the scientific method, statistics, and analysis, I peruse fascinating studies that reveal insights and much to mull over. I try to consider as much as I can when designing instructional events. I'm truly grateful to all those conducting research and those working to be sure we are all aware of the findings. Please don't stop.

But . . .

There's a big "but" here: Until I've witnessed findings in application, I remain skeptical (but hopeful) regarding many conclusions represented as "fact." *It's true. It's based on science.*

There are faults in studies, to be sure. Sometimes faults are hard to recognize, even by the most objective scientist. I don't suggest faults are intentionally hidden (although that does happen), but it can be very hard to identify all the possible confounding variables, especially regarding instruction of humans, let alone control for them. It's not unusual that a confounding variable is discovered later, months or even decades later, to invalidate a conclusion that has become well entrenched.

Science Flip-Flops

As it should always, scientific findings will sometimes need correction as we seek the truth. Indeed, researchers themselves (at least the most respected ones) remain skeptical, even, perhaps especially skeptical, of their own findings. They properly insist on multiple concurring studies for assurance, and even then, they continually probe for deeper understanding and possible alternative explanations.

Let's review a couple of primary cautions.

Myriad Variables Influence Learning

In research involving instruction and learning, there are countless variables that influence how different people respond to instructional paradigms. There are so many differences in so many different situations with so many different interests, attitudes, goals, and prior learning. As practitioners, we must be keenly aware that humans are complex; their minds behave in surprising ways to influences we sometimes don't even consider or know how to sense.

Overgeneralization

Understanding the big picture should make us particularly cautious about generalizing results as prescriptions for instructional design. I suspect all of us have fallen into this trap.

My Story

As we were working on a project for one of the world's largest automotive manufacturers, our client wanted all on-screen text narrated. We objected on research grounds that when displayed text is read, people tend to focus on comparing the narration to the text. In doing so, they comprehend the messages less well. The scientific literature told us text should either be displayed or spoken, but not both. So, we pushed back.

After field testing a version without narration and getting feedback learners weren't comprehending the text as well as expected, the client insisted we add the narration as originally requested. Still somewhat hesitant, we experimented with an on-screen button that allowed learners to either listen or read. This provided both options but allowed only one mode at a time. That seemed more in line with what research studies recommended. That didn't satisfy anyone!

Learners select either audio narration (Figure above) or on-screen text (Figure below).

Then we tried automatically displaying the script after the narration finished. Bingo! Learners expressed appreciation for the ability to review and verify what they thought they heard. And they thought having heard the narration first made the text easier to read afterward. During audio narration, they could concentrate on the visual graphics and animations without worrying that they might have missed something. Having given learners the choice also racked a sense of our appreciating them as adults. We saw increased comprehension across the board. Research provided the direction but not a complete solution.

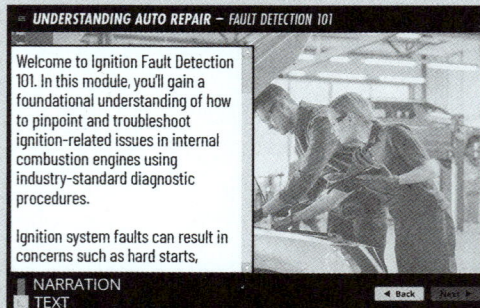

On Intuition

So, here's the flip side:

Intuitive notions are hit and miss. Sometimes I look at instructional designs and can hardly keep from rolling my eyes. How would anyone think that would work? What's happened to common sense? And yet, sometimes principles that seem obviously valid turn out not to be.

When we first started experimenting with computer-assisted instruction (CAI), one of the forerunner terms for what's now called elearning, it was possible to give learners immediate feedback. This was in great contrast to students submitting their homework or test papers and waiting some time, perhaps several days, for feedback. Immediate feedback was touted as a major advantage of CAI and became standard practice. It still has strong advocates in many quarters.

It took perhaps more decades than we can explain to discover that immediate judgmental feedback isn't always best practice. Why not? Here are two of many reasons:

Problems with Immediate Judgmental Feedback

1. Immediate judgmental feedback absolves learners of the valuable cognitive exercise of reflecting on and evaluating their work. In multistep performance, as most real-world tasks are, immediate feedback identifies errors before learners can recognize for themselves how an early mistake is causing downstream problems. Becoming able to recognize their faults on their own leads to deeper and more valuable learning.

2. Immediate judgmental feedback induces learners to take shortcuts that are detrimental to their learning. Instead of thinking carefully before acting, making a decision, or submitting

an answer, learners find they can quickly give random responses for the purpose of getting immediate guidance. Instead of thinking things through and responding to the confronted challenge (the very exercise required for learning), learners simply get corrective feedback to a guess or nonsense answer, copy it, and submit the correct answer. They essentially use feedback as a crutch to move along as quickly as possible. They take advantage of its readiness to advise them on what to do and, without much thought, learn little as a result.

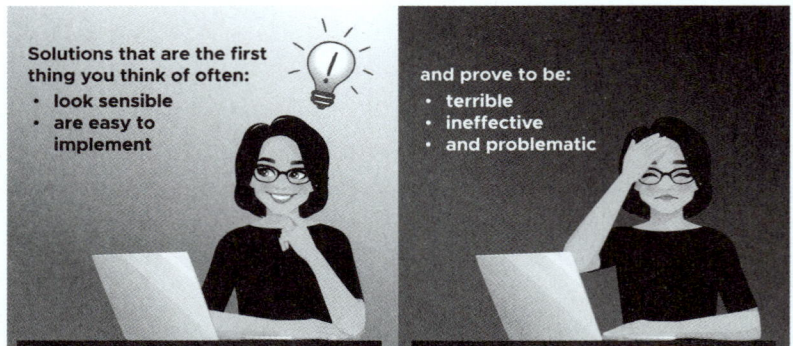

Trust Your Experience

Having stated concerns relative to opposite ends of the continuum, the center position is, as usual, smart to consider. Experience advised by both research on one hand and intuition on the other is likely to be a superior guide. That's not to say experience is always more accurate, but when experience contradicts research or intuition, I would recommend moving ahead cautiously with its guidance.

As practitioners, we don't have to know why things work or don't work; we just need to know the difference. Obviously, it's more comforting to know why. And knowing why can help us reason out when something that's worked in the past might not work again in a somewhat different situation.

My conclusion is that there's no fail-safe method of designing great learning experiences, but when all three—research, experience, and intuition—are consulted, we're likely to make good choices.

Get to Know Your Learners

It's easy to assume we know our audience; they're people. We know people. They're just like us. But we'd be wrong to think so. Well, most probably we'd be wrong if we thought we knew enough to train them optimally without learning anything about them individually. Yet trainers, subject matter experts, and yes, we instructional designers, and pretty much everyone is quick to make assumptions about other people. One big assumption is that learners will think and feel like we did before we learned what we know now.

Some of the many assumptions we make about learners involve their . . .

- Desire to learn this content and learn it now
- Time available for training
- Experience in prior efforts to learn this content, if any (or a lot)
- Perceived relevance to current issues and aspirations
- Feelings about prior experiences with elearning
- Desire to learn via elearning
- Expectations about their ability to learn
- Self-assessment of current skill level
- Actual entry skill level

There are, no doubt, many other attributes of individual learners that will affect the impact and whole of the experience you are creating. As we go forward to design learning experiences, we need to continually reflect on how our decisions may lead to varied outcomes given the many potential individual differences among the learners.

Do We Have to Be Concerned About Individual Differences?

No. We don't want more things to deal with. We've been getting by for a long time with our assumptions that all our learners are pretty much alike, so we could continue treating all learners as if that were true. Nobody expects otherwise. The work of designing and building instructional programs can sometimes feel overwhelming, and we're often working under time and budget pressures and possibly also short on resources.

But we want to be successful, greatly successful. We want to help each and every one of our learners raise their skill proficiency and realize their full potential. We don't want any of them to waste their time because of our choices.

If we have to compromise, where would be the best place? Although conventional, maybe ignoring learner differences isn't the best place to compromise, especially in elearning where one of its greatest strengths is its ability to adapt to individual learners.

Our work is all about getting our learners to a point of competency. At least that's how we've seen it. But is that really the end point? Perhaps just as important is getting learners to a point of performance *confidence* as well—and even feeling joyful about performing their skills so well. If we want sustained performance improvement, our best bet is taking learners not just to a point of skills development but all the way to enjoying their performance and feeling proud of it.

SKILLS   COMPETENCE   CONFIDENCE & JOY

Basic Training   **High-Impact Training**

Focusing on learners up front and continuously is the key to high-impact instructional programs.

The Practicality Excuse

Recognizing we differ from each other in many ways, we might feel adapting to individual learners suggests too many alternative learning experiences to design and build. Too much work. Too little time. Too much expense. But let's set such concerns aside for a moment. What if it were more practical than it appears?

Let's think what a personal mentor might do, because isn't that the model to aspire to? Wouldn't we all love to have expert mentors working with us personally, privately, quietly to guide and help us do, well, pretty much everything we want to do well? As mentioned previously, the model I aspire to in elearning is exactly that of a great mentor. Something far more powerful than a book or a video can be. Something that picks me up when I fail and encourages me to do even better than I think I can.

Thinking about what a personal mentor would do, even about what we would do as a personal mentor ourselves, reveals important insights on how to make our training excel. I think we know more about what constitutes great learning experiences than we realize.

Sales Skills

Solution Selling

I'm glad you asked!
As your coach, I suggest the following:

> **DONE**
>
> I sense your frustration as you watch the 'Customer Interest' dropping. It's not too late to save this opportunity.
>
> Remember, you've already had several conversations with this customer already. Show your customer she is a priority by acknowledging any info you have gathered previously.

Customer Interest

⊕ Add a Note

≡ Transcript

📋 Scenario Background

❔ Ask Coach

What would you say?
Click the best option, then watch the video to see the customer reaction.

Perfect. So, last time we chatted you mentioned that men's fragrance sales were lagging in certain markets. That must be very frustrating. Can you tell me a little about how you will be measuring success for this upcoming launch?

Perfect. Can you tell me about your success metrics for this launch?

Perfect. Can you tell me more about what is driving the need for this men's fragrance launch?

Perfect. So, last time we chatted you mentioned that men's fragrance sales were lagging in certain markets. I was a bit surprised to hear about this launch for a new men's fragrance. Can you tell me more about what is driving the need for this launch?

Coach/Mentor in a Simulated Sales Call

Coaching

EXAMPLE

Coaching Support. *"This module simulates over 80 different sales call scenarios, all with coaching support. It allows learners to make mistakes and receive guidance from their mentor rather than only corrective feedback. This supportive approach allows the learner to apply knowledge with assistance and insights in addition to receiving specific feedback."* **Allen Interactions Inc.**

CHAPTER 21

THE MENTORSHIP MODEL
ASK AND OBSERVE

Question: What would a great mentor do when meeting a learner for the first time? Would the mentor immediately launch into delivering content? "I'm going to begin by covering 10 foundational principles. Listen up. Take notes." No, I don't think so. A classroom teacher? Yes, too often. In elearning? Also, too often.

Good mentors are constantly pulling in information, asking, and watching. And then deciding what would be the best and most helpful feedback and follow-on experience.

Current Skills

A good mentor is going to be interested in the level of skills the learner has currently and also perceives themselves to have. A good mentor would likely ask the learner to demonstrate their current skills. "Play your favorite song for me."

Aspirations

A good mentor is also going to ask what aspirations the learner has for advancement—why the learner is signed up to learn the skills at hand and what the learner hopes to accomplish with those skills. "Do you want to be a stage performer or just play to relax?"

Setting Challenges

The mentor is then going to select a task that's likely to interest the learner and not likely to be far out of scope, neither too hard nor too easy, based on how the learner has described current abilities, and then say, "Let's see what you can do. I bet you'll do well with this."

Observing and Guiding

The mentor is going to watch carefully, observing strengths and weaknesses. The mentor is going to compliment the learner on whatever things were done well, recognize attempts to apply good form or procedures even if not fully successful, and make notes on what needs to be improved (although not necessarily verbalizing such assessments immediately).

Self-Efficacy and Adaptation

The mentor is going to ask the learner how they felt about what was just done to see if a valid set of principles and criteria had already been internalized. And then the mentor would likely select another task for the learner to perform, perhaps a task that is appropriately easier or harder than the first one, which would build on current strengths and also provide an opportunity to help the learner improve or acquire new skills.

How can we best help each learner if we don't know anything about them? Neither mentorship nor elearning can be of most help without learning about the learner and adjusting appropriately.

So, the very practical and very necessary first steps are to . . .

First, Ask Learners

Ask about their current level of competency. It doesn't actually matter as much about how accurately learners assess themselves as it matters that we ask. We will be observing performance behaviors and adjusting as needed. Asking not only gives us a place to start; it also tells us some helpful things about each learner, such as performance confidence, self-efficacy, risk-taking preferences, and personal goals. In addition, asking communicates our recognition that the learning experience is all about helping the learner as best we can. Such communication can help build a partnership with learners and ramp up the effectiveness of everything we do instructionally.

⊙ Help

WELCOME

By sharing our personal experiences, NAMI In Our Own Voice (IOOV) presenters improve attitudes and increase knowledge about people with mental health conditions. We're thrilled that you're participating in our movement to improve the lives of people impacted by these conditions. Thank you - your story makes a difference!

Welcome Video

EXPLORE OUR FIT

NAMI presenters describe the reality of living with mental health conditions by sharing their powerful personal stories, using a unique structure for a specific purpose.

Are We a Good Fit?   NAMI Background

DRAFT YOUR WORDS

IOOV presentations influence the way people think about mental health conditions. Let's get started on your first draft.

Overview   Making "I" Statements

Finding Your Own Voice

Mental Health Onboarding

Ask Learners. *"This course is intended for individuals interested in working on suicide hotlines or supporting people with emotional issues. An important part of this training involves assessing potential volunteers' suitability by evaluating their mindset, strengths, and areas for growth. The success of the program depends on aligning the training with the learners' needs."* **Allen Interactions Inc.**

First, Ask Learners

EXAMPLE

Second, Get Learners Active

Even if learners indicate having no related skills at all, perhaps especially when that's their assessment, they're probably underestimating their abilities. Of course, a learner might be accurate, but that doesn't really matter. What we're hearing in this case tells us that we should start with the most basic of exercises for the learner to attempt, offering all the help that may be needed. If the learner handles it easily, we can congratulate the success enthusiastically and point out capabilities the learner hadn't recognized and valued. It's all positive from here on.

On the other hand, if the learner claims advanced capabilities, we have a green light to suggest a task of at least somewhat advanced challenge. If we're hearing strong confidence, then perhaps we excitedly suggest, "Let's go for it!" to indicate we're listening and hoping the learner is exactly right.

Again, if the learner does well, we will have saved time on the journey to competency, potentially a lot of time otherwise spent on boring and wasteful attempts trying to teach the learner skills already developed. With early performance success, we can congratulate enthusiastically and move ahead, perhaps risking a significant jump forward if not concluding the entire course.

If, in any of these cases, the learner needs help, hey, that's what a mentor or our program is here for. We'll help as needed or abort if it's clearly way over the learner's head and select a simpler exercise. Behaving just as a good mentor would creates excellent chemistry for learning, shortens learning time as much as possible, and keeps learners focused and on task.

That's a lot of benefits. eLearning was made for this!

Iterate

Objectively observing performance and continuing to ask how the learner assesses the learning experience is foundational throughout instruction, not just at the outset. Happily, this paints an iterative structure that makes design and development a well-defined process. It simplifies and speeds the work, while creating learning experiences that are anything but boring. The CCAF model, explored in the next chapter, is a well-articulated and generally applicable framework for doing all of the above.

CHAPTER 22

THE AWESOME CCAF MODEL

1. **A MEANINGFUL SITUATION**

2. **A STIMULUS OR URGENCY TO ACT**

4. **CONSEQUENCES OF USER ACTIONS & GUIDANCE**

3. **A PHYSICAL GESTURE IN RESPONSE TO THE CHALLENGE**

The CCAF model provides an organized and structured framework for designing great learning experiences composed of Context, Challenge, Activity, and Feedback components—the essential components of active learning. It is not restrictive like a template, but rather very flexible while still providing a functional and discerning way to think about learning events. You might think of it as both an aid to brainstorming learning activities and a checklist of the elements necessary for active learning.

We refer to this model repeatedly because of its broad applicability, simplicity, and power to achieve performance-based outcomes. And also, because CCAF provides a built-in framework for assessing learner capabilities and easily adjusting to them as well. What more could we ask for?

First, some basic definitions of the components:

Context is a portrayed place, time, or situation the learner could reasonably be expected to be in when performing a task.

Imagine you're . . .

- A paramedic at a car accident site
- A store employee at a service desk
- Having a sales conversation with a prospective buyer
- An anesthesiologist in the operating theater of a hospital
- A project manager conducting a budget review
- An HR director interviewing a candidate for hire

Challenge is a problem to be solved or a task to be performed. It's a stimulus for the learner to think, analyze, and decide what's best to do and then perform the steps required to meet the challenge or solve the problem. Examples:

- Decide whether to hire an employment applicant
- Mix in the appropriate number of eggs
- Calculate the quantity discount price
- Take emergency resuscitation measures
- Accept or reject a product return
- Modify a project budget and timeline

Activity is what the learner does to meet the Challenge. In today's elearning, these activities are typically performed through gestures using the computer's mouse and/or touch screen, but may include voice entries, eye tracking, taking photos, or using simulator controls. We don't generally consider selecting an A, B, C, D multiple-choice answer to be an Activity; that's just answering a question.

Feedback can be one or a combination of several types: judgmental/ extrinsic, consequential/intrinsic, or instructive.

Judgmental or "extrinsic" feedback

Tells learners whether their actions were effective/correct or not but not necessarily why.

Consequential or "intrinsic" feedback

Simulates outcomes of learner's actions, showing without judgment what happened.

Instructive feedback

Explains why and how the learner's response was appropriate and effective, the opposite, or something in between. And may provide hints, instructions, or a demonstration of correct actions, especially after repeated learner failures.

Of interesting note: Although derived from the separate paths of interactive game design and interactive instruction, the two primary types of gamification—intrinsic and extrinsic gamification—correspond directly to intrinsic and extrinsic feedback used in elearning.

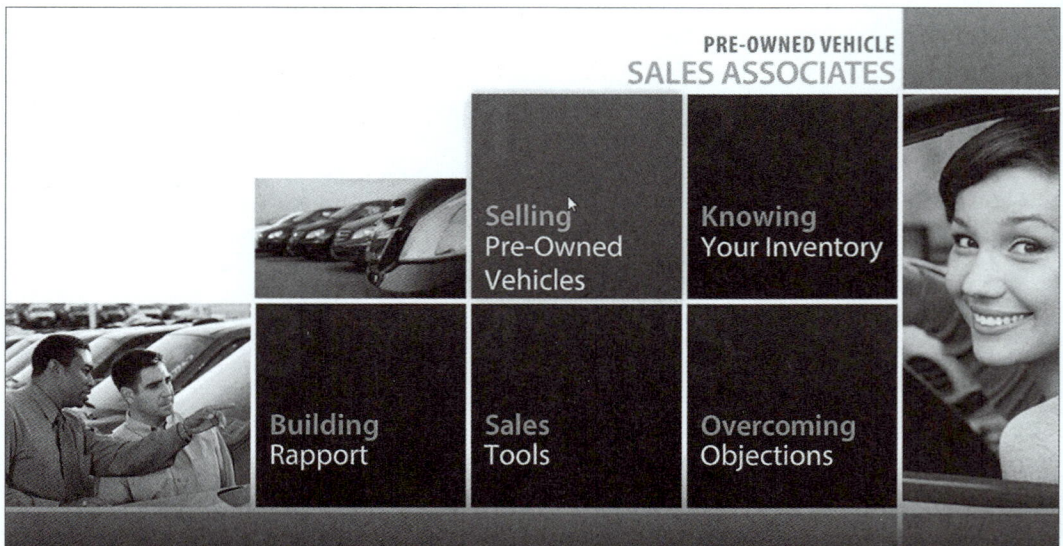

Using the CCAF Model for Simulations

Using the CCAF Model for Simulations. *"Automotive sales simulations helped Sales Associates improve their performance through practice in a series of realistic, motivational challenges. The activities included advanced role-plays and feedback on both interpersonal and non-verbal communication skills. The course includes spaced repetition to enhance performance confidence and retention."* **Allen Interactions Inc.**

CCAF Model

EXAMPLE

The Role of Feedback in CCAF

With CCAF, we begin interactions with very little instruction, if any. Instead, we trigger interactivity almost immediately. Instructional information and guidance are delivered primarily via feedback—in response to observed learner attempts to meet challenges. This placement of content presentation is very significant. First, it's presented in the context of the learner's need for it. As such, it's a form of help and performance assistance. Its value is apparent to the learner. Second, if a learner doesn't need it, we don't waste time and the learner's energy presenting it for study. Conditional presentation of content is a method of individualization built into and natural with CCAF.

Instructional feedback can take a wide range of forms, such as hints, questions to stimulate thought, reminders, examples, and many other forms all the way to the rare "extreme" in the CCAF framework of instructing the student explicitly what to do.

Visualized consequences make feedback memorable.

It's often as important to associate negative outcomes with inappropriate decisions and actions as it is to link positive outcomes that result from better decisions and actions.

The primary principle for designing instructional feedback in CCAF is determining what will most effectively cause learners to (1) identify various actions they could take and (2) accurately anticipate the outcome of each possible action. It's often as important to associate negative outcomes with inappropriate decisions and actions as it is to link positive outcomes that result from better decisions and actions. Developing expertise is generally a process of developing a robust set of associations between different possible actions to take in meeting challenges and the outcome to be expected from taking each action.

We'll detail the options and related pros and cons of CCAF feedback in later chapters.

An Interesting Design Note for Instructional Designers

Coincidentally (and helpfully), the three components of Mager's performance objectives foundational to many schools of instructional design are reflected directly in CCAF:

Performance Objective Component	CCAF Component
Conditions under which performance is to take place	Context
Level of performance perfection required	Challenge
Observable behavior that can be measured	Activity
N/A	Feedback

If you are familiar with—or, better yet, even skilled in creating—Mager-style performance objectives, you're almost thinking in CCAF constructs already. CCAF tightly links design to performance objectives and in so doing takes great advantage of the clarity and focus provided by performance objectives.

CHAPTER 23

GAMIFICATION VIA CCAF

We return here to gamification and the two primary types: intrinsic and extrinsic.

Extrinsic Gamification

The weaker of the two types of instructional gamification is external to or not integrated with the content. It's a generalized format like *Wheel of Fortune* or *Jeopardy!,* Tic-Tac-Toe, or card games in which any topic can be plugged into the framework. Play is usually based simply on right or wrong answers to questions, which determine scores or what the learner can do next.

In extrinsic learning games, learner focus tends to shift to learning the rules of the game, game strategy, and winning. While injecting appreciated fun and energy into the event, these games also redirect focus away from learning the content and useful skills. Learners don't necessarily practice transferable skills to mastery or delve deeply into the content beyond exposure to facts. They rarely perform multistep tasks since maintaining a fun pace requires quick responses. Extrinsic gamification can provide some helpful motivation and a sense of playful fun, surely much more than passive "tell-and-test" instruction, but we can do much better.

Intrinsic Gamification

Intrinsic gamification is the stuff of which popular video games are made. In contrast to extrinsic gamification, intrinsic gamification is usually simulation based. Learner motivation focuses on achieving success with the content-based simulation not on learning unrelated game rules and skills as with extrinsic gamification.

The CCAF components of Context, Challenge, Activity, and Feedback (see Chapter 22) demonstrated so successfully in video entertainment games work beautifully for learning games as well. But rather than mythical contexts and fabricated rules and tools, intrinsic learning games set the stage for authentic challenges that learners actively address (usually without magic wands). We're looking for skills that transfer readily to real-life responsibilities. Feedback comes in the form of real-world consequences to actions and inactions as would actually happen.

While sometimes instructional gamification is defined as "applying game mechanics to instructional interactions," it's quite possible to employ those mechanics and not create successful learning events. It's not just the presence of game mechanics that qualifies as instructional gamification, but rather their effectiveness in motivating thinking and practice of transferable skills.

Game mechanics used well can help create awesome learning events. They are often used in creative combinations. Mechanics include:

- **Random pop-up incidentals**, such as unexpected barriers or new options, can require learners to compare alternative solutions or remember what they were about to do while they attend to something else. Incidentals can cause learners to reflect on what they've learned, put it in line with other solutions, and learn which action is best under specific circumstances. Interruptions can make learning experiences more authentic as we often experience interruptions in life. They facilitate more effective transfer of learning to on-the-job performance. Interleaved recall and practice exercises can help seat new learning in long-term memory.

- **Competition**, such as competing for the highest scores or fastest task completion, can be fun and motivating. Learners can compete with others or themselves, trying to beat their best previous score. Competition with others is usually best in practice mode rather than in initial learning. Competing first with your own baseline capabilities keeps focus on learning enough to be competitive, builds confidence to compete, and makes competitors more fun to play with. After reaching ascending levels of competence, learners can be matched with other game players who have similar levels of skill, which contributes to all players benefiting and having fun.

- **Risk**, such as limiting the number of errors allowed before learners must start over or increasing penalties for repeated errors, keeps learners intensely engaged. It's one of the primary characteristics of video game play that makes the games so addictive and fun. No risk, no fun.

- **Level-Ups.** Of the various kinds of rewards serious learning games use, perhaps nothing is more effective than being escalated to higher levels that offer both greater challenges and also enhanced resources and options (think a knowledgeable executive assistant or artificial intelligence robot) that can provide helpful assistance on request. For learning, level-ups keep learners focused on advancing skills, perhaps learning to delegate and use their time more productively.

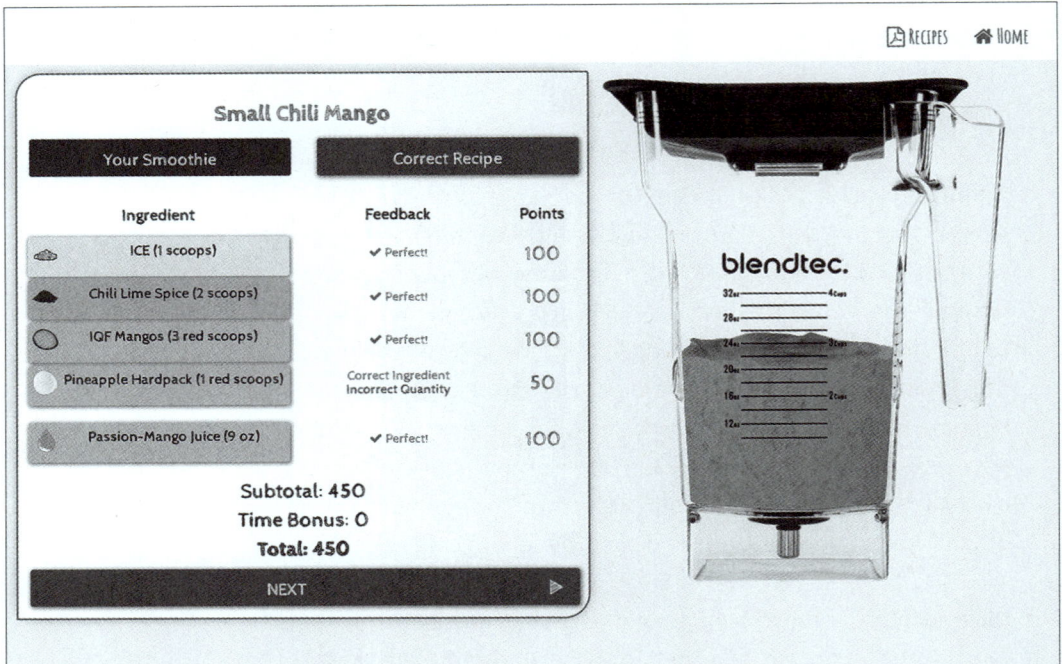

Preparing Juice Drinks

Level-Ups

EXAMPLE

Level-Ups. *"This game challenges learners to build their skills and confidence. The first scenarios allow use of job aids. After successful performance with aids, timing is introduced followed by the removal of job aids and addition of challenges for faster performance and handling increased complexity. This progression aligns with real-world performance expectations. The game challenges participants to advance their skills with clear progress indicators."* **Allen Interactions Inc.**

In general, intrinsic gamification is a double win: It's much more fun and also far more instructional than non-gamified elearning and extrinsic games. It motivates learners to practice not only to mastery but even beyond mastery (sometimes called "over learning") to gain a strong sense of ability and performance confidence. Most importantly, with game rules based on real-life restrictions and possibilities rather than artificial rules injected just to create a game, it transfers skills to real-life application directly.

XEL and Simulations

Many games are based on various sorts of simulations, whether buying properties to create monopolies, surviving in futuristic worlds, or experimenting with business models to create successful enterprises. Within these contexts, designers create rules or algorithms that govern how the game works and what players can and cannot do.

One could just as well use the terms "simulation-based" or "game-based learning" for eXperience-based ELearning (XEL) as both simulations (rudimentary or sophisticated as they may be) and game-playing elements are essential to creating the experiences we need. Indeed, the components of XEL include:

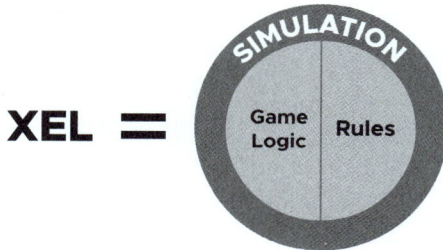

1. Game logic, such as stratified levels of challenge and performance criteria need to "level up"

2. Means of input communication with the game, such as keyboard, joystick, voice, touch, and/or mouse

3. A scoring and/or timing system, such as declining achievable points as a learner delays action

4. The rules players/learners must abide by, such as staying within budget

5. Simulation logic, such as accruing employee contentment as HR helps everyone keep their résumés current

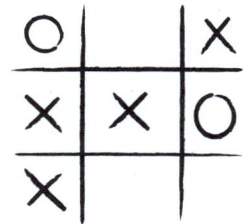

Critical XEL Concept 1: Logic rules are the core of the experience.
Rules govern *what* players/learners can do and *when* they can do
those things. Rules determine the *outcomes* of player/learner actions
and inactions. Rules determine not only whether the experience is
interesting and fun, but also whether there are takeaways worthy of
the time invested in play.

Whereas rules in entertainment games can be novel, arbitrary, and
imaginary, at least some of the rules in instructional simulations must
parallel actions people can and cannot take in real life. Another set of
rules governs attributes of the simulation, how it works, and determines
what happens when specific actions are taken. It's the quality of the
rules that determine the quality of the game and learning.

**Critical XEL Concept 2: All these rules, taken together, comprise the
content to be learned** and applied in post-training performance. This
profound concept deserves restating: **The rules are the instructional
content**—they define what is to be learned and understood. They
get learners to (1) practice performing actions, such as selecting a
candidate to hire or setting a sale price, and (2) associate expected
outcomes with those actions.

More simply stated, rules define the relationship between learner
actions and outcome consequences.

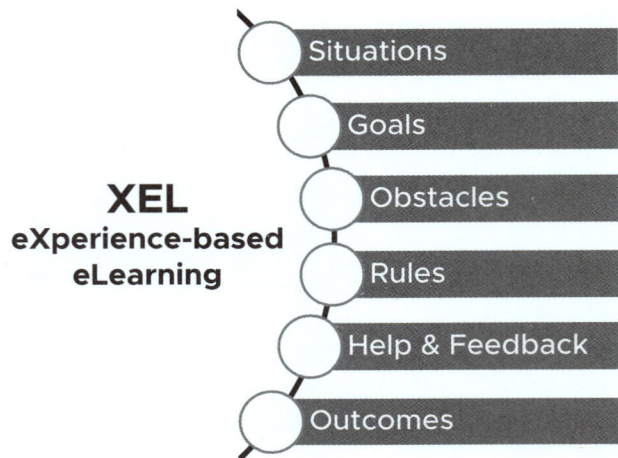

XEL
eXperience-based
eLearning

- Situations
- Goals
- Obstacles
- Rules
- Help & Feedback
- Outcomes

Good rules can make any content interesting, overcoming what might otherwise appear to be boring content.

In rethinking our design process and giving initial attention to the experience itself, we focus on the primary goal of capturing and maintaining the learner's attention and involvement. This is what deserves primary attention at design launch, not something to be tacked on after we've laid out our content discourse.

FINALIZING THE DECISION

After a lot of hard work and many hours, it's time to present the final project to the client. The team is struggling to choose what angle to take in the final ad campaign. Anxiety is high because of the client's reaction to previous presentations.

How can you help your team make the best choice?

1. Keep working with y... have to work into the...
2. Present two ideas to... would appreciate tw...
3. Explain to the client... but they need more... getting everything ju...

CAMPAIGN SUCCESS   TEAM MORALE

CONSEQUENCE

2. Present two ideas to the client. They seemed to like small pieces of ideas in the past; maybe they would appreciate two different examples.

Giving the client a choice not only shows them the talent the team has but also that you care about their opinion. Your team is excited to see their recommendations valued in this way.

CAMPAIGN SUCCESS   TEAM MORALE

CONTINUE

Motivation Skill Builder for Pryor Learning

Motivating Teams. *"This course contains a series of microlearning modules on how to motivate teams. Each has several short videos providing content, followed by a skill-builder challenge in which the learner is put in a situation where they have to make a series of choices. As they participate two meters provide feedback, showing the impact their choice has on campaign success and team morale."* **Artisan Learning**

Building Motivation

EXAMPLE

CHAPTER 24

THE 3M'S MEET CCAF

Several times now, I've alluded to the three essential characteristics of effective instruction—Meaningful, Memorable, and Motivational—the 3M's. As a quick refresher, it's easy to agree that instruction needs to be:

The 3M's

 **Meaningful** because if you don't understand it, *what* can you be learning? If you don't see any use for it, *why* would you be learning it?

 **Memorable** because if you quickly forget what you learned, you might as well not have learned it at all.

 **Motivational** because if you don't use what you've learned, again, you might as well not have learned it.

The 3M's Equation

Successful training doesn't come from just one or even two of the M's. It requires all three. Always. Think of learning outcomes as a product of the 3M's:

Learning = Meaningfulness x Memorability x Motivation

If any M = 0, Learning = 0

But now we have the question of how to cost-effectively design and implement MMM or 3M Learning.

Designing and Implementing 3M Learning

It should come as no surprise that if the most effective instruction is characterized by the 3M's and CCAF is a powerful framework for designing experience-based learning, the two concepts snap together, hand-in-glove. Let's see how this is the case.

Meaningful *Learning with CCAF*

Context is the foundation of CCAF designs. When the context is a situation learners can readily imagine themselves in, it establishes relevance for learners instantly. In contrast to content-focused design, CCAF urges designers to think about learners and the situations in which this training will be valuable. When the value of learning is clear, a big step is taken toward meaningfulness.

The Challenge component of CCAF cements the deal. Based on a relevant Context, the addition of a Challenge further communicates the relevancy of the learning event by its implication that you are about to learn to meet this type of Challenge.

Of course, it's important to use language understandable to learners, avoid undefined jargon, and introduce a level of complexity appropriate to the learner's knowledge and skill level as all individualized instruction seeks to do. But the addition of an authentic Context and Challenge make learning far more meaningful and obviously valuable to learners than programs who sidestep these elements.

Memorable *Learning with CCAF*

Will Thalheimer astutely observes, "Sadly, most training is designed to support understanding but not remembering."[16] What makes things memorable? Strong associations with things of value already implanted firmly in memory created through practice, novelty, or emotional attachments.

Financial Planning

Creating Memorable Experiences. *"The course incorporates an online card game designed to train financial advisers to help clients identify their primary reasons for investing. The deck consists of cards focused on fear, happiness, and commitment. Advisors are challenged to seek and understand clients' human factors beyond just quantitative data. The learner interacts with two individuals to gather personal information and develop a specific recommendation."* **Allen Interactions Inc.**

Memorable Learning with CCAF

EXAMPLE

---

16 Will Thalheimer, *The CEO's Guide to Training, eLearning & Work: Empowering Learning for a Competitive Advantage* (Work-Learning Press, 2024).

In almost all performance training, we want learners to be able to assess a situation and identify effective and appropriate actions to take because they know what outcomes to expect. For learners to choose those appropriate actions, they must first become able to identify relevant alternative actions and evaluate the likely outcomes of each.

SITUATION	CONSIDER	EVALUATE	CHOOSE
Context & Challenge	Action 1 →	Outcome 1	Not Good
	Action 2 →	Outcome 2	Not Good
	Action 3 →	Outcome 3 ←	Good
	Action 4 →	Outcome 4	Too Hard

Learners identify desired outcomes and take corresponding actions.

Because Context and Challenge establish relevance and value, when designed well and appropriately for the learner, they set the stage for memorable learning. When learners decide how to respond and actively do so, feedback in the preferred form of consequences (presented dramatically wherever possible and appropriate to do so) strengthens the association of situations with actions and with outcomes.

Further, by delaying judgmental feedback and allowing learners to evaluate the appropriateness of their actions, make corrections, or try again, the resulting practice provides yet another memorability boost.

Motivational *Learning with CCAF*

When we talk about CCAF motivation, we talk about two critical motivations:

- The motivation to learn
- The motivation to apply what's been learned

Motivation to learn in general and to learn a specific ability varies among people as well as within ourselves from time to time, even moment to moment. Recognition of this is essential as, without motivation, little learning occurs. *There are exceptions, such as learning from vicarious traumatic events.*

Thankfully, because levels of motivation vary, we have opportunities to influence it through a variety of means. See Chapter 25, "7 Magic Keys to Motivation."

Motivation to apply learning is also essential if we are to realize goals of improved performance. While motivation to learn is often given insufficient attention, motivation to apply newly learned skills is as well. Both tend to be considered outside the realm of instructional design responsibilities, perhaps falling to HR to provide performance incentives. But given how essential motivation is to training success, it seems we should be giving it top priority.

In addition to the "7 Magic Keys" to motivational learning, which work well within CCAF, CCAF itself can contribute to both learning and performance motivations in several ways.

Using CCAF to Full Advantage

The full advantage of CCAF comes not from just having the four components present, but also from their quality and how they are used.

Authentic Contexts and Challenges

When the Context and Challenge pose a situation learners can see themselves facing and having responsibility to solve, they can be thankful this is a simulated event. They have an opportunity to safely attempt to handle it without fear of embarrassment from failure. They often appreciate the opportunity to deepen their knowledge and skills by exploring different actions to see what happens.

As the saying goes, "When it's time to perform, it's too late to practice." See Allenism #36. By revealing the kinds of situations learners can expect to face and providing a risk-free place to practice, learners become comfortable learning from private failures.

Practice

Practice is essential to learning, of course. It's also essential to building the confidence that one can handle learned situations effectively every time. By placing learners in a representative series of different situations and having them practice, learners can gain the confidence to perform newly learned skills—even in situations that aren't identical to any previously simulated situation. I stress building confidence, as with performance confidence people can become motivated and eager to demonstrate what they can do. Conversely, lacking confidence, people often shy away from unknown risks of public failure.

Jump In Immediately

In CCAF, we minimize instruction prior to presenting the first Context and Challenge. We are, in fact, hesitant to do anything before saying something like:

> Welcome, Winston! Imagine your first client wants you to represent her in a legal dispute involving intentional damage to boundary fencing.

This one sentence says a lot. It implies what you're going to learn to do and avoids saying so in stilted outcome objective lingo. It instantly gets you thinking about what relevant knowledge and experience you have, if any. You might be thinking, *This is totally new to me*, or *I've got this! No problem.* In either case, learners are likely to be intrigued to learn more about the case and see if they can handle it. Those who can will be quickly advanced to more complex challenges, while those who can't will be given hints, feedback, and/or pertinent instruction, along with as much practice as needed to build competence and confidence.

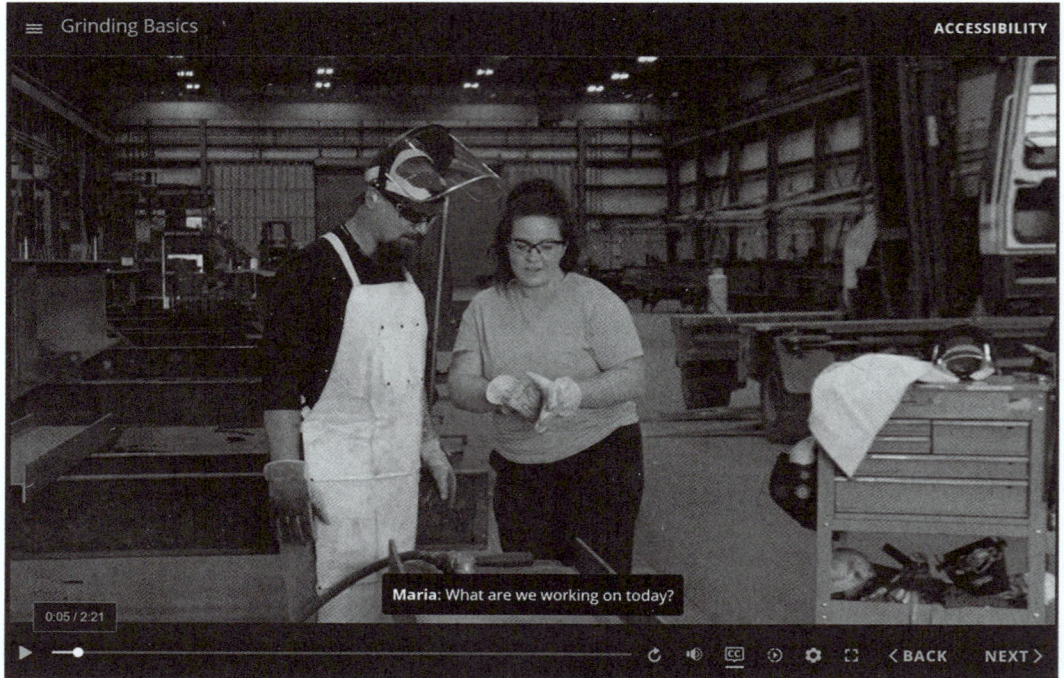

AISC Steel Fabricator Education

CCAF Engagement

EXAMPLE

Engaging Learners Immediately. *"This curriculum is for new steel fabrication workers in an industry that had significant retention problems in the first few days and weeks on the job. The target audience included recent high school students (maybe graduates, maybe not) who had not yet committed to the industry or even the job. Each module started by going directly into the story."* **Artisan Learning**

Helping vs. Presenting

I don't want you to miss this: What is often thought of as teaching happens in a very different way in CCAF. And at a different time.

It's not until the learner has encountered a Context and Challenge and made some attempt at solving it that we consider how best to help the learner. If we don't know anything about a learner, we'd be shooting in the dark and not able to provide any individualization at all. And we'd probably have learners unsure what this course will really be about.

So, we need to get to know each other.

As soon as learners begin taking action, which could well be asking for help, we'll begin to know how best to use their time. No up-front course promotion is as genuine and meaningful as stepping right into CCAF with all the interactive individualization it offers.

What is often thought of as teaching happens in a very different way in CCAF. And at a different time.

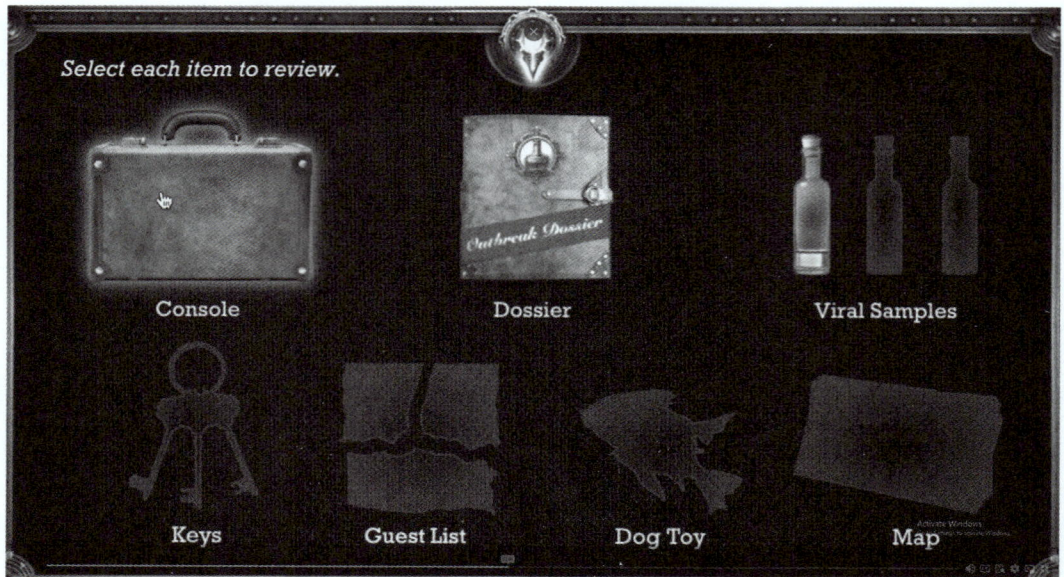

Select each item to review.

Console

Dossier

Viral Samples

Keys

Guest List

Dog Toy

Map

RSV Awareness

Real-Time Challenges

EXAMPLE

Actions & Consequences. *"In this course players are immediately immersed in a narrative-based sorting game where they explore the Chateau Goldwater, interact with staff, and gather information to solve a mystery. The game emphasizes the CCAF model by minimizing upfront instruction and presenting learners with real-time challenges, encouraging them to make decisions, see consequences, and adjust their approach. This approach, combined with detailed instructional feedback, enhances engagement and knowledge retention surrounding respiratory syncytial virus."* **ELB Learning**

CHAPTER 25

7 MAGIC KEYS TO MOTIVATION

Motivation to learn is essential. Without it, training is up against a brick wall upstaged only by conflicting beliefs as a show stopper. See Chapter 10, where we explored how beliefs dictate behaviors.

MOTIVATION LEVEL

Not interested. No attention.	Willing to attend (nice break).	Some interest, desire to do well.	Interested. See value.	Committed to improvement.
No learning even while going through the motions.	Respond to novel items, ignore others.	Prepare to pass test, forget everything afterward.	Attend fully to presentations, persist through confusing or difficult material.	Monitor own accomplishment; find missing info; rehearse, practice, organize as needed.
No behavioral change	No behavioral change	No behavioral change	Some behavioral change	Behavioral change!

BEHAVIORAL IMPACT OF TRAINING

I've detailed powerful ways to motivate learners in previous books, papers, and presentations, especially in *Michael Allen's Guide to e-Learning, 2nd Edition.* While this book adds insights arising from the many projects we've done since then, all the material in the *Guide* remains solid.

The Keys are very briefly described and updated here with additional insights that reinforce their importance. Be sure you don't overlook these powerful ways to ramp up the effectiveness of your designs.

Michael Allen's Guide to e-Learning

OVERVIEW OF THE 7 MAGIC KEYS

1. Establish Relevancy

The first Key was originally "Build on Anticipated Outcomes," which is still at the heart of the matter. One important way to motivate learning (or any other motivation) is to build on motivations people have already—in other words, what is *relevant* to the goals people are interested in pursuing. If learners don't see what value learning the content of a course has for them, they're not going to be energized to learn. The easy way to create relevancy is by creating a Context and Challenge the learner will face first up and reveal what the learner will be able to do upon course completion.

2. Put the Learner at Risk

In all performance training, we want learners thinking about alternative actions they can take and then evaluating the likely outcomes each action would cause. So, when are we going through such a process with our fullest attention? When we're at risk.

Railway Safety for Drivers

Avoiding Truck/RR Accidents. *"This game addresses the real-life risks associated with the profession of truck driving. The rules serve as educational content, providing opportunities for practice and engaging challenges such as handling trespassers, avoiding tickets, and dealing with distractions such as phone calls. Progress within the game is contextualized appropriately by authentic-feeling consequences and successes."* **Allen Interactions Inc.**

Create a scenario in which doing the wrong thing results in some form of simulated (but as authentic as possible) disaster. If that's too hard or impossible, then think about requiring the learner to start over or lose game points on taking the wrong path.

Put the Learner at Risk

EXAMPLE

3. Create Intrigue

The third original Key was, "Select the right content for each learner." Indeed, to create continuous value for learners along their learning path, we want to be sure we are employing the right content at each step. This is definitely a positive. But being too obvious about it doesn't really ramp up motivation as does intrigue. In fact, intrigue is one of the most powerful ways to get people engaged.

Related to risk, you might use the framework of a story in which unknown information will determine either a positive or negative outcome. As the learner decides what to do (or have a character do), give the learner the means to gather relevant information. You'll benefit from the identification of information the learner thinks is relevant, and the learner will learn what must be considered to do the right thing. The resulting tension and intrigue can be highly motivating and make learning fun.

4. Use an Appealing Context

I've mentioned context often as it's so important. Often people say, when it's clear someone hasn't understood, "Let me put that into context for you." We know context is clarifying. But context is important in multiple ways, such as establishing relevancy, conveying what a course teaches, and making a course pleasant to interact with.

On this latter point, clean screen layouts, crisp supportive media, and fascinating animations (especially when they illustrate a point that would otherwise require a ton of words) can convey a sense of quality and even respect for learners. If learners find the context appealing as a whole, they will be motivated to stay with it even if just to see what's next.

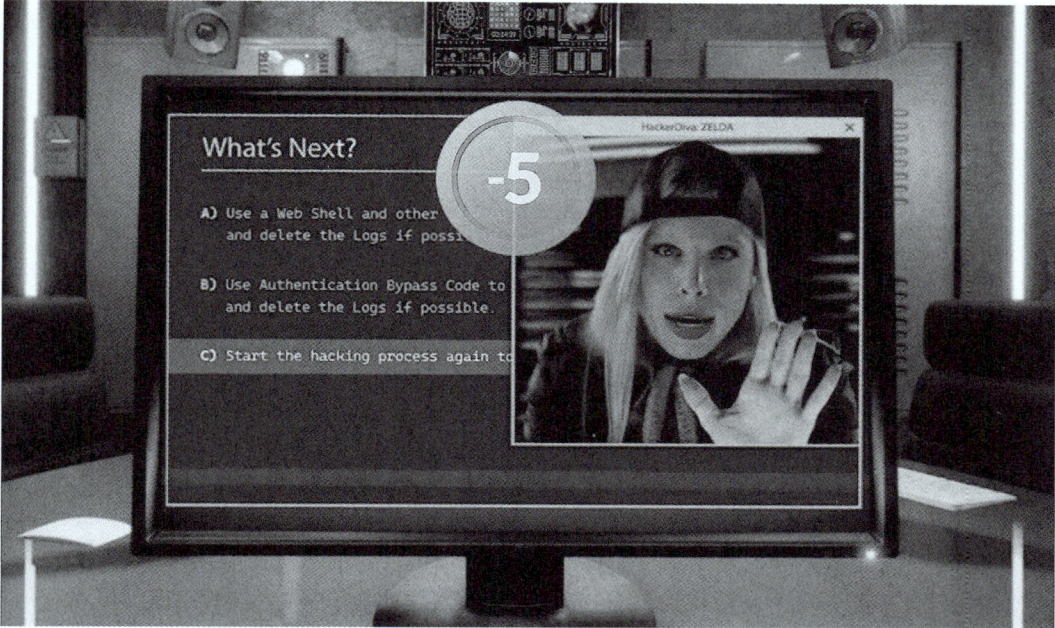

HackOps: Understanding Cyber Attacks

Hollywood Style Adventure. *"Learners role-play as undercover operatives to understand cyber attackers' tactics, techniques, and procedures (TTPs) for breaking into networks, stealing data, and installing ransomware. The game establishes relevancy by immersing learners in real-world cyber-attack scenarios, putting them at risk with simulated disasters if they make wrong decisions. Intrigue is created through a storyline with unknown outcomes, and learners perform multistep tasks to complete exercises from a hacker's perspective. The game provides intrinsic feedback and delays judgment, enhancing engagement and knowledge retention, culminating in a 'Hollywood' movie-style surprise ending."* **ELB Learning**

Intrigue

EXAMPLE

5. Have the Learner Perform Multistep Tasks

In trying to provide good learning experiences in elearning, in contrast to just asking questions to be answered, we want to mimic the performance of real tasks. Most real tasks require the performance of multiple steps. We look at whether we're satisfied with our performance on the first step, and if so, we go on to the next step. If not, we try to rectify our error before going on.

Product Popularity

One of Artie Guy's handbags was recently spotted on the shoulder of a famous actress. When asked about her unique purse, she raved about her obsession with Artie Guy handbags. Demand for the handbags has increased based on her endorsement.

What do you do?

> Increase inventory by 5% to minimize stockouts.

> Increase inventory by 50% to minimize stockouts.

> Do nothing, order same as usual

◄ BACK

SUPPLY CHAIN DASHBOARD

29% 71%

8%
Transportation

Total Cost   Total Profits

100%
Customer Service

6%
Labor

On Hand Inventory
1,000,014 units

Planned Order
600, 014 units

15%
Inventory

Selling Handbags

Have the Learner Perform Multistep Tasks

EXAMPLE

Multistep Tasks. *"In contrast to just asking questions to be answered, we want to create better learning experiences by mimicking the performance of real tasks, including the performance of multiple-step tasks. We ask learners to decide if they're satisfied with their performance on the first step, and if so, we go on to the next step. If not, as in real life performance, we ask learners to try to rectify errors before going on."* **Allen Interactions Inc.**

Multistep tasks are much more engaging than single-step tasks and certainly more than question answering. They are especially motivating when learners are given an opportunity to determine their satisfaction with each action and the ability to backtrack to correct a previous error when they suspect it is causing a problem.

6. Provide Intrinsic Feedback

Visually, or verbally if necessary, communicating the consequences of the learner's decisions and actions pushes learners to assess their performance. Learning this ability is often overlooked but important to achieving full mastery. It also makes learning experiences more cognitively and emotionally engaging, with learners motivated to achieve satisfying outcomes.

Intrinsic feedback is particularly effective when combined with multistep tasks.

7. Delay Judgment

Because technology enables it, it would seem that immediate appraisal of each learner's actions would be ideal. But, in fact, immediately learning whether your decision, action, or answer is correct invites a strategy of casually responding without thought just to get judgmental feedback that might reveal the correct answer.

If elearning isn't engaging and we aren't ramping up the motivation to learn, learners will use any device they can imagine to speed through as fast as possible, learning little, if anything. Delayed judgment makes it faster to think and learn, especially when combined with multistep tasks and intrinsic rather than judgmental feedback.

All Seven?

Just incorporating a few of the Magic Keys will pump up learner motivation and engagement. It's not necessary and quite a reach to apply them all, but it's definitely possible as the example on page 197 demonstrates and designer/developer Dr. Pooja Jaisingh notes:

Inbox Zero Hero touches each of the seven keys.

- *Welcome and Briefing:* *Sets a relevant tone and introduces the challenge. This aligns with Keys* 1: Relevancy, 3: Intrigue, *and* 4: Context.

- *Interactive Elements:* *Learners will engage with multiple interactions that immerse them in an authentic environment. These interactions require judgment across multistep decisions with delayed, meaningful, intrinsic feedback and opportunities for reflection. This covers* 1: Relevancy, 2: Risk, 4: Context, 5: Multistep Tasks, 6: Intrinsic Feedback, *and* 7: Delay Judgment.

- *Self-Check:* *The course closes with a self-check to reinforce learning with intrigue and reflection. This ties into* 1: Relevancy, 3: Intrigue, 5: Multistep Tasks, *and* 6: Intrinsic Feedback.

Inbox Detective: Urgent or Not?

Review all six emails. For each one, toggle the button to mark it as 'Urgent' or 'Not Urgent.' Once all messages are labeled, click **Submit Choices** to proceed.

	Sender	Subject	Preview Text	
☐ ☆	Priya Malhotra – Mega...	**Need Your Thoughts ASAP** - Can you take a look at the latest deck before noon?		Urgent
☐ ☆	Tina - People Ops	**Quick Check-In** - Are you joining us for lunch on Friday?		Not Urgent
☐ ☆	Kevin Sharma (Manage...	**Client Call Prep** - Let's finalize your slides by EOD.		Urgent
☐ ☆	Learning Digest	**Fresh Ideas Just Dropped** - You'll love this month's lineup of reads.		Not Urgent
☐ ☆	Kavya – Marketing	**Small Change?** - Should we tweak the CTA on that page?		Not Urgent
☐ ☆	Finance Team	**Revised File Attached** - Please confirm receipt before Thursday COB.		Not Urgent

Submit Choices

Inbox Zero Hero

Inbox Zero Hero. *"This example covers all seven of the magic keys. In the demo we explain how they each apply across the welcome, interactivity, and self-check sections."* **Pooja Jaisingh**

All 7 Magic Keys Tasks

EXAMPLE

CHAPTER 26

BASIC INDIVIDUALIZATION CONCEPTS

No, No, No. Who Did We Lose This Time?

Let's view each course of instruction as a journey on which learners begin with whatever knowledge and skills they have as they head out. Given an effective instructional program plus sufficient attention, engagement, and effort on the part of the learners, teachers expect some learners to cross the finish line with some new knowledge and skills in tow. But probably not all learners, unfortunately.

With unindividualized delivery, whether classroom or digital, some will get lost on the journey. *Well, they just weren't giving it their all. Not much I can do about that.*

It's a simple, clear, and accepted depiction of education and training. For practicality, everyone is treated as if they're starting from the same place (although surely that's not where everyone is) and will benefit from taking the same path to arrive at the same end point at the same time (although that never really happens).

Prior to instruction, some may have already advanced to different points along the path or even reached its conclusion, but practicality demands starting all learners from the same point—a starting point as far removed from the end point as is needed to be sure very few, if anyone, is unable to track from there. If the starting point is too advanced, some learners may never be able to catch up. And clearly, that is undesirable. But then so is boring all those who are already much further into the journey.

Learners left behind   Learners waiting for others to catch up

Nice and Neat

By treating all learners alike, the lockstep process coordinates nicely with school calendars, product rollouts, fiscal calendars, and other organizational constraints and demands. Its fixed dates for start and conclusion are handy, without doubt. But on the other hand, it's necessary to have groups of learners available to start at the same time and available for all scheduled learning activities, which, of course, isn't always optimal for ongoing organizational operations.

Treating Everyone Alike Isn't Fair

Treating all learners as novices to avoid anyone being left behind has always been annoying and time-wasting for the learners who aren't novices. There are much better solutions for both individuals and organizations.

To be fair and provide equal benefits to learners, we have to differentiate instruction based on readiness, needs, and abilities. Let's look first at optimizing instruction for the benefit of individuals through individualization.

Individualizing for Individuals

If we want to optimize the journey for each learner, instructional programs must factor in learner variables—the characteristics that define the individual persons that learners are. We want eager participation and energized focus. We want learners purposely gaining from every morsel of what we have to offer. That's not going to happen if the program is a poor fit.

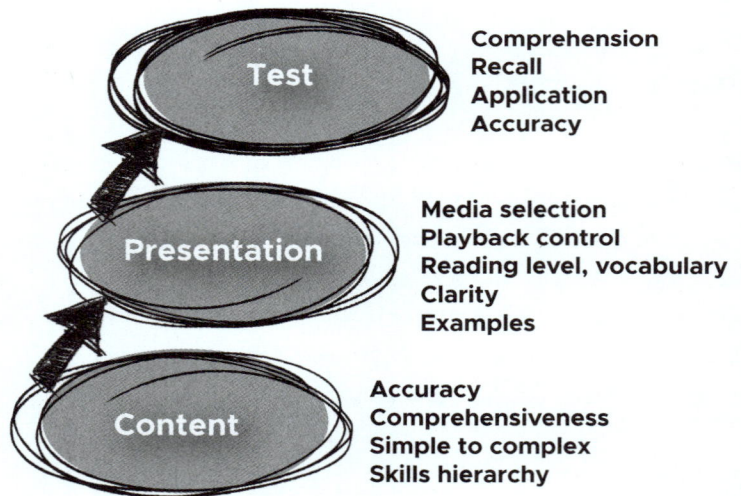

Figure 26.1. Typical Design Sequence Makes Individualization Difficult

At the start of the design process, rather than concentrating on content presentation, clarity, and accuracy to the relative exclusion of considering differences among learners (as is typical—see Figure 26.1), we need to be thinking about how we can make sure the instruction is right for the full range of our learners. If we don't start with this, we would be trying to individualize too late in the process—if, in fact, we ever got to it, as few do. By making individualization considerations foundational, we have the greatest possibility of doing what would be best.

In rethinking elearning, we want to take full advantage of the technology's ability to deliver unique experiences to every learner as may be needed.

In rethinking elearning, we want to take full advantage of the technology's ability to deliver unique experiences to every learner as may be needed.

Individualizing for Organizations

Individualization of learning has awesome benefits for organizations just as it does for each learner. Perhaps most obvious among them is the prospect of shortening learning time.

Shorten Learning Time

When staff are away for training, they aren't addressing their responsibilities and contributing value to the organization. The ideal length of a training program for most organizations is zero minutes. They dream of taking a blue pill and instantly becoming a skilled helicopter pilot.

But when training is critical to realizing consistent performance of best practices, it can't be skipped entirely. The faster it can be done, the better—as long as it enables learners to perform at the desired level and perhaps motivates them to do so continuously as a bonus outcome. Individualization allows learners to complete training as fast as they are individually able. Faster learning trainees can immediately get on the job without having to wait for slower learners.

Among other benefits provided to organizations from individualization of instruction are learner appreciation, performance confidence, and even joyful performance.

Learner Appreciation

It's widely documented that the more organizations invest in training, the lower the attrition.[17] Employees feel valued when high-quality training is provided and feel even more valued when the training recognizes their current skills, their aspirations, and how they feel about the appropriateness of training programs. Individualized training recognizes individuals instead of delivering standard programs everyone has to slog through. Individualized recognition transfers to appreciation for the organization, which leads to a plethora of positive outcomes.

Performance Confidence

We all tend to shy away from the risk of making mistakes, especially in front of others. Many instructional programs teach people to answer questions correctly about how something should be done, but that doesn't mean people are now prepared to do it. Further, even if learners demonstrate an ability to perform a task in training, it doesn't mean they've reached the level of confidence needed to perform those new skills on the job or while being observed by others.

Well-designed individualization strives not only to build skills but also works to address performance fears and build strong confidence. These programs don't conclude until there is both objective evidence a learner is capable and the learner rates themselves as being ready and confident to perform in post-training situations.

17 Laetitia Samuel-Owusu, "Employee Training Statistics: The Value of Good Training," Intellum, June 6, 2024, https://www.intellum.com/resources/blog/employee-training-statistics.

Agile Project Management

An Individualized Adventure. *"This course on agile project management is a choose-your-own-adventure in which learners navigate various scenarios based on their choices. The simulation includes distractions and decision points, leading to positive, neutral, or negative outcomes. Learners appreciate the personalized experience and gamification elements such as points and a static leaderboard."*
Don Becker, University of Houston

Personalized Experience

EXAMPLE

Joyful Performance

Habits are powerful things. They hold strong sway over what we do. Even when we've learned better methods and we've become confident we can perform them, what will motivate us to change our ways? Organizations implement various incentives, which sometimes work but fail all too often. One of the primary reasons this happens is that we like to do what we enjoy doing and don't like being manipulated into doing things in ways we don't enjoy and bring discomfort. It's not that complicated.

The challenge is to help learners become joyful in new performance patterns. Once again, individualization comes to the rescue by adapting to individuals:

1. Reducing the risk of failure through "overlearning" and developing a strong sense of confidence is a first step.

2. Using CCAF to demonstrate the positive consequences of excellent performance of the new skills and the negative consequences of disapproved or inferior behaviors can help as well.

3. Suggesting learners ask others in the organization, "How would you feel if I changed my performance (in a certain way)? Would you appreciate that? Would it make things better?"

Ask learners how they might become joyful in making performance changes.

One technique that's been particularly effective is to ask learners how they might become joyful in making performance changes. The answers can be matched to the same answers given by people who felt the same way initially but went on to become very pleased they made the changes. Watching video clips of such kindred spirits and those who now joyfully broke with old habits and successfully perform in preferred ways can make a learning program uniquely successful.

CHAPTER 27

WHAT CAN BE INDIVIDUALIZED

Creating a unique experience for each learner in order to maximize effectiveness and engagement while speeding learners toward competency and confidence as quickly as possible may sound beyond reach. Let me assure you that it isn't and, further, that **not doing so is very expensive** (even if accounting hasn't realized it yet).

There are many ways to individualize—some are trivial; some require artificial intelligence. It's probably the case that the greater the individualization, the more valuable the elearning is. But there are clearly intermediate steps that are valuable and much better than doing nothing.

Here's a list of ways to consider individualizing your learners' instructional experiences.

Basic Forms of Individualization

1. **Self-pacing**
   The ability of learners to work as fast or as slowly as they wish or need to is an obvious benefit of elearning afforded by its very nature. Pretty much a freebie.

2. **24/7/365 accessibility**
   eLearning adjusts to the learner's schedule, being ready and waiting with unlimited patience between periods of availability. A valuable advancement allows learners to either return to the

exact point of progress after taking a break or go back to a menu to review or select a topic of urgent need. Not quite a freebie, although a Learning Management System (LMS) can help with this.

3. **Differentiated feedback**

   In the earliest elearning, learners would get the same feedback for any answer: *"The correct answer is . . ."* Learners were tasked to compare their answer to the correct one but often didn't and just moved on. An advancement provided one feedback message for correct answers and another for incorrect answers—often the dreaded and unhelpful "No. Try again." As is typically done now, systems analyze answers and respond differentially. It takes more work, but this is much better. Artificial intelligence helps here.

4. **Self-selected sequencing**

   While many designers have required learners to work through content in a fixed sequence, some have seen the advantage of providing content menus. Learners can directly access a list of microlearning modules. Self-selection can sacrifice transitions from topic to topic and risk learner frustration from not having prerequisite understandings, but also gives learners appreciated options. Interdependencies within the content or lack thereof help determine best practices here.

5. **Test out**

   Learners who feel they already have some or all of the skills addressed in a module or the whole course can opt to take a pretest (which is often just the post-test offered early and the best use of a post-test—see Allenism #19). If learners do superbly well, they can be given completion credit and exit. If they do well in some areas, those course modules can be made optional while the remainder are required.

6. **Help on request**

   Hints, examples, lists of steps, applicable principles, and other

forms of help can be made available on request. Various designs withhold some or all forms of help until the learner has made some attempt, either successfully or not. To assure mastery, learners may be required to repeat exercises until they can be performed without accessing help.

7. **Practice to mastery**
Instead of a fixed amount of practice for all learners, learners continue to practice until mastery criteria are reached. Criteria usually include the maximum number of errors allowed, amount of help accessed, and number of sequential exercises performed successfully. They may also include response time or the time needed to complete an exercise.

8. **Pattern recognition**
It's surprising to many that detecting learner response patterns and addressing them was fundamental in very early elearning. In the early 1960s, Patrick Suppes of Stanford University was developing elearning to teach children mathematical concepts and procedures. By looking for error patterns, such as not subtracting from the tens column when necessary, Prof. Suppes was able to detect specific misunderstandings and provide the specific individualized instruction needed.

Contemporary Individualization

1. **Practice to confidence**
Confidence is a subjective state that only learners can assess and report. Even if we see perfect performance in every practice exercise, learners may need more practice to reach a reported level of confidence that will enable them to put their new skills into use.

2. **Practice for long-term retention**
Learning can decay quickly if it's not exercised over time. How much practice sustained retention requires and over how many

weeks or months of distributed practice is needed depends on individual attributes and other things that are happening in the learner's life during this time.

3. **Challenge adjustment based on performance**
Learning challenges that are beneath a learner's capabilities (whether acquired in current training or previously) quickly become boring while challenges that are too great frustrate learners—an emotion that easily becomes a blockade to learning.

4. **Challenge adjustment based on self-efficacy**
A learner's self-assessed competency may have little correlation with actual competency. Responding by adjusting challenge levels can help get these states aligned, making learners either open to more learning or ready for post-training performance.

5. **Activity modification based on affective state**
We all have a host of affective attributes that direct our attention, attitudes, energy, decisions, and behaviors. After asking learners how they're feeling, we can adjust learning events in many ways, such as by providing a demonstration on how to perform a task, providing hints along the way, or ramping up a challenge by imposing a time limit—challenging learners to beat their previous best time. Such individualization can optimize instructional effectiveness and make learning truly learner-centered.

6. **Personalized goal setting**
Allow learners to set specific, measurable goals within the elearning environment and track their progress against these goals. After meeting their own goals, elearning can report the value of the level of competency attained and suggest, if appropriate, shooting for higher levels if necessary for specific role responsibilities.

Emerging Individualization

1. **Use video to detect affective states**
   Detect emotions via live video of facial expressions and posture.

2. **Interact with spoken language**
   For those with minimal typing or spelling skills, natural spoken language can help both speed up learning experiences and make them more comfortable. An additional instructional advantage comes from requiring learners to think of actions to take rather than just selecting them from a prompt list.

3. **Use AI to converse with learners**
   AI can query learners, challenging their skills and understanding as might a live tutor.

4. **Use AI to construct CCAF components in real time**
   Although AI is used by many authors today to help construct the CCAF components, it's possible already to let AI construct CCAF cycles in response to detected needs and projected benefits for individual learners.

5. **Cultural and language customization**
   Adapt content to the learner's cultural context and preferred language to enhance relevance and accessibility.

6. **Preferred learning modality**
   Offer content in multiple formats (e.g., video, text, interactive simulations, or auditory narration) so learners can choose the method that matches their preferences.[18]

---

18 There's been much made in research about the lack of evidence of learning styles. But it's quite another matter to consider the affective states produced by pushing learners into types of learning experience they dislike versus providing ones they prefer and engage them fully.

7. **Role and interest customization**
   Provide activities and examples that adapt to the learner's industry, role, or personal interests to increase relevance and engagement.

8. **Gamification customization**
   Design tailored rewards or individualized challenges to keep learners motivated.

Individualization Summary

Here's a quick reference to help you decide what, why, and how to individualize.[19]

Component	Features	Purpose	Challenges	Implementation Strategies	Examples
Learner Access and Scheduling	□ 24/7 Accessibility □ Self-Pacing □ Free Navigation	Provides flexibility to accommodate different learner schedules and promotes engagement by fitting into their lives	Connectivity issues, procrastination, or skipping critical content	Use LMS/LXP, design modular units, and offer interactive navigation with progress tracking	□ Downloadable resources □ Interactive menus □ Seat time estimates
Sequencing and Pathways	□ Self-Selected Sequencing □ Test-Out Options □ Challenge Adjustment (Triggered or Role-Based)	Ensures learners focus on relevant content, increasing motivation and reducing time spent on unnecessary material	Overlooking foundational content, misinterpreting learner needs, or inaccurate assessments	Provide content maps or dashboards, integrate pre-assessments, and use AI or manual adjustments for difficulty	□ "Choose Your Own Adventure" □ Branching scenarios with progressive difficulty

---

19 Special thanks to Ann Iverson, Sr. Instructional Strategist and Executive Producer, Innovative Learning Solutions LLC, for constructing this great summary table.

Component	Features	Purpose	Challenges	Implementation Strategies	Examples
Mastery and Retention	☐ Practice to Mastery ☐ Practice to Confidence ☐ Practice for Long-Term Retention	Guarantees deeper learning and skill retention while fostering learner confidence and readiness	Time-intensive mastery requirements or subjective confidence evaluations	Set mastery thresholds, include self-assessments, and implement spaced repetition through scheduled reviews	☐ Scenario-based simulations with mastery checkpoints ☐ Confidence checks embedded in activities
Feedback and Challenge	☐ Differentiated Feedback ☐ Challenge Adjustment Based on Performance ☐ Feedback Based on Preferences	Enhances engagement by addressing learner needs and improving understanding through personalized feedback	Potential for overwhelming feedback or inconsistent challenge adjustments	Develop detailed explanations, track performance data, and use AI or manual adjustments to align feedback with learner personas	☐ Progressively harder tasks unlocked as learners master easier ones ☐ "Your choice indicates a misunder-standing of X concept; here's a refresher."
Emotional and Cognitive Adaptation	☐ Activity Selection Based on Affective State ☐ Challenge Adjustment Based on Self-Efficacy ☐ Emotion-Aware Learning	Boosts learning effectiveness by responding to emotional states and aligning learning tasks with emotional readiness	Privacy concerns, emotional mismanagement, or misalignment with actual competency	Incorporate emotion-based check-ins, pre-task self-assessments, and manual or AI tools for real-time adaptation	☐ "Feeling confident? Try this advanced scenario." ☐ "Looks like you're stuck—here are a few options for you to try."

CHAPTER 28

PRACTICAL CONTENT INDIVIDUALIZATION

Content individualization is generally easy for elearning as long as the learning experience is modularized. Again, the CCAF framework is perfect for this, providing a module for each set of Context and Challenge together with provisions for Activity and instructional Feedback as may be appropriate. For content individualization, the question is how to select modules.

There are three types of content individualization techniques:

1. Learner-controlled content selection
2. Software-controlled branching
3. Mixed initiative control

Learner-Controlled Content Selection

I've heard students using elearning report they felt trapped, almost like hostages. They couldn't browse. They couldn't review. They could do only what the current screen allowed. And they had to work through those screens in the order the author placed them. Feeling like a victim doesn't inspire engagement and enthusiasm for learning.

Browsing

Few authoring systems make it easy to allow learners to browse, look ahead to see what's coming within a current module, or skim through and maybe even sample components anywhere in a course just as you might look through a book to see if it would be the right one for you. Even without an authoring system in the way, it's not particularly easy to create such elearning capabilities when going straight to programming either. But it can be done, and it's worth it. A good LMS can help a lot.

Once you have created the framework for browsing, you can use it for all the courses you create. It's definitely worth it.

What's for Dinner?

Providing learners a menu from which to select topics is a helpful technique used fairly often in elearning. It requires authors to give away some of their control, but it doesn't mean learning outcomes will suffer. Quite the contrary, instead of serving only one preset meal, providing choices to learners extends a partnering hand and creates a sense of joint responsibility. It moves from the thought *we're here to make learning happen* to *we're here to help you learn and reach your goals.*

We need learners to be constantly doing all they can to learn. If they don't feel the responsibility—that it's somehow the responsibility of the elearning to make it happen—we will all have a hard time succeeding. But, not to worry. In my observations, learners frequently work through content in the order listed in the menu even when they have the choice. Learners generally expect the order provided to be the one you've optimized. Their expectations are most likely correct, but having provided learners the options of jumping ahead or reviewing sends the right message to learners and gives them agency.

Testing Out

Another learner-appreciated option allows learners to skip modules by demonstrating their abilities. It means you have to create a reliable measure of student abilities that is sufficiently comprehensive, but you should do that anyway. We're not talking about multiple-choice questions here unless you're teaching learners to correctly answer multiple-choice questions. It's rare that's the case. Almost universally, we're looking to be sure learners can perform job-related tasks proficiently. So, to facilitate skipping modules appropriately, we need to measure the learner's ability to perform the tasks taught in them.

Caution!

Studies over decades have shown learners tend to make poor decisions regarding their learning. It seems we often don't know when we're learning as opposed to when we just think we are.[20] So, the design challenge is to give learners respectful controls while also giving them the guidance that will help them use their time and energy effectively.

Software-Controlled Branching

Given the practicality and advantages of structuring courses from microlearning modules, especially CCAF modules (although CCAF isn't a requirement), there are two types of software-controlled branching to consider:

- Branching among modules
- Branching within modules

Branching Among Modules

When we see students performing at the high end of proficiency, it's an opportunity to jump them ahead to greater challenges, and when

---

20   Peter C. Brown, Henry L. Roediger, and Mark A. McDaniel, *Make It Stick: The Science of Successful Learning* (Cambridge, MA: Belknap Press of Harvard University Press, 2014).

we see students struggling and needing a lot of help, the software can branch to remediation and more practice on the basics.

A simple journey map may look like the following:

Learner's Journey

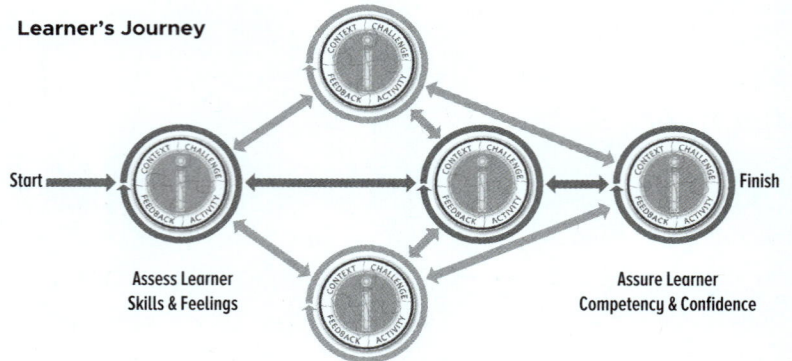

Microlearning modules are represented here by CCAF modules, although other module structures can be used. What's essential is that modules are collecting learner performance data on which to decide, among other things, if the current module is the appropriate one or if branching to another would likely serve the student better.

The last module before the course finish line is designed to require learners to perform all skills learned in the course to at least the minimum required proficiency. If learners fail in any one aspect or more, they are branched to a relevant module or modules before eventually returning to the final module to verify proficiency.

Individualized Branching Among Microlearning Module	
Measures and Indicators	**Possible Branches to Alternate Modules**
On learner making successive ineffective decisions*	• Branch learners to an entry-level module for foundational learning • Branch learners to part-task exercises to rehearse solution components
On learner repeating the same error or type of error*	• Branch learners to part-task exercises to rehearse solution components • Present worked examples to study, perhaps via video walk-through • Present incorrectly worked examples and ask the learner to identify the errors made
On learner giving quick, excellent solutions	• Branch to more advanced or other topics
* Try not to jump in fast with directions or corrective information. We want learners thinking and evaluating. A little frustration can be motivating, but too much is debilitating. If frustration is high, suggest breaking the challenge into mini challenges.	

Branching Within Modules

In well-designed interactive learning programs, we're frequently, if not continuously, measuring student proficiency. There are many decision points at which software can make helpful things happen within modules and even within interactions.

Individualized Branching Within Microlearning Module

Measures and Indicators	Possible Software Decisions
On learner making immediate requests for help	• Advise or require learners to attempt a solution before help is made available • Limit the number of help requests allowed, perhaps with a countdown display
On learner finding only incomplete solutions[21]	• Ask learners if they think their solution was successful/complete • Ask learners if they can think of more to be done • Ask learners if they can think of additional steps to take
On learner finding only an ineffective solution*	• Ask learners if they're satisfied with their solution • Ask learners to try something different to see what happens
On learner repeating the same error or type of error	• Branch to part-task exercises to rehearse solution components • Ask if learner can identify the most likely first point of their first error
On learner's response latency increasing (rather than decreasing) to equal challenge difficulties	• Ask the learner if there's a distraction or if something has become unclear or concerning
* Try not to jump in fast with directions or corrective information. We want learners thinking and evaluating. A little frustration can be motivating, but too much is debilitating. If frustration is high, suggest breaking the challenge into mini challenges.	

---

21 I use the word "solutions" instead of "answers" to emphasize the value of task performance over simple question answering.

Mixed Initiative Control

We have mixed initiative individualization when learners and the instructor (or elearning) collaborate, with each having the option to take control on various conditions. It's probably the most effective and comfortable form of individualization, and also one most similar to in-person mentoring. For example, learners can opt to review and continue practicing before moving ahead or conversely jump out of a module to another. The system can similarly suggest doing the same thing or holding off for a little while to complete a current exercise.

To make the experience comfortable and effective, rather than confusing and disruptive, justification and permission should be sought and received. Examples:

Individualized Mixed Initiative Branching	
Initiation	**Permission**
System: "You handled the last few challenges perfectly. We could jump to a new set of challenges now unless you want to practice a bit more."	**System:** "Please let me know what you prefer: • More practice. • Let's jump."
System: "You're requesting a lot of help, which is what it's <u>here</u> for. But perhaps you'd now like to see what you can do fully on your own."	**System:** "What do you think? • Remove help access and see how it goes. • Let me have only one help next time. • Just give me hints instead of help. • Leave help services on, but I'll try to use them less."

Individualized Mixed Initiative Branching

Initiation	Permission
Learner summons a menu or control panel in the midst of a module then clicks to jump to the next one.	**System:** "You haven't completed the current module and could find the next one confusing because of material we haven't yet covered. But you can certainly try it if you wish. I'll mark your place so you can resume the current module later. • Let's jump. I'm finding this pretty easy. • Let's jump. I just want to see where this leads. • Uh, no. Maybe I'll just stay here."
Learner summons menu or control panel in the midst of a module and then clicks to abandon it and return to a previous one.	**System:** "No problem to back up if you wish. To be of most help, please indicate what you're thinking: • I think I missed something important in a previous module. • I just liked that other module and want to review it. • No big reason. I just want to go back. • On second thought, I'd like to continue here."

Aviation Training: ATC 600A

Learner-Controlled Branching. *"This module offers aviation students a multi-level training experience. Learners can start with any of the levels, Demonstration, Practice, or go right to Test based on their perceived needs. The simulation then provides feedback on their accuracy. This approach aligns with the concept of individualized learning by offering self-pacing, differentiated feedback, and personalized goal setting. It ensures learners can progress at their own pace, receive tailored support based on their needs, and achieve competency and confidence efficiently."* **Karl M. Kapp, Commonwealth University's Institute for Interactive Technologies**

Personalized Experience

EXAMPLE

CHAPTER 29

PRACTICAL AFFECTIVE INDIVIDUALIZATION

Self-Efficacy Woes

We've mentioned the importance of affective influencers on learning, such as fears and aspirations. Self-efficacy is also one of those affective states that has been researched extensively and found to have profound impact on learning.[22]

Bandura discovered long ago that with a very low assessment of their abilities in a specific area—writing, math, art, for example—learners are not able to learn those skills well. They've often given up and tuned out even as a course of instruction began. They basically just wait for the course to end while thinking of other interests, learning little if anything, and feeling they have substantiated their claim that they can't learn these sorts of things.

ACTUAL COMPETENCY   SELF-EFFICACY

TOO LOW →
• Won't try
• Doesn't improve
• Uses familiar methods

TOO HIGH
• Bored during training
• Doesn't recogize needs
• Makes no changes

Surprisingly, there's a similar outcome for those whose self-efficacy *exceeds* their current level of abilities. In this case, learners also tend to tune out because they don't feel they need instruction. They feel

22   A. Bandura, "Self-Efficacy: Toward a Unifying Theory of Behavioral Change," *Psychological Review* 84(2) (1977): 191–215, https://doi.org/10.1037/0033-295X.84.2.191.

the course is for others who don't have their skills and experience. Even if the course contains important and useful updates, these learners are likely to miss them because they're also thinking about other things and fully intending to continue performing tasks as they have been.

What can we do? Is it really practical to be concerned with this?

Helping Learners Who Don't Need Help

We can address the issue head-on, again by first asking learners how they feel and then adapting. It's simple enough to ask learners through an interactive dialogue or even via AI conversation. Figure 29.1 shows one such dialogue in which, from the very first sign-on, learners are asked how they feel about taking this course.

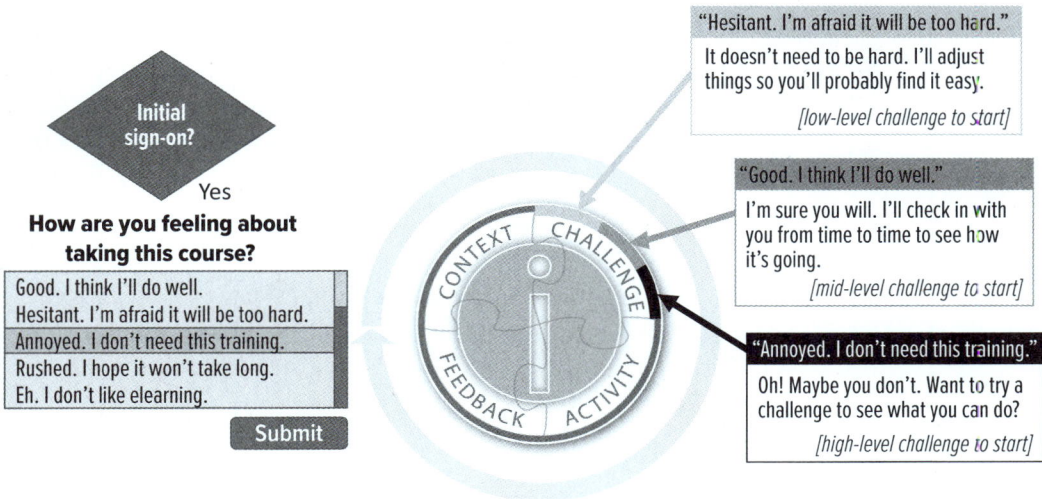

"Hesitant. I'm afraid it will be too hard."
It doesn't need to be hard. I'll adjust things so you'll probably find it easy.
[low-level challenge to start]

"Good. I think I'll do well."
I'm sure you will. I'll check in with you from time to time to see how it's going.
[mid-level challenge to start]

"Annoyed. I don't need this training."
Oh! Maybe you don't. Want to try a challenge to see what you can do?
[high-level challenge to start]

Initial sign-on?

Yes

How are you feeling about taking this course?

Good. I think I'll do well.
Hesitant. I'm afraid it will be too hard.
Annoyed. I don't need this training.
Rushed. I hope it won't take long.
Eh. I don't like elearning.

Submit

Figure 29.1. Assessing and Responding to Affective States

Alternate designs use a slider to report feelings or a set of emotive faces. These reporting methods can be made active at all times so learners can seek support in early phases of growing discomfort. See the following example user interfaces as well as the empathetic responses from the instructional software as it adapts to the various reported affective states.

Perpetual Slider—Self-Reflection

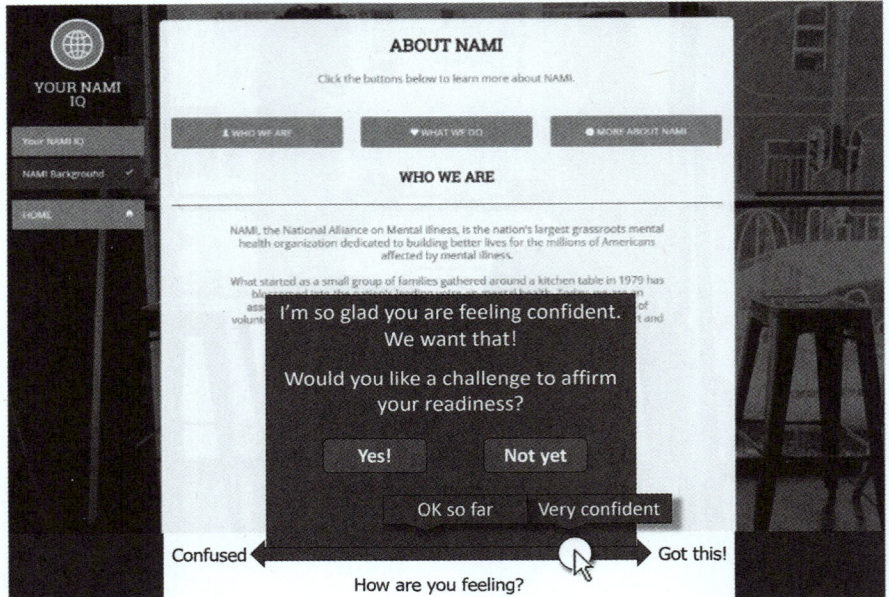

Figure 29.2. A Perpetual Slider Eases Reports of Feelings at Any Time

Perpetual sliders can appear in many forms. Having them always on screen provides comfort to learners who, by the presence of the slider, know they can and are invited to report their feelings at any time. Movement of the slider can trigger any type of response the designer thinks would be helpful.

Adaptive Trigger

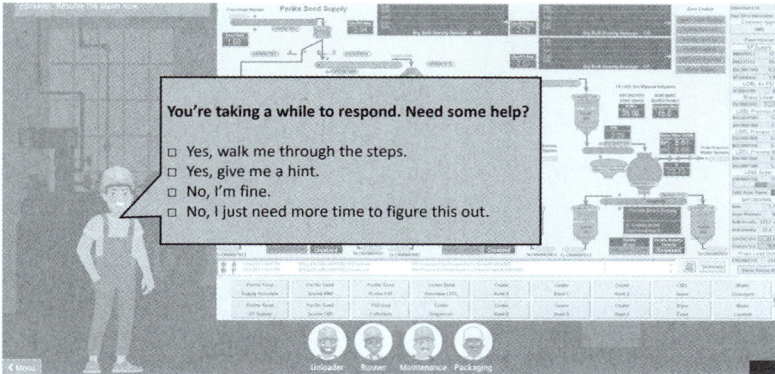

Figure 29.3. Adaptive Triggers

Adaptive triggers are constantly monitoring learner activity. If it varies from normal on such attributes as speed of responding or accuracy, a pop-up message alerts the learner of concern and desire to help. Options allow learners to indicate that everything is fine or that help would be timely.

Emotional Identification

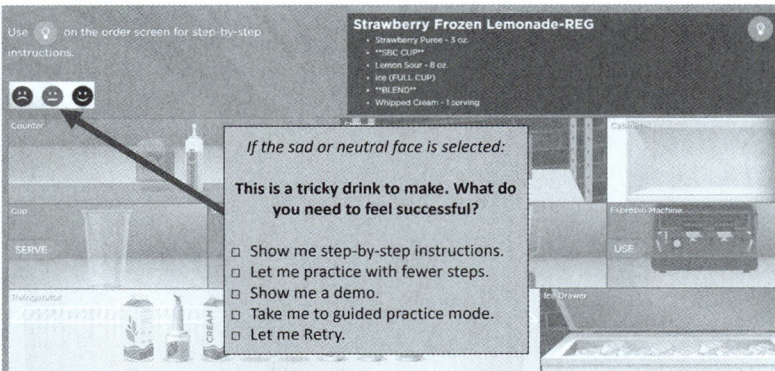

Figure 29.4. Emotional Identification

Perpetual icons represent various emotional states learners may be in. These also recognize that the learner's feelings are important and that at any time we are wanting to help. A menu lists ways our program can help.

Periodic Check-In

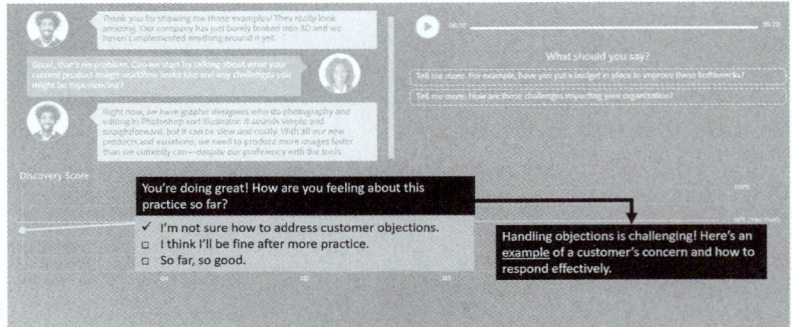

Figure 29.5. Periodic Check-In

Similar to Adaptive triggers, Periodic triggers are spaced through the learning content to pop up with somewhat regular frequency to check with learners to see if all is going well from their perspective. Once again, options are available to learners based on how they're feeling.

When learners realize their feelings matter, we can partner with them to make learning experiences more effective. Just asking how they feel enhances learning prospects.

Consider self-efficacy again. For those learners with an inflated assessment, we can invite them to try their hand at an advanced challenge, perhaps at the level of the final activities in the course to be done without hints or feedback until completion (or aborting). This experience can confirm their skills and award completion. Or it can help high-self-efficacy learners see how course content will help them—calming their initial doubts and making it easier to focus.

For those learners with a notion of inability, noting expectations of difficulty or failure can suggest a range of helpful responses. After reassuring those learners that plenty of assistance will be forthcoming (which, in itself, can lift expectations a bit), adjustments can be made by providing worked examples, hints, and incremental positive feedback—all of which are valuable to have in elearning anyway.

While inviting learners to report their affective states can be used with many instructional paradigms or frameworks, CCAF makes this valuable structure easy and practical, as we'll see in Book 3.

DESIGNER'S NOTEBOOK #5

Self-check: See if you garnered these takeaway principles and are ready to use them.

☐ A combination of theory, research findings, and experience, mixed together with cautious regard for intuition and "conclusive" science, produces the best guidance.

☐ Learning science is difficult because of the myriad influencers of learning always present and the complexity of human behavior. It's tempting to generalize but often a mistake.

☐ Individual differences, including states of anxiety and other fluctuating affective conditions, require adaptive individualized learning experiences.

☐ There are affordable, practical ways to create highly effective elearning that goes beyond basic skills training to achieve competency, confidence, and a joy of performing well.

☐ A good mentor's continuous appraisal of understanding, performance level, and affective states is an excellent model to achieve in elearning.

☐ Motivation is essential for learning. It's risky not to ramp up learning, such as with the 7 Magic Keys to Motivation, and let the potential lack of motivation negate all your otherwise great design work.

☐ The CCAF model provides an organized and structured framework for designing great learning experiences from the essential components of active learning: Context, Challenge, Activity, and Feedback.

☐ Context helps establish content relevance for learners, enabling them to imagine a situation they might expect to be in.

☐ Challenges present a problem to be solved or a task to be performed.

☐ A range of possible learner actions, simulated as authentically as possible, allows exploration of various solutions.

☐ Feedback in combinations of illustrated consequences, judgments, and instruction complete the CCAF cycle. Cycles are often repeated with adjustments to one or more components until mastery is reached.

☐ We can't individualize anything if we know nothing about our individual learners, so the initial CCAF module is as much about meeting our learner as our learner finding relevancy in what we have to teach.

☐ Implementation of CCAF is often most effective by jumping directly to CCAF modules without much, if any, preface, introduction, or hype. CCAF better communicates the learning objectives (being able to meet challenges such as those presented), including where course content is applicable (the Context).

☐ Learning events must be Meaningful, Memorable, and Motivational (the 3M's) to be effective. Lacking any one of them compromises learning outcomes.

☐ There are many components of learning interactions that can be adjusted to achieve effective individualization (see Chapter 27 for a list and Chapters 28 and 29 for example implementations).

BUYER'S CHECKLIST #5

To ensure a great investment in training and ROI, be sure to ask the following questions.

☐ People are different, so there aren't instructional experiences that are optimal for everyone. Are you examining how a proposed elearning program is sensitive to learner differences and responds to them?

☐ eLearning is most powerful when it is designed to respond to each person's needs as they proceed through a course. We call that individualization and have pretty simple and practical means of achieving it. Be sure to inquire what kind and how much individualization you're buying.

☐ One of the ways we differ from each other is how capable we think we are. That's called "self-efficacy." If a person's self-efficacy is low ("I'll never be good at math.") or higher than their actual skill level ("I should be teaching this course, not taking it."), they will not do well if the course doesn't individualize instruction. Does the proposed course inquire about the learner's self-efficacy and respond differentially to high and low levels?

☐ Motivation is essential for learning as we can't do the learning for others, and not much learning happens if people aren't interested in learning. Intrigue, game-like risks, and realistically simulated challenges requiring multistep tasks keep learners engaged. Are they present in the prospective elearning you're considering?

Book 3

HOW TO BUILD eLEARNING

BUILDING HIGH-IMPACT INSTRUCTIONAL PROGRAMS WITH SAM

Every elearning project is an opportunity to be creative and innovative. And it needs to be.

We must never abandon the important commitment to always make the best use of each learner's time.

And we also need to stay within budget and timeline. This is no small order.

After a brief callout to the family of legacy models all called ADDIE (see Chapter 30) in Part 6, we'll jump into iterative models that are working better to address the budgetary and time constraints while promoting creativity and innovation. At times, one has to be amazed at how well iterative models address the daunting collection of challenges each elearning project faces. But at other times, one can be brutally reminded of the discipline it takes to stick to a process when there are so many masters to satisfy.

Agile and Yet Not

With dissatisfaction of the content-centered learner-agnostic courseware commonly generated by the pedantic ADDIE model and its many variations, we developed a bold breakaway from that widely entrenched legacy in the creation of the Successive Approximations Model (SAM). After its invention, there was an unexpected, coincidental, and very welcome validation of SAM from the field of software engineering. Although SAM was developed independently decades earlier, the Agile model for software engineering was created in 2001 to address almost exactly the same problems elearning developers were facing. It arrived at very similar conclusions and promoted some very similar concepts and procedures that are fundamental to SAM.

Nevertheless, in-house experiments to substitute a pure Agile model for SAM found the models have substantive differences, with Agile not able to grapple as effectively with some of the challenges faced in elearning design and development. We'll discuss these issues in Part 6.

CHAPTER 30

THE (SHORT) ADDIE CHAPTER

Everyone Knows What ADDIE Is

Pretty much everyone who has been in training, even if for only a short time, knows ADDIE stands for Analysis, Design, Development, Implementation, and Evaluation. It's a handy acronym for the categories of major tasks involved in creating training programs. There's no dispute that all the tasks traditionally itemized for ADDIE are good, appropriate, and necessary things to do. There are a lot of them.

Figure 30.1. Phases of ADDIE

No One Knows What ADDIE Is

There's not a great consensus about whether ADDIE is a framework or still (as it was initially) a process, although there are many manuals for applying ADDIE as a phased approach—performing analysis first, then design, then development, and so forth—whether circularly, iteratively, or otherwise.

In any case, ADDIE is often considered to be a process, but the implied if not mandated flow of steps has many drawbacks such that most organizations make modifications. And yet they still claim to use ADDIE. And that's the real problem.

When someone says, "We're an ADDIE shop," they haven't told us much. Which ADDIE is that? What process model do you use? If this one process is different from that one, but they are both called ADDIE, what is ADDIE? Pretty much all we can deduce is that any process that includes the ADDIE-listed tasks is ADDIE.

My Story

Some three decades ago, as president of an organization called the Association for the Development of Computer-Based Instructional Systems (ADCIS), I suggested we put ADDIE on trial. I was personally convinced, as I am today even though at one time I was a supporter and even taught ADDIE in graduate school, that ADDIE was the root cause of hundreds of poor elearning courses. Correct in the eyes of an ADDIE advocate but boring for students and great wasters of student time.

The problem? I easily found prosecutors and witnesses for the prosecution, but not one single defender. But why, then, was there so much ADDIE (whatever it was) going on, and why did people stick with it?

It remains a mystery to me today, so many years later, that some still proudly claim to be ADDIE-proficient or members of ADDIE shops, especially when there's widespread experience favoring less tedious and more effective methods. But its legacy roots run deep in some quarters. About that, I hasten to say three things:

1. It's a shame to stick in a rut—stonewalling your potential. ADDIE is tedious and boring too. Experimenting with alternatives yields insights that lead to better outcomes.

2. On the other hand, if you have an approach that produces awesome learning experiences on time and within your budget, stick with it regardless of what I or anyone else says about it.

3. If you are extrapolating and exploring new models, that's awesome. Sometimes a small change can have big benefits. But please give your modified model a unique name.

For much more on the problems with ADDIE and solutions offered by the Successive Approximations Model (SAM) we've been continuously validating and improving since about 1980, please see our book published by ATD, *Leaving ADDIE for SAM*.

While you'll find more details in that book, an overview appears in the following chapters—enough to get you on your way to creating awesome learning experiences.

Another important source is the Serious eLearning Manifesto. Endorsed by professional designers and developers, this online resource contrasts typical elearning with what professionals produce when a project seriously embraces the need for high-impact effective training. It lists both values and principles essential to great learning experiences.

Leaving ADDIE for SAM

MANIFESTO

Serious eLearning Manifesto

| The Manifesto | Manifesto Premiere | Become a Signatory | Signatories | Trustees | The Instigators |

The Manifesto

typical elearning	**SERIOUS eLEARNING**	eLearning Manifesto
content focused	Performance Focused	
efficient for authors	Meaningful to Learners	
attendance-driven	Engagement-Driven	
knowledge delivery	Authentic Contexts	
fact testing	Realistic Decisions	
one size fits all	Individualized Challenges	
one-time events	Spaced Practice	
didactic feedback	Real-World Consequences	

Serious eLearning Manifesto. Source: https://elearningmanifesto.org

CHAPTER 31

12-STEP MASTER PLAN

So, again, "How to do it?"

Learning to create great learning experiences is a bit like learning to play the piano. You can learn how to hold your wrists, curve your fingers, find middle-C, stop holding the sustain pedal down, etc. But you need to get some experience to become able to think, hear, and feel the music you are creating. As with all learning, knowing how something is done is quite different from being able to do it.

Working as a junior member of a team is a very good way to build your own skills, but even if that's not an option, following the 12 steps of the Master Plan will give you many advantages over legacy approaches. Give it a try. There's no substitute for "doing it." Just remember, concentrate on the "music." Think about your learners and the experiences you're creating for them, not just the task you're on.

The Master Plan

The primary steps listed below are detailed in subsequent chapters. They are in the sequence generally preferred for creating contemporary elearning that focuses on learners and learning experiences first. Consistent with principles presented in previous chapters, the plan notably infuses subject matter content into a learner-centered framework and not the other way around. It breaks strongly from getting content developed first and then creating presentations and quizzes afterward.

Conditional factors always need to be considered and may suggest, if not actually force, steps to be taken in a different order. That doesn't justify resorting to a "tell-and-test" approach and abandoning experience-based learning.

STEPS	DESIGNER NOTES
1. **Gather background information** What performance is desired and why? Who is leading the charge? Is training already in place or previously tried? How effective was it? Is there a deadline? What job title or responsibilities do trainees have? How receptive to training are people likely to be? What incentives for good performance are in place? Will people be receptive to performance change? Etc.	The more you can know starting out, the better. But this shouldn't be an extensive analysis effort. Don't get bogged down. Get to know the situation and key people. Talk with supervisors of people to be trained, if you can.

STEPS	DESIGNER NOTES
2. **Conduct a Savvy Start** See Chapter 34 for details. Key data to be gathered include: • What constitutes success and how it will be measured? • Who is the point person and who has decision authority? • What capabilities and restrictions are there in the delivery platform? • How much time do we have? • How much access will there be to subject matter experts (SMEs) and typical learners? Sketch one or more CCAF modules, concentrating on what could be imagined as the final module(s) in the course in which the learner's proficiency (or lack thereof) would be demonstrated.	Ideally, a first draft Behavior Catalog (see Chapter 16) and some functional prototypes will be built during the Savvy Start in response to the discussions. Based on the prototypes, the group can then respond to the "big" question, *"Why shouldn't we do this?"* The Savvy Start is the basis for generating a Statement of Work (SOW), further design sketches and prototypes, and a detailed project plan.
3. **Identify additional sources of approved content** Are there industry standards, proprietary methods, online resources, or other places from which acceptable content can be gleaned?	Interactive learning always requires more content than presentation-based instruction as is found in books, online, etc. Find what's available and trusted to discover what additional content needs to be developed.
4. **Create a Statement of Work (SOW)** The SOW documents what's been discovered so far and lays out the program of work to be done. Additional sketches, prototypes, proposed communications, project management, timeline, and budget are essential components.	This isn't usually the fun part of a project. It's hard work. Yet skipping over a documented understanding on key principles makes for problems ahead.

STEPS	DESIGNER NOTES
5. Get the SOW approved	
You need overall budgetary approval as well as an established means of getting approvals for deliverables along the way. It's important to have identified the people authorized to give approvals for the following items along with the amount of time the approval process can take.	Approvals can delay projects as it sometimes feels the project client is giving up control, but without the commitment to process and timely approvals, projects can be at great risk. SAM does a lot to keep clients informed and in control. Be sure to point that out.
• Budget, timeline, and itemized deliverables • Process for escalating concerns • Media styles and instructional approach • Interface requirements to an LMS, LRS, and/or other data tracking systems • Budgetary safety reserve	
6. Generate an Objectives × Treatments Matrix	
Referencing the Behavior Catalog to generate a list of performance objectives and adding the instructional model proposed for each objective creates the Objectives × Treatments Matrix (see Chapter 38), which, among other things, becomes a great to-do list.	This handy tool becomes not only an invaluable design aid but also helps make the best use of time, effort, and budget by identifying reusable structures or learning objects (RLOs).
7. Prototype treatments	
The treatments needed are identified in the Objectives × Treatments Matrix where the potential for multiple applications is noted. Prototypes are constructed to test ideas and propagate new and better ones. Build with minimal effort and have no hesitancy to discard and replace them. In fact, even if you like your first ones, set them aside and try coming up with something better. It's often possible even if you don't expect you'll be able to.	Specification documents are notorious for creating mixed, even conflicting, expectations. Ironically, storyboards also fail to communicate important design details adequately. Prototypes do much better because they provide just enough functionality to convey the essence of proposed learning experiences.
8. Create special-purpose prototypes	
Functional prototypes are indispensable for evaluating interactivity. Other components, such as graphic style, reading level, accessibility, performance of video, and LMS interface, need to be tested as well.	Overall, we want to minimize the time and effort put into creating prototypes as they're just a test, but don't fail to produce them and verify that all is good before developing content. Late surprises can be costly.

STEPS	DESIGNER NOTES
9. **Test prototypes with learners** Learners who are typical of the target audience are the real experts. It's easy to inaccurately assume the user interface is intuitive, that graphics are understandable, and that wording is clear and at the appropriate reading level.	It's sometimes quite difficult for organizations to free up people for testing, and it can feel unnecessary and an unwelcome delay to do it. But it's invaluable in the ways it contributes to success.
10. **Create and test a Design Proof** The Design Proof (see Allenism #27) pulls together all the design decisions into a functional slice of a course—preferably the ending slice. It is essentially a visual, functional demonstration of the proposed training that integrates samples of all components to test and prove viability.	Getting a Design Proof approved is an important milestone. It represents a transition from design exploration to focusing on efficient product production with only errors expected to be corrected.
11. **Create the final CCAF module** Start by first developing the end of your course, where you will want learners demonstrating their performance proficiency. If they can't, of course, their learning isn't complete and you will want to send them to remedial or part-task learning modules.	By designing and developing the last CCAF module or modules in your course first, you will have components you can extract and reuse to create part-task CCAF modules, which learners will encounter earlier in their learning journey or take as remedial experiences based on demonstrated need.
12. **Create the learning path** Work backward from the final CCAF module, extracting components to train learners on subtasks until you create an opening module that will help with learner placement along the path.	Make the module that opens the course sensitive to entry-level skills and feelings (see Chapter 29). Make sure relevancy is clearly established through a Context and Challenge all learners can imagine themselves facing (see Chapter 22).

CHAPTER 32

ITERATIVE DESIGN AND DEVELOPMENT

Because of the numerous and multifaceted challenges of designing and creating an interactive learning program, it's very easy to get off track. Without constant vigilance, it's all too easy to dive deeply into one task or subtask and then realize only minimal attention can be given to others.

Project Enemy #1: Last-Minute Changes

Discovering the need for additional content and receiving requests for last-minute changes is one of the most frequently reported problems. In response, we're tempted to start modifying quickly, probably with good reasons at the time, only to discover downstream we're running short on time. If only we'd known about desired corrections early on. But we know it's hard for clients to know at the very start of a project exactly what they will want at the end.

We need a process that identifies initially unknown needs and desires as soon as possible. We certainly don't want to wait until we've produced a "final" product to learn it isn't what it should be. And we can't afford to start all over.

Pragmatically, our process really must expect outliers, both good ones and bad, and plan to narrow in on success rather than expecting to shoot the bull's-eye in one straight shot. We'd like, and really need, the opportunity to align our arrow and shoot several times before locking in a trajectory.

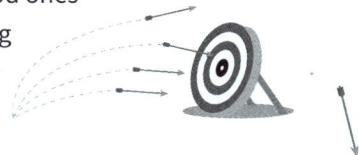

Our Defense

Project Enemy #1 needs to be addressed at the start. Although at the outset of a project we must define success criteria, the long-distance view doesn't easily spot every need and opportunity ahead.

Discovering better solutions downfield shouldn't be viewed as either a surprise or a fault. Indeed, new insights are to be expected when we're in a better position to see opportunities. And we want to incorporate as many of those good things as possible; we just don't want them becoming a new requirement late in the process. How can we get the good without the bad?

Iterations to the Rescue!

A linear path of working once through the content, completing the design, and then passing it off to developers to build sounds simple, manageable, and efficient. But rarely does it result in a creative learning masterpiece that engages, motivates, and leads learners to confident competence.

In contrast, the Successive Approximations Model, or SAM, is highly iterative. It doesn't expect design perfection before any development is undertaken. It actively looks for alternative ideas to consider. It doesn't hesitate to throw out parts that aren't working. And yet it manages to make the best use of the time, resources, and budget allowed to produce the best possible product within given constraints.

How is this possible?

Why Shouldn't We Do This?

With SAM, we don't start out asking, "What should we do?" That's a hard question, and it generates a lot of opinioned responses; perhaps at least as many opinions surface as the number of people asked. Instead, we take our first quick shot based on initial understandings, needs, and expectations. We build rapid prototypes. And then, as we evaluate the prototypes, we ask a simpler and far more constructive question: "Why shouldn't we do this?" See Allenism #9.

Perfection is too hard, too expensive, impossible. With SAM, we don't try for perfection at each iterative attempt. Rather, we try to make things better as our vision becomes clearer and we get the clearer vision early through iterative rapid prototyping.

The essence of the concept is repeatedly looking at possibilities to evaluate them, designing what might work, developing ideas as minimally as possible—developing them just enough to evaluate them, and then repeating. In a nutshell, it looks like this:

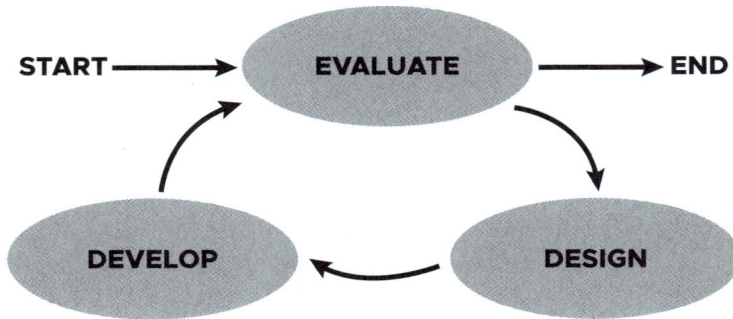

Little SAM

Of course, there are many steps and tasks to be performed in creating an instructional program. The diagram above minimizes those details to convey the essential concept of iterating interleaved evaluation, design, and development. We will expand the diagram and walk through the process in detail, but before we get ahead of ourselves, let me say more about what the Little SAM diagram introduces. Its simplicity betrays its power.

Little SAM

Little SAM is almost exactly the process I'd prefer to use if I had a small team and everyone could be on the project together throughout. It coincidentally mirrors many of the foundational principles in Agile software development. After completing small sprints of work, the team steps back and appraises the product. The highest priority inadequacies are identified, additional sprints of work are completed, and the process continues. The product grows in function and refinement.

SAM is always looking to make the best of a fixed budget and timeline. Considerable up-front effort goes into determining criteria to be met and how success will be measured. We insist on iterations and revisions but limit them knowing that there will be diminishing returns from doing more. And we apply a discipline to cover all content once over before perfecting segments as we go.

I've advocated this process for a long time and found it very successful as long as you have a team of multi-skilled individuals who can remain available, focused, and productive for the project's duration. There's little handing off to specialists, so not much time is spent writing detailed specifications, making sure everyone is on the same page, and rectifying problems due to miscommunication. This is a major advantage and time-saving attribute.

Little SAM vs. Time Limits

One of the concerns raised most often by people first considering Little SAM is that iterations could go on forever. They've wisely identified the risk of endless ideas for improvement and feature additions. The work could be iterating forever. They're right!

There will always be another way to make a project better. Always. Count on it. But what makes Little SAM so great is that, given whatever time you had, you built the best product possible. If you have to stop, you stop. Even if your work is cut short due to unforeseen circumstances, you'll have on your hands the best functional product you could have developed in that time frame. Conversely, if you get the gift of an extension, you can do more, should you choose to do so. You don't have to redraft the product definition or do anything differently than you would have done in your next sprint. You just keep going.

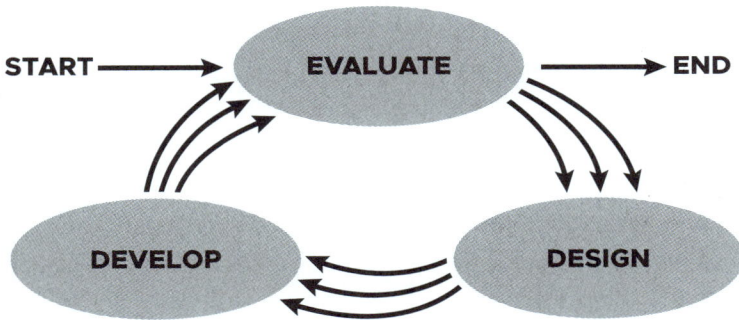

Little SAM Iterations

Little SAM done right is amazing in its ability to conform to time and budget constraints.

So, contrary to first impressions, Little SAM done right is amazing in its ability to conform to time and budget constraints. When the budget has been exhausted, you've developed the best project you could with the money available.

Does This Really Work?

Yes. But *only* given a few critical things:

1. **You have a small team** as mentioned above—a multitalented team of individuals capable of doing both instructional design *and* instructional writing or building with an authoring tool *and* a graphics creation tool.

   It's invaluable to Little SAM to have a team of versatile people devoted to the project so you won't have delays waiting for someone to be available or so that people not familiar with the project's goals, history, and discussions will have to be switched in and out and get up to speed.

2. **You maintain functionality** of the product from the start so it can be tested frequently, if not continually, and appraised by everyone on the team and the supporting stakeholders.

   While it's important to realize that discarding some work can be a form of progress, it's also important to keep functionality alive so the work can be evaluated by almost everyone. We don't want evaluations based on labored documents that try to paint a picture of what to expect—documents that are not only hard and time-consuming to write, detailing every aspect, but are also too easy to misinterpret (despite best efforts for clarity and comprehensiveness) and lead to a surprising and problematic range of varied expectations.

3. **You adhere to the principle of *breadth before depth*** (see Allenism #33). Perhaps most important of all, you must not stall out on one objective in an attempt to perfect its treatment before moving on to other content.

Let an initial treatment suffice until all content has been covered once, then return to a second pass, continuing in layer-wise fashion until time runs out or you're satisfied with the product as a whole.

Big SAM

We'll detail the many aspects of Big SAM in the following chapters, but we'll take a moment here for a quick look ahead. It's helpful to remember that Big SAM is a process articulated primarily for larger projects or those in which designers and developers can't work simultaneously, shoulder to shoulder.

Big SAM is based on the very same principles—the very important principles—as Little SAM. The primary difference is that designs are taken to a more complete stage before being handed off to a separate team of developers.

Big SAM is empowered by iterations for creativity, productively and quickly exploring alternatives, and creating consensus on design, just as Little SAM is. The "Big" difference is that for large projects it's usually necessary to have separate design and development teams.

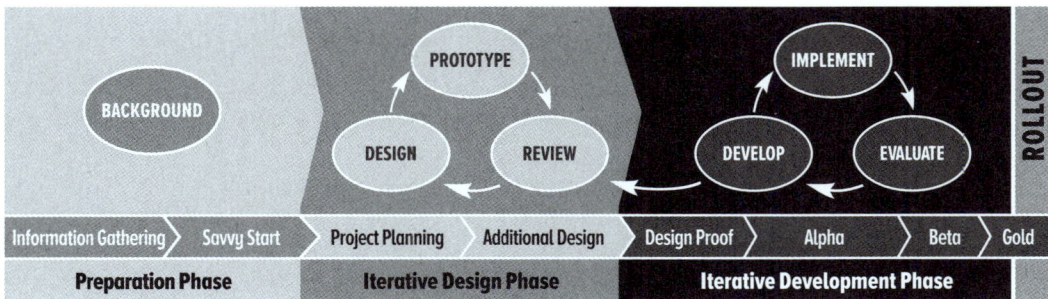

Big SAM (Successive Approximations Model)

To complete large-scale projects in as little time as possible, there may even be multiple design teams and development teams. So, communication becomes more formalized, budgeting more difficult, and coordination essential. To support all these needs, the process as a whole is divided into three iterative phases: Preparation, Iterative Design, and Iterative Development.

We devote the following chapters to detailing this process.

BIG SAM: PREPARATION PHASE

In this chapter, we're focusing on the first of Big SAM's three phases, the Preparation Phase, which includes background information gathering and the Savvy Start.

Backgrounding

We don't recommend spending a lot of time in up-front analysis with SAM as you might in other approaches, such as is often recommended with ADDIE (a legacy alternative to SAM). There are two primary reasons we minimize time and effort in the Preparation Phase.

1. As Allison Rossett delineates in her book *First Things Fast*,[23] there is no end to the things one could examine in preparatory analysis. After looking at a few obviously relevant things, additional items of possible relevance appear, and those lead to still others. Much time and effort can be spent pursuing information that ultimately turns out to be irrelevant. So, we need a process that directs us to using our time most effectively.

2. In iterative design, we throw out design possibilities and ask the big question: "Why shouldn't we build this?" Answers to the question identify needs, problems, and questions that have to be

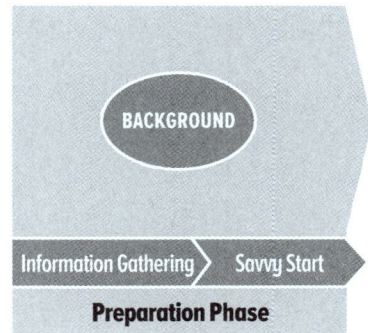

---

23   Allison Rossett, *First Things Fast: A Handbook for Performance Analysis* (San Francisco: Pfeifer, 2009).

considered and therefore give direction for gathering additional specific information, if indeed any is needed.

Initial Information You Need to Know

Some of the most helpful information you really need to know appears in the following checklist. What you are unable to determine prior to the Savvy Start should be discovered in the Savvy Start if at all possible. The following checklist will help you track what you've learned and what you have yet to find out.

Backgrounding Checklist

		Answered Prior to Savvy Start	Answered in Savvy Start
1.	Who is sponsoring the project (i.e., who has budget authority)?	☐	☐
2.	Who cares most about success, and how would they measure it?	☐	☐
3.	Why is a learning program being developed now?	☐	☐
4.	Who is the intended audience?	☐	☐
5.	What behaviors need to change or what skills need to be developed?	☐	☐
6.	What continuing performance support will learners have?	☐	☐
7.	How often will learners perform the tasks they are learning to perform?	☐	☐
8.	What delivery means can be used? (For example, instructors, self-study, distance learning, elearning, and so on.)	☐	☐
9.	What's been tried in the past? What were the results?	☐	☐
10.	What content currently exists, and what form is it in?	☐	☐
11.	Is the budget preset? If so, what assumptions is it based on?	☐	☐
12.	Is there a critical rollout date? When? Are there advantages to early completion?	☐	☐
13.	Who needs to be involved (and why)?	☐	☐
14.	Who is available to help? (For example, content experts, supervisors, learners, media artists, writers, or reviewers.)	☐	☐

Guideline: To minimize potentially wasted effort, limit up-front analysis and data gathering to the information that's relatively easy to acquire. If some seemingly desirable instructional designs or approaches appear to be obvious contenders, it's worth digging deeper, asking more questions or more people, and collecting more data about them. You can do a better job of scrutinizing past history and future possibilities if you know specifically what you're looking for. A prospective approach provides that guidance.

CHAPTER 34

THE SAVVY START

What Will It Cost and How Long Will It Take?

Almost as soon as there's a thought about developing a training program, you get a question pretty much in the form of:

> ### "We need a training program for our people three months from now.
>
> ### How much will it cost?"

You reply, "Okay, great. But I need to know a lot more before I can estimate costs."

You then hear, "Oh, sure, sure. But, I mean, just typically, what does it cost?"

There can be a lot of frustrating exchanges on both sides of this conversation. It seems reasonable to ask about the "typical cost." But just as it's not reasonable to ask, "I want to build a new house. About how much will it cost?" a responsible answer can only be of such a wide range of possible costs that it doesn't really answer the question.

The Savvy Start is an invaluable and highly productive event that helps projects succeed from Day One. It provides answers to critical questions while alerting clients to the wide range of options they are probably not considering. Ideally, projects aren't budgeted, scheduled, or otherwise mapped out before a Savvy Start occurs.

A Little SAM in Big SAM

The Savvy Start is a structured meeting for key stakeholders that uses the iterative process designers and developers will use throughout project development. It's basically a Little SAM exercise that stops short of doing actual product development. Instead, it produces sketches and prototypes to help stakeholders express their opinions and experiences and come to a consensus on the instructional approach to be taken.

This unique two-day, sometimes three-day, event has great benefits:

- It acquaints stakeholders with the nature and benefits of an iterative process.

- It helps determine whose voice may be the loudest in terms of in-process decision-making. And whose may be most important.

- It brings values and experiences to light that can help the project avoid pitfalls and avoid stepping on mines.

- It pushes for agreement on the criteria for project success.

- It provides answers to key questions that are necessary for project planning, including schedule, resources needed, and budget.

The Agenda (and Sticking to It)

Even though the Savvy Start is a creative brainstorming session, an agenda or a plan of action is important and necessary. Because everyone is encouraged to discuss their ideas, past experiences, and expectations, an agenda is needed to keep the sessions on track.

The Savvy Start usually begins with a review of the process, expectations of outcomes, and examples of good and bad instruction related to the subject matter. It then focuses on the definition of success and how it will be measured, after which the fun of iteratively brainstorming, sketching, and prototyping commences. The meeting should conclude with a discussion of the Savvy Start Summary Report and how the project will proceed following the Savvy Start.

Leaving ADDIE for SAM

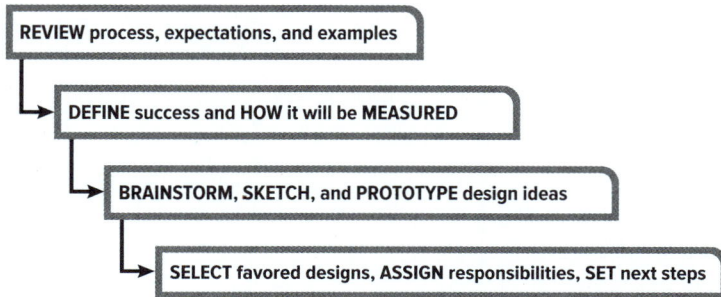

REVIEW process, expectations, and examples

DEFINE success and HOW it will be MEASURED

BRAINSTORM, SKETCH, and PROTOTYPE design ideas

SELECT favored designs, ASSIGN responsibilities, SET next steps

Field Guide

Suggested Savvy Start agendas appear in *Leaving ADDIE for SAM* and in the corresponding *Field Guide.* Agendas can and should be modified given special circumstances. Savvy Starts can be very successful in a variety of formats, such as in person or via Zoom.

Savvy Start Summary Report (SSSR)

The Savvy Start provides critical information for planning the entire project. Identified are:

- Who is going to be trained
- How success is defined
- How the success of the project will be measured
- What knowledge and skills must be learned and mastered
- What resources (human and materials) will be needed
- Proposed workflow and timeline milestones for deliverables and feedback cycles
- QA and acceptance testing plans
- Required branding standards
- Who the client's project point person will be

- What delivery platform(s) are available or must be used
- When the project must be completed
- How learners needed for review and testing will be made available
- Client preferences (such as style, uses of media, etc.)
- Design sketches and prototypes
- Accessibility requirements

All this information is organized and documented in the Savvy Start Summary Report (SSSR) and provides the basis for generating a proposed Statement of Work (SOW), which provides the following:

- Timeline/schedule
- Budget with safety reserves
- Assumptions
- Process for Change of Scope (COS) requests, problem resolution, and use of reserved funds
- Style and media guidelines
- Project Management Plan (see Chapter 39)

PROJECT PLANNING OVERVIEW

After the completion of the Savvy Start, it's time to begin developing a formal project plan.

Initial Planning

Rapid collaborative design is the foundation of the successive approximation process. Bringing a team together to create quick, ugly, and disposable prototypes starts the ball rolling toward an effective and engaging learning product. Sharing constructive thoughts and reactions with each other allows rapid and invaluable consideration of alternatives at minimal expense. Iteration, as always, is the strategy from beginning to end; however, this flexible, creative process must produce a product by a certain date within a budget that delivers meaningful on-target results.

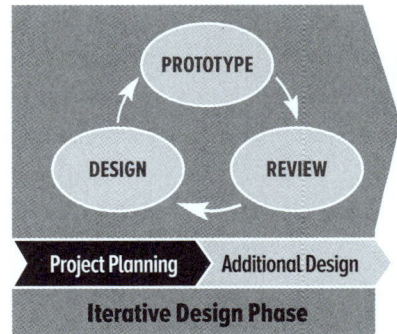

The role of planning is to:

- Identify the resources needed to achieve each goal,
- Communicate those requirements to the team, especially to the identified decision-maker, and
- Obtain a commitment to providing the resources required.

While there may be pressure—as there is in many organizations—to determine a budget early in the process, even before the Savvy Start, doing so is truly unwise. It's like asking how much a wedding will cost without knowing how many attendees are expected, where it is to be held, whether it's formal or informal, whether dinner is to be served, and so on.

Nailing Down the Budget

The Objectives × Treatments Matrix (OTM—see Chapter 38) is a great help to budgeting because with it you will know how many different types of interactions you will need to create, how complex and varied content information is, what media will be essential, and so on.

A common practice for estimating treatment costs is to consider the complexity of the interaction or interactions each needs. Conveying just a range of possible costs is tempting, but the wide range you'd need to share is simply too large to have much value. The Savvy Start is done quickly to provide answers that, together with backgrounding information, a commitment of critical resources (such as SMEs, supervisors, and learners), and the prototypes, narrow the range of possible costs and make it possible to provide well-founded estimates.

While SAM is extremely good at fitting projects to preset constraints and producing the best possible products within them, it cannot overcome totally inappropriate constraints. Sometimes it's best to go back to the drawing board and start over, rethinking who to train on what.

The completion of the Savvy Start Summary Report and project plan presents a prime decision point. Can and should the project be properly funded and resourced? Or should less (or more) ambitious goals be set? Or should the project be aborted?

Although there needs to be flexible creativity in the project, successful management depends on a structured plan that clarifies what needs to happen, when it will happen, and who will make it happen.

1

DEFINITION OF SUCCESS:
Increase in same-store sales
HOW IT WILL BE MEASURED:
• Total tire sets sold • Measured by differences in store sales, by quarter • A/B testing of training treatments

2

BEHAVIOR CATALOG

BUSINESS OBJECTIVE:			REVENUE OUTCOME:		
Increased tire sales			$60,000K per month, per store		
Behavior	**Performance Outcome**	**Assessed By**	**Performed By**	**Headcount**	**Frequency**
Recognize tire sale opportunity	Remember and follow instructions	Service Manager	Car Intaker	400 Nationwide	.5x/day/= 200x/day
Measure tread wear	Remember and follow instructions	Service Manager	Service Technician	520 Nationwide	200x/day
Verify stock	Remember and follow instructions	Parts Manager	Service Technician	520 Nationwide	60x/day
Offer best current price	Following offer, guide instructions	Sales Manager	Service Rep	280 Nationwide	60x/day
Close sale	Perform expertly	Sales Manager	Service Rep	280 Nationwide	54x/day

3

OBJECTIVES × TREATMENT MATRIX

INSTRUCTIONAL TREATMENTS & EST. DEVELOPMENT COSTS			
	A	**B**	**C**
Objectives	$0.00	$0.00	$0.00
1	X	X	
2		X	X
3			X
4	X		
5	X		

Figure 35.1. Basis for Budgeting

			Factor	Units	Subtotals	Budget Remaining
Starting Budget	$ 175,000.00					$ 175,000.00
Contingency	$ 25,000.00					
Total Budget	$ 200,000.00					
Preparation Phase					$ 2,000.00	$ 173,000.00
Information Gathering						
Logistics						
Content Review & Ananlysis						
Iterative Design Phase						
Savvy Meetings					$ 3,000.00	$ 170,000.00
Savvy Report/Project Planning Design > Mockup					$ 1,000.00	$ 169,000.00
Activity Design > Prototype > Review Cycle 2						
Level 1	$ 1,000.00		1.00	2.00	$ 2,000.00	$ 167,000.00
Level 2	$ 2,000.00		1.00	6.00	$ 12,000.00	$ 155,000.00
Level 3	$ 3,000.00		1.00	2.00	$ 6,000.00	$ 149,000.00
UI Design > Prototype > Review	$ 1,000.00			1.00	$ 1,000.00	$ 148,000.00
Fixed above -- Variable below						
Iterative Development Phase						
Design Proofs - Development and Representative Content						
Level 1	$ 2,500.00		1.00	2.00	$ 5,000.00	$ 143,000.00
Level 2 + Passive Video	$ 6,000.00		1.00	6.00	$ 36,000.00	$ 107,000.00
Level 3	$ 8,000.00		1.00	2.00	$ 16,000.00	$ 91,000.00

Figure 35.2. Example eLearning Budget Calculation

Compromises

With only a month to complete a project, it probably couldn't have many highly complex learning events. With a limited budget, the team may have to choose between professional illustrations and clip art. Multiple and maybe even suboptimal uses of treatments may be necessary. When learners speak different languages or are a part of different cultures, localization is a requirement. But when costs of performance errors are high, impact is essential. What to do?

Trade-offs are nearly always necessary, even in the best of circumstances. Will it be high-end media, numerous unique interactions or a small number reused, professional writing, or any number of other project choices? All need to be considered carefully and factored in.

Priorities

Realistic plans are built on compromises, and priorities are vital to making the right ones. Setting priorities early in the project is also a great way for everyone on the design team to create and maintain expectations. To begin formalizing what is known about constraints and declaring priorities, necessary qualities or parameters of the following key components should be defined and then placed in rank order, such as:

Priority	Success Factors
1	Partnerships (collaboration)
2	Performance improvement / error reduction goal
3	Knowledge improvement goal
4	Budget
5	Timeline (schedule)
6	Content scope
7	Reviews and approvals
8	Instructional design
9	Spaced practice to keep skills honed
10	Type and quantity of media—e.g., illustration vs. photography

The team should be sure to add missing components that are important to the particular project and circumstances. Weighing these often-conflicting success factors is difficult, to be sure, but listing and ranking them help build successful partnerships.

Expectations

Hopefully, by this point in the process, everyone is convinced that creating something ineffective will be the costliest path to take. Unfortunately, there may be a predetermined and inappropriate budget that's too small. If the budget cannot be expanded, it's back to the priorities and compromises to find the means to do something effective.

Sometimes small budgets stimulate creativity that produces great results that might not even have been achieved otherwise. A workable solution may be to reduce content to the core of what's really needed, but hopefully not less. Alternatively, a phased approach may be the best option. Each phase might be done well enough to achieve effectiveness on selected topics, with remaining content to be covered in subsequent projects.

When schedules and costs are not predicated on a Savvy Start, guesswork is at play and some red flags should be raised. Of course, it's possible to build learning solutions within a very wide cost range, but the solutions at opposite ends of the range do not usually have equal effectiveness, nor the same return on investment. Significantly underestimating costs will likely create solutions that are so ineffective the entire investment is at risk. Consequences include wasted learner time, lost opportunities to iterate and implement effective solutions, and learners becoming frustrated or disengaged with the effort needed to succeed. Launching an ineffective program is damaging and expensive.

Calculating Production Costs

Actual costs for a project vary depending on many factors, some pertaining to content availability and complexity, SME availability, your relationship with the project sponsor, your experience with this type of content, and so on. Your history will be an important guide.

The following pro forma cost calculator will help you think about your Iterative Development Phase costs, especially if you are new to this work.

Design Proof Costs

CCAF Construction & Representative Content Development	Number Required	Cost Each	Line Total
Level 1 Interactions	1	$	$
Level 2 Interactions + Passive Video	1	$	$
Level 3 Interactions	1	$	$
Reuse Level 1 Interactions	1	$	$
Reuse Level 2 Interactions	1	$	$
Reuse Level 3 Interactions	1	$	$
Video—interactive (includes reedits)	1	$	$
Design Proof Cost Subtotal			$
Alpha Content Development Costs			
Level 1	1	$	$
Level 2	1	$	$
Level 3	1	$	$
Video Scripts	1	$	$
Alpha Review and Corrections	No. of CCAFs	$	$
Beta Review and Corrections	No. of CCAFs	$	$
Subtotal			$
Safety Reserve		10%	$
Phase Total			$

More on Project Planning

Project planning in SAM cannot be done well without a full understanding of iterative design, and iterative development—the tasks at hand, the things they depend on, and the things they produce. The following chapters interleave these topics to help draw connections.

As you study these final chapters and complete your understanding of the SAM process, you might want to refer back and forth to the example project plan table of contents in Chapter 39 to see how all components come together in a project plan.

CHAPTER 36

ITERATIVE DESIGN PHASE

Additional Design

Although some genuine design work is typically accomplished in the Savvy Start, the purpose of that exercise, as described in Chapter 34, has more to do with an analysis of the situation, including the identification of responsibilities, expectations, requirements, and limitations or constraints.

The Iterative Design Phase, which is staffed typically by design experts and others as needed (such as subject matter experts, media designers, instructional writers, etc.), is where the majority of the design work is accomplished. The previous design work from the Savvy Start will have been done in concert and in real time with stakeholders to set standards, values, and expectations.

It's important for evolving designs to be consistent with the sketches and prototypes approved by the Savvy Start team, but they are just the starting point. Many more sketches, prototypes, and detailed decisions need to be made in the process of generating and reaching a final design to be implemented in the Development Phase.

Iterations in Detail

We've mentioned many times the invaluable benefits of iterative design in previous chapters and how it works to support creative design and development of effective learning experiences while also working within the constraints of time and budget. It's almost a sure win as long as (and this is very important):

- The number of iterations is controlled
- You avoid quickly going with your first idea
- Designs for all types of content are created before polishing and finalizing any design
- Key decision-makers are identified and stay involved at appropriate levels
- Success and measures of success are well defined at the outset and kept in mind
- Rough disposable prototypes are created for review and to convey design ideas in action
- Prototypes are tested with representative learners

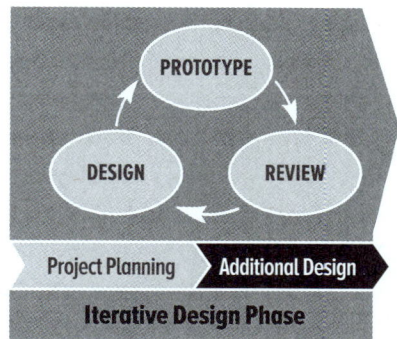

Since we're now in the "How to Do It" section of the book, let's examine each of these principles in some detail:

Limiting iterations to three is trickier than it may seem. Reliably, each iteration will spawn new ideas for creating an extraordinary learning event. But the returns on time and effort invested will be diminishing while other content lies in wait. Three iterations seem to be the magic limit. You can always come back to polish here and there after you have devised individualized interactions for all types of content.

Not going quickly with your first idea is also a challenge and sometimes the most difficult temptation to be managed. It's not a rare feeling that your first idea is pretty great. Excitedly, everyone is ready to invest in it. You might be absolutely right to do so, but it's best to be sure. How to do that?

It's pretty simple, actually: **Deliberately pretend you cannot go with your first design** and force your team to come up with an alternative. It may seem at first that you can't, but with some persistence, you can always come up with an alternative. When you do, compare its pros and cons to your first idea. What have you learned? Trying one more time, using ideas from Design One and Design Two, along with some new components, may well produce Design Three—the best design so far and one worth pursuing. With three designs in hand, step back, evaluate, pick one, and move on to new content. It's a tried-and-true process.

Designing treatments for all content before finalizing any yields the opportunity to (1) revise all designs for consistency with each other and (2) retrofit into earlier designs any great design ideas that have emerged in subsequent design work.

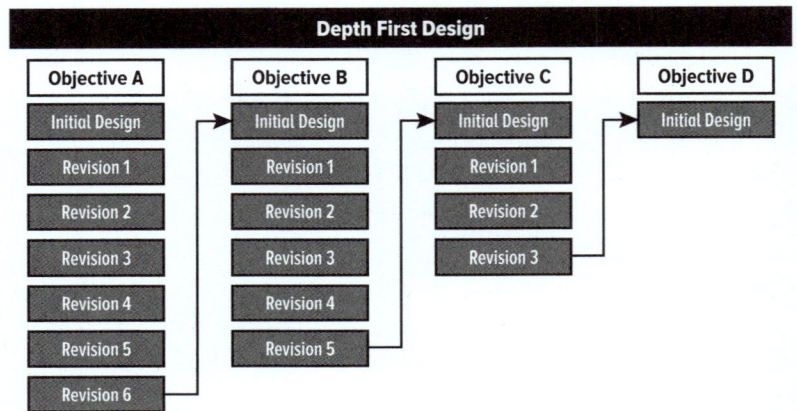

Figure 36.1. Depth First Design Distributes Efforts Unevenly

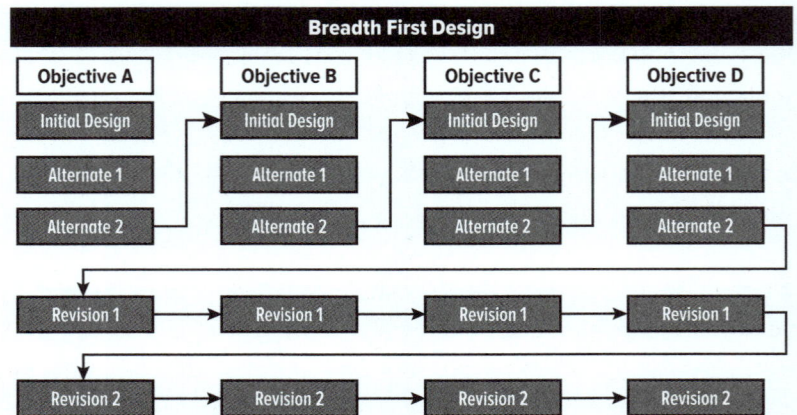

Figure 36.2. Breadth First Design Promotes Quality and Design Consistency

As shown in Figure 36.1, repeatedly giving in to the excitement of "just one more iteration!" often results in less and less attention being given to subsequent content areas, whereas addressing each content area more briefly and then returning repeatedly to run through all designs as shown in Figure 36.2 gives each objective equal attention, allows new insights to be incorporated throughout, and prevents content for the later parts of the course getting insufficient attention.

Identifying and keeping key decision-makers involved may seem like the least of your concerns, especially as the project proceeds and is dealing with design and implementation details. But projects have a way of evolving. That's often a very good thing, and something we foster, but leaving key decision-makers in the dark isn't. We don't want to surprise key decision-makers with a product that diverges from their expectations and risks rejection of potentially a lot of invested work.

Defining success and measures of success are essential to assure success. The alternative is something like shooting an arrow without knowing where the target is. It's a super high and unnecessary risk.

Creating rough disposable prototypes provides an invaluable way to convey design ideas in action. Even experienced experts misjudge static designs intended to represent interactive learning experiences. To fully convey design ideas for active learning requires the opportunity to *experience* the key interactions. Until all members of the team can witness the interactivity, it's likely they will all be imagining and expecting something quite different from each other. Further, just as with sketching, prototypes inspire consideration of alternatives. But note, it's important not to invest too much in these disposable prototypes lest they become too expensive to discard.

Testing prototypes with representative learners is sometimes a logistical challenge, but who are the real experts who can determine how good an instructional design is? It's learners—learners who represent those for whom the instructional program was created. Their voices trump those of all the rest of us, and it's their feedback we need before it's too late to identify and correct mistaken theories, assumptions, and design flaws.

With the background information reviewed and used to guide initial designs, and the Savvy Start Summary Report generated and approved, we're ready to set out on the journey of designing interactive learning events—backwards!

CHAPTER 37

YOUR DESIGN JOURNEY (BACKWARDS!)

It helps to picture the journey as a collaboration of you and your learners.

- Where are your learners starting from? (They might be starting from very different places.)
- Where do they want to go? What do they want to be able to do?
- How do you get them to want to be where they need to be?
- How do you get them to where they need to be?

To know your learners have arrived at the target destination, what's the last thing you want learners doing before you award them a gold star—their badge of readiness? Demonstrating proficiency by confidently doing well the tasks we're training them to do, right?

Even if the final learner challenge(s) were defined in the Savvy Start, Additional Design work would be required to build the interactions. That should almost always begin by focusing on the end of the journey first. We need to be sure the final module requires learners to demonstrate their proficiency on all skills taught.

Let's Think About Failures

Look first, as always, at the Context and Challenge. Instead of, for example, asking airport ticket counter trainees about verifying reservations at a quiet desk, think about the Context in which they perform their tasks and the Challenges they have to overcome. Play loud airport noises. Create interruptions such as when another traveler steps in to ask about a flight or where to check a bag.

Instead of supplying needed information in the Challenge, make agents request it as they normally would. Supplied information might be incomplete or be inaccurate in some way as it sometimes is. The combined final Context and Challenge need to be as authentic as possible and demonstrate all the skills needed for performance success.

It helps to ask supervisors what mistakes they see, how learners can detect they've made a mistake, and how they can correct them.

Where Are You Starting From?

While design and development start with creating the final experience, the learner's journey treks toward the goal of solid performance proficiency and confidence from wherever they may be. It sure helps to know where they're starting from.

We gain important information regarding learner abilities, or lack thereof, from the first Challenges they encounter. We'll talk about structuring those first encounters later, but based on the strength of their initial performance, some learners can jump ahead quickly. Others would be guided stepwise through a comprehensive line of instructional experiences, while still others would branch selectively to only a few needed microlearning modules—all determined by the individual learner's performance and requests.

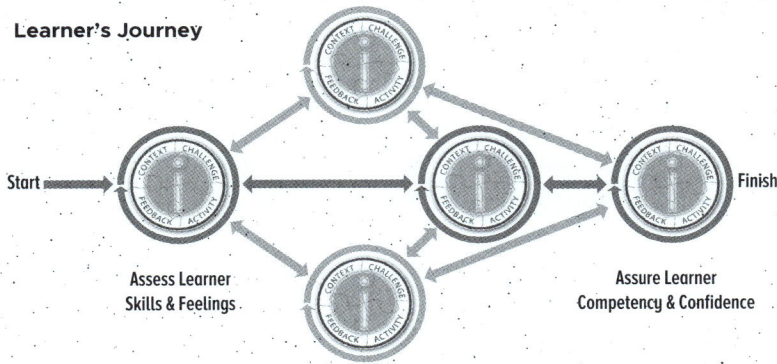

Figure 37.1. Individualized Learning Road Map

Instructional Advantages to Being Contrary

Contrary to typical approaches and what might seem most natural, instead of designing CCAF modules in the sequence most learners might encounter them, there are great advantages to working backward from the journey's final destination. To do this, we think first about where we want to take our learners. What's the target destination?

The target destination has responsibility to assess and hopefully confirm performance mastery and affective readiness based on:

1. **Outcome performance objectives**, which specify:

   a. Observable performance (the A in CC**A**F)
   b. Conditions under which the observable performance is to be given (the Context component of **C**CAF)
   c. The quality or effectiveness of the performance (meeting the Challenge in C**C**AF)

2. **Affective outcome objectives**, which specify:

   a. An acceptable level of reported confidence
   b. A minimum correlation of confidence with performance accuracy (a learner knowing what they know or can do and what they don't know or can't do)
   c. A minimum reported desire to perform the new skills or level of skills as soon as possible

Keep in Mind

Knowledge about how a task should be done is different from being able to do it. Knowledge is a journey enabler, not the destination.

The final learning module can be one (or more) CCAF modules to put learners in Contexts and give them Challenges that are as realistic as possible and represent what learners will encounter in their real-world responsibilities. We call them "authentic" learning experiences because, to the extent possible, they feel like being on the job and having the full responsibility to not only decide what would be the best action to take and when to take it, but also the ability to take the right steps in the right order.

Development Advantages to Being Contrary

Designing the final module(s) gives you, the team, and stakeholders an early opportunity to sense what the whole of the training program will be like, what it will emphasize, and how you will target identified goals. It also challenges your creativity at a time when everyone is fresh with their initial energy and enthusiasm. You aren't locked into constraining decisions that might otherwise have consumed resources and left little for these, the most important components of the course, forcing you to take shortcuts in a mad dash to finish up.

In this "last first" journey from end to start . . .

- After you've created the last module(s), step back to ask: If my learners make mistakes on this final exercise, what mistakes am I likely to see?

- Create training experiences that allow those mistakes to be made and can address them when and if they occur, perhaps by calling up a remedial exercise or module.

- Then, continue backing up from the final goal toward the basics, and think about the mistakes learners might make when going through the second-to-last learning experience. And third-to-last. And fourth-to-last . . . When you feel you've designed CCAF components for the most novice learner you might have, you've reached your stopping point—which is the starting point for learners (refer back to Figure 37.1 Individualized Learning Road Map).

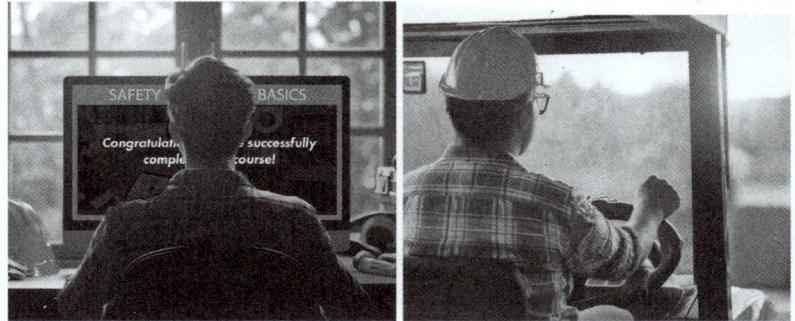

CHAPTER 38

PROJECT PLANNING: OBJECTIVES × TREATMENTS MATRIX

The Objectives × Treatments Matrix (OTM) is an important project planning tool just as it is an indispensable instructional design tool. It maps treatments to objectives so that we can identify necessary interactive components that need to be developed.

What's a Treatment?

Good question. Treatments can be any reusable objects, including algorithms, types of feedback, a means of accessing reference resources learners can use from time to time, CCAF components, or a complete set of interdependent CCAF components that comprise an interaction.

Here are some example treatments:

Example Treatment 1: Learners correct entries in a cost-accounting spreadsheet. Totals and all dependent cells update instantly as values are edited. Feedback is delayed until the learner indicates everything has been corrected.

Example Treatment 2: Learners perform a simulated chemistry titration by selecting and placing equipment properly, using correct quantities of titrant and analyte, and selecting and adding an appropriate buffer solution to the titration chamber or a masking solution to the reaction chamber.

Example Treatment 3: Learners observe a video of a process being performed, stopping the video immediately when an error is observed and then identifying the error.

When and How Is the Objectives × Treatments Matrix Created?

Construction of the OTM is begun in the Savvy Start and completed in the Iterative Design Phase of SAM as part of Project Planning and Additional Design.

The designer begins by analyzing the final instructional objective (or cluster of objectives) to determine what would be the best CCAF experience to enable learners to perform authentic transferable tasks from beginning to end while also assessing the learner's proficiencies. That design is entered into the matrix as Instructional Treatment A (the final treatment).

	Instructional Treatment Uses & Estimated Cost		Treatments
	A Full Service (Final CCAF)	B Previous CCAF . . .	A. Trainee must provide complete service including welcoming diners, suggesting beverages and hors d'oeuvres, through to promoting desserts and collecting payment.
Objectives	$0.00		
1	X		
2	X		
3	X		B. When welcoming diners . . .
4	X		
5	X		

First Entries in an Objectives × Treatments Matrix

The final learning activity isn't always constructed to teach every component objective directly or even any component objective. Some objectives may be "enabling" objectives for which mastery is evident when learners are able to successfully perform the terminal objectives that depend on them. Microlearning modules that some (or all) learners will encounter or be steered back to if higher order performance difficulties arise will address enabling objectives directly. We document all this by completing the matrix.

	Instructional Treatments + Estimated Costs				
Objectives	A Full Service Simulation $0.00	B Flag Video Model $0.00	C Advice Model $0.00	D Task Model $0.00	E Conversation Model $0.00
1	X	X	X		
2	X		X	X	
3	X			X	
4	X	X			
5	X				X

A	Full Service Simulation	Trainee must provide complete service simulation including welcoming diners, suggesting beverages and hors d'oeuvres, through to promoting desserts and collecting payment.
B	Flag Video Model	Play video of table waiter providing service. Learner must flag and identify service errors as they occur.
C	Advice Model	Several "seasoned waiters" provide advice on handling customer complaints. Learner applies selected advice to witness outcomes.
D	Task Model	Learner enters orders on tablet. Learning "gadget" delays specific feedback, but displays "hot," "warm," or "cold" as learner works to indicate progress and to see if learner can correct own errors.
E	Conversation Model	AI-based conversation with diners asking questions about menu and placing orders, some with requested substitutions.

Adding Treatments for Enabling Objectives

Whether any treatment will be used more than once is unknown at first until all objectives have been assigned treatments. Listing all treatments keeps them in mind and builds a task list that's invaluable for project management. If it is appropriate to use a treatment again, that's very good news. Multiple uses minimize time and effort. And costs!

In addition, by extracting components of downstream modules to create more basic ones, it's much easier to maintain user interface consistency and reduce the number of conventions learners have to confront. Treatment components are often recombined to create new treatments that address a broader scope of objectives.

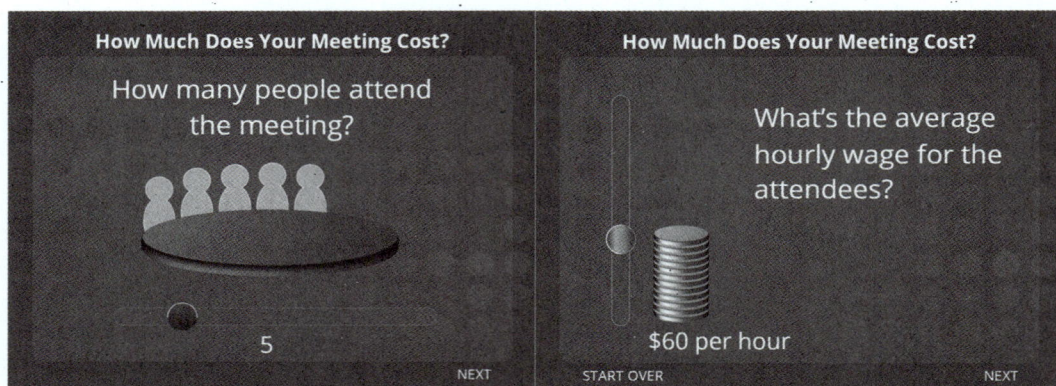

Meeting Calculator for Pryor Learning

Microlearning

EXAMPLE

Pryor Learning Solutions Meeting Calculator. *"This microlearning course focuses on building the need for effective meeting management. It features a meeting cost calculator that allows learners to input details of recurring meetings (such as number of participants and duration) to compute the annual fiscal impact. This tool is designed to highlight the cost implications of inefficient meetings and change learner behavior. It can be paired with a companion resource, the 'Do You Need a Meeting?' flow chart."* **Artisan Learning**

CHAPTER 39

PROJECT PLANNING: PROJECT PLAN TOC

The following table of contents for a project plan provides a checklist of elements to consider, especially if you're planning on your own or as part of a new team. Many organizations have their own versions, of course, but this is a good plan to consider.

1. PROJECT OVERVIEW

    1.1. Organization's Vision / Mission Statement
    1.2. Business Problem
    1.3. Performance Gap
    1.4. Definition of Success
    1.5. Measurable Criteria for Success
    1.6. Proposed Solution
    1.7. Satisfaction Checklist

2. DESIGN AND DEVELOPMENT PROCESS (SAM)

    2.1. Objectives × Treatments Matrix
    2.2. Instructional Treatments
    2.3. Cost Estimates

3. MANAGING SCOPE

    3.1. Scope of Content, Required & Nice to Have
    3.2. Scope Change Management

4. QUALITY

    4.1. User Testing Plan
    4.2. Quality Assurance / Quality Compliance
    4.3. Scope of Quality Assurance

5. PROJECTED MILESTONES & DELIVERABLES

6. ROLES & RESPONSIBILITIES

    6.1. General Responsibilities—Who Is Accountable, Consulted, Informed
    6.2. Project Sponsor
    6.3. Development Team

7. DECISION-MAKING

    7.1. Authorized Approvers (Named)

8. COMMUNICATIONS PLAN AND ISSUE RESOLUTION

    8.1. Primary Contact Responsibility
    8.2. Project Status
    8.3. Email Protocol
    8.4. Course Comments & Fixes
    8.5. Meeting Planning
    8.6. Responsiveness & Best Practices
    8.7. File Transfer
    8.8. Project Webpage
    8.9. Issue Resolution

9. PROJECT RISKS

10. SATISFACTION GUARANTEE

CHAPTER 40

ITERATIVE DEVELOPMENT PHASE

Big SAM differs mostly from Little SAM by separating development work into its own phase. This is done mostly for larger projects with larger and more specialized teams. The rapid design prototypes produced earlier prove their value once again in this phase of SAM. They are far more valuable than specification documents that describe what needs to be built and storyboards that never seem to capture the critical essence of interactive experiences. (Despite common practice, I recommend not using either specification documents or storyboards.)

Nevertheless, even with prototypes and the intent to be quite detailed, questions will arise and need to be addressed during Development, where we will often see ways to save time and effort through some design modifications to address both unforeseen roadblocks and opportunities for more sophisticated individualization. For this reason, the Development Phase follows exactly the same pattern of iteration used in the Design Phase.

Design Proof

All work preceding this point has been leading up to production of the all-important Design Proof. This product of the first Development cycle is a full implementation of at least one instance of each type of interaction planned. Its purpose is basically to test everything before going too far and finding out that something fundamental to the instructional approach is not in the cards and must be done differently.

The Design Proof gives everyone—stakeholders, designers, and developers—the clearest view of what the final product will be like if it stays on the current path. Some modifications may need to be made, although hopefully steps have been taken to make sure the design is good and solid at this point. But now is the last time to make easy, low-cost adjustments before full content development begins.

What's the Problem?

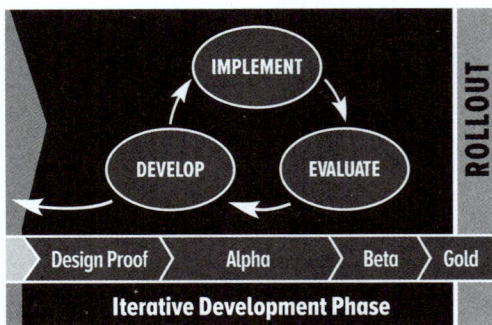

There are many potential problems such as rights to a needed video are out of budget, a series of interactions are beyond the capabilities of the authoring tools available to the project, or delivery on mobile devices is now required contrary to earlier thoughts. We obviously want to discover such problems as soon as possible—as early in the process as possible. The Design Proof helps us do just that.

The Design Proof is generated using a familiar cycle:

- **Content Development**
  Preceding design work hasn't written all the text, generated all the graphics, developed all other media, and so on. At least it shouldn't have been. When we come to Development, we expect to have only sketches and prototypes. But now for the Design Proof we need to develop selected, representative content to final production quality. Not all the course content yet, but enough content to be sure we will be able to evaluate all types of content to be incorporated.

- **Implementation**
  Next, at least one representative component of all types of expected media and interactions is integrated into the delivery platform using whatever programming language(s) and/or

authoring tool(s) will be used for production. Further, integration with the LMS, if one is to be used, will be accomplished so it can be tested as well, including data collection and module routing. Other delivery factors will be set up for evaluation, such as communication with the variety of digital delivery devices to be supported and response speeds.

- **Evaluation**
  Finally, the Design Proof is tested. It's important to involve people who represent learners who will be using the final product, not just the designers and developers. They shouldn't know more or have more experience than the targeted learners. They should be as similar to them in all relevant aspects as possible.

Every effort is made to be sure all the elements in the Design Proof will perform as expected and represent a model for all further development, implementation, and evaluation. But the process is kept iterative, because experience shows us that despite even extreme efforts to perfect all elements in the Design Proof, there will inevitably be surprises and changes that must be made.

So, instead of feeling that we've somehow failed, we succeed by planning for the need to make some changes. Being in that situation amplifies productivity, professionalism, and satisfaction among all stakeholders.

Developers' Perspective

Before our process evolved from a linear, "waterfall" process into an iterative one, developers—i.e., programmers—insisted they should not start work until the design was 100% complete. "*To be efficient with our time and build a robust, properly performing program, we need to know exactly what functionality is needed. Making changes midstream,*" they asserted, "*may well require restructuring to the point we must effectively start over. You can't afford that.*"

It was a pretty intimidating perspective. Designers were usually dependent on programmers to bring their ideas to life, so they did everything they could to oblige. But try as everyone did, once the program started to function, designers saw problems and opportunities. "*Is there any possibility we could add a BACK button here? I'll try not to make any other requests if you can do this one small thing for me.*"

Of course that one request always mushroomed into more. In truth, programmers often saw the need to make changes themselves. Sometimes they went ahead and made them, proudly revealing their contributions afterward. Sometimes they were good changes; sometimes not, leading to, "*Well, I thought you'd really like this. For me to take it out now is going to cost us some time here.*"

This perspective is the antithesis of SAM and the iterative approach that can efficiently produce superior products. Changes are progress and the order of the day. Within limits, of course.

What SAM Needs and Expects

Rather than employing a process that expunges emerging ideas, we want to be in a position to celebrate and incorporate them.

Instead of trying to freeze designs prior to implementation, experience tells us that great designs evolve through experimentation. We need to see, touch, and feel our initial ideas in action. We expect these experiences to generate new and better design ideas—which are to be encouraged as long as they don't arrive at the last minute.

Rather than employing a process that expunges emerging ideas, we want to be in a position to celebrate and incorporate them.

How to do that? Flexibility achieved through using the best tools and planning for changes.

Authoring Tools

Authoring tools came about in large part because programmers tired of having to make change upon change and because designers feared exasperating programmers. The primary goal of advanced tools was to make it fast and easy to make changes of many types, ranging from simple text modifications to algorithmic changes to enhancing dynamically animated simulations. Ideally, designers could create and modify their designs themselves.

Some authoring systems achieved much of this goal and even enhanced interactive capabilities in the process. Others settled for easy development of simplistic presentations and quizzes, effectively limiting the author's ability to create respectable elearning.

Some offered template-based development, which had advantages and disadvantages. If a template was exactly what was called for, then great! But experience teaches that while a template may look perfect at the outset, it will often need modification. In further concern, templates are often based on a very rudimentary appreciation of instruction and learning (anyone want yet another multiple-choice question editor?) and push instructional designers in directions that are suboptimal. We have enough challenges designing learner-centered individualized learning experiences without having the authoring tools fighting against us.

Unfortunately, even today the current trend seems to be moving toward reducing the capabilities in order to make editing simpler. *"Create great elearning in minutes, not hours or days."* I haven't seen any of those "great" ones yet. This will change with artificial intelligence, although it's unfortunate that some AI vendors are prematurely claiming extremely rapid production of sophisticated elearning that is anything but that.

We want to see interactive capabilities advance by leaps and bounds. We want powerful, intelligent ways to individualize learning experiences, and we want to be able to experiment with them quickly and easily to achieve fantastic learning outcomes. Artificial intelligence is a welcome tool to aid us, and I hope we're seeing a new "golden age" of fun and effective elearning just around the corner. I welcome it on behalf of learners everywhere.

Planning for Change

Regardless of the tools, programming language, or AI platform used, the surest requirement is always flexibility to make modifications. Separating content and data from logic is fundamental. Making nearly all values variable from the start means that even surprising needs for change can be accommodated. So, rather than letting designs be implemented in fragile, fixed ways, we must go in the opposite direction: achieving functionality as soon as possible so ideas for improvement can be inspired from initial forays and so those ideas can be implemented quickly and easily to inspire yet further ideas for improvement.

It's an iterative world! (Where have we heard that before?!)

CHAPTER 41

FINAL DELIVERABLES

There's just one more "just to make sure" iteration. Unlike the previous iterations, the series of iterations is limited to a single pass. They're even named. And if all is looking good, only one cycle is necessary; the sequential releases are precautionary—just in case. We want to get things right!

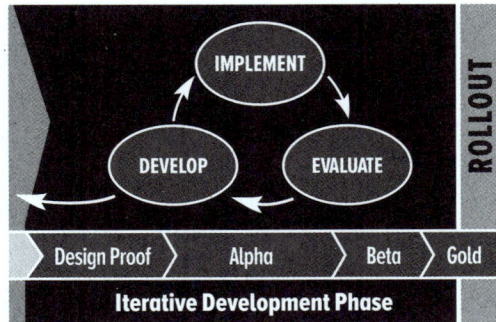

There are two planned releases ahead of the final "Gold Release," at which point the course is out the door. They are called the "Alpha Release" and the "Beta Release."

Alpha Release—No Unknown Errors

The goal of the Alpha Release is to have no undocumented errors or omissions. It is a complete version of the instructional application ready for validation. All content and media are implemented. If problems exist—and they well might because it is often important to begin Alpha evaluation before all issues can be rectified—those known problems are listed. No major, undocumented issues are expected to be found, but it is nevertheless common for them to surface despite everyone's best efforts.

Evaluation of the Alpha Release identifies deviations from style guides, graphical errors, text changes, sequencing problems, missing content, lack of clarity, and functional problems.

Beta Release—Gold Candidate

Because errors are nearly always found in Alpha Releases despite everyone's best efforts, this second validation cycle is scheduled as a practical precaution. The Beta is a modified version of the Alpha that incorporates the needed changes identified. If all goes as expected and corrections were made carefully, the Beta review would discover very few if any errors. Whatever errors may be discovered should include only very minor errors, such as typos or mislabeled graphics. The Beta Release is sometimes also called a "Gold Candidate," meaning that if no errors are found (as is the goal), the Beta becomes the Gold Release and is rolled out.

What if errors are found, either significant errors or a lot of minor errors? This is a possibility despite all process precautions. We fall back on our favorite weapon, iteration, and produce Beta 2. That should certainly do it. Unless we've gotten sloppy or had to work around unmanageable disruptions, we should rarely need to produce a Beta 2, much less a Beta 3. But things happen. That's why we always keep a safety net in our budget.

Gold Release

Construction of the Gold Release is the final phase of development. At this point, while no project ever reaches perfection, the courseware becomes fully usable within the parameters of previously approved project guidelines.

An important perspective is that since there always remain ways to improve an instructional product, a Gold Release launched for learner access is still something of an experiment. Feedback from learners in the field can be invaluable. It's always best to reserve enough resources so at least one more round of improvements can be implemented.

DESIGNER'S NOTEBOOK #6

Self-check: See if you garnered these takeaway principles and are ready to use them.

☐ ADDIE is hard to define because many adaptations go by the same name. Given the rapid modifications today's technologies permit, even for unplanned needs, more well-defined and Agile methodologies provide great benefits.

☐ The Successive Approximations Model (SAM) is based on iterations successively asking, "Why shouldn't we do this?" until concerns and objections are resolved.

☐ The Serious eLearning Manifesto is an online guide to the principles and values for contemporary elearning excellence: https://elearningmanifesto.org/.

☐ The primary steps for creating excellent elearning experiences are:

1. Get some background information.
2. Conduct a Savvy Start.
3. Identify additional sources of approved content.
4. Create a Statement of Work (SOW).
5. Get the SOW approved.
6. Generate an Objectives × Treatments Matrix.
7. Prototype treatments.
8. Create special-purpose prototypes (color palette, narration, etc.).
9. Test prototypes with representative learners.

10. Create and test a Design Proof.
11. Create the final CCAF module (if not done for Design Proof).
12. Create the learning path.

☐ Budget is derived from the measurable definition of success established in the Savvy Start, the Behavior Catalog, and the Objectives × Treatments Matrix.

Alpha Release

☐ The second production cycle (the first of which created the Design Proof) produces the Alpha Release from approved designs.

☐ Full content development integration occurs in this cycle. Samples no longer suffice.

☐ The Alpha is nearly the final version of the complete instructional program to be validated against the approved design. All content and media are implemented.

☐ Completion and approval of the Alpha signals the beginning of the validation cycles.

☐ Review of the Alpha is expected to find only minor deviations from style guides, writing issues, graphical errors, and functional problems.

☐ Known errors and omissions are documented and corrected in creation of the Beta Release.

Beta Release

☐ The Alpha Release is modified to reflect errors identified in its evaluation. The resulting Beta Release is viewed as a first Gold Release candidate. There should be no functional errors at this stage.

☐ If errors are detected, another iteration may be necessary to produce a second Beta Release, Beta 2, and additional prospective releases if significant errors continue to be found.

☐ Not only subject matter experts but also learners representative of the target population should assist evaluation of the Beta Release.

Gold Release

☐ If problems remain in a Beta Release, they must be rectified before the Beta Release can be given the gold crown. A modified version of a Beta, "Beta 2" (sometimes called "Gold Candidate 2"), and, if necessary, a succession of numbered candidates is produced until all problems are resolved.

☐ When the Beta Release performs as expected and no additional problems are identified, it simply becomes the Gold Release without further development and is ready for rollout implementation.

☐ Hopefully, but all too rarely, Rollout signals the beginning of an evaluation study to determine whether targeted behaviors are actually achieved and whether these new behaviors secure the performance success expected.

BUYER'S CHECKLIST #6

Part 6 is concerned with the details of developing a custom training program. As a buyer, you don't have to know how to do the things listed below, but you need to be sure your vendor does. Here are some questions you might ask vendors as you go about selecting one.

☐ Do you generate prototypes for us to evaluate before launching into full-scale production?

☐ How do you individualize learning experiences so that each learner has an optimal pathway to competence and confidence in the shortest amount of time?

☐ Have you developed simulation-based training previously on content similar to ours?

☐ How can you give us confidence that the rollout of a new training program you've produced will go smoothly?

RETHINKING—AGAIN

And so, we come to the end of today's rethinking, but not tomorrow's. When at any point we think we've got a total handle on elearning— "What works. What doesn't. What's missing."—we just might be missing some golden opportunities to be of more service to our learners.

We always want to intrigue learners, spur them on to more learning and realizing more of their potential. You might consider taking up the Allen Interactions motto:

"We will ever strive not to waste one moment of a learner's time."

"We will ever strive not to waste one moment of a learner's time."

If that means having to work overtime to create great learning experiences, we will strive always to do it with empathy and innovation.

Whew! That's it, folks!

Thank you.

AFTERWORD

In 1994, I was working as a layout designer for a textbook publisher and was asked to create an "interactive supplement" for a higher-ed textbook. There were two software programs available: Macromedia Director and Authorware. Director would be used to create the media elements and Authorware would be the development platform. I chose to become the Authorware developer, while a colleague went with Director. My choice of Authorware changed the trajectory of my career and life. Becoming a developer of educational material opened me up to the world of corporate training—a practice I didn't even know existed! After we published the supplement, I joined a company that designed and delivered computer-based training for technology companies in Silicon Valley. When I dove into Authorware to create my first learning product, I was entranced with the power the program gave me to build deeply immersive interactivity. That moment was the catalyst for me to leave behind publishing and become a learning and development professional. Talk about timing: I was in Silicon Valley and the internet boom was exploding. Tech companies were looking for new ways to rapidly train their workforce, so armed with Authorware, I started my own training development company.

Starting my L&D career as a tools developer using the software that Dr. Allen created gave me a broad perspective on how to truly build impactful learning. Once I became fluent in Authorware, I trained over 1,000 L&D professionals to use it. I built amazing learning products with it, including an award-winning ergonomics training for Stanford University, deeply technical satellite training for the Department of Defense, and highly interactive telecommunications training for AT&T. As Dr. Allen reinforces in this book, learning happens through experience, not passive consumption. His emphasis on active learning and practice reflects his decades of research and experience showing that "when it's time to perform, it's too late to practice."

Dr. Allen conceived Authorware to enable a more visual approach to unlocking educational experiences. Before Authorware, what I call the "BA years," developing interactive educational content was overly complex and often a programming-intensive process. By creating an icon-based, WYSIWIG (what-you-see-is-what-you-get) interface, Dr. Allen democratized the process of building interactive training and single-handedly expanded the universe of instructional design and reshaped how we envision, design, develop, and deliver digital learning experiences.

In reading this, his tenth scholarly book, I was struck by his ability to take the complexities of designing instructional materials and break them down into bite-size nuggets of knowledge that we can all leverage in our day-to-day work. Gems such as:

- *Practical Insights on Learning Design.* He highlighted the critical importance of establishing relevance and responding to learners' emotional states. And he shared that although he thought he had a "reasonably complete understanding of what elearning was, could be, and should be" he had moments of realization that his view was incomplete. This humility and continued growth is remarkable after decades of leadership in the field. And one highlight for me in reading this book was the undercurrent of curiosity that he sees is of the utmost importance in the work we do.

- *Designing Experience-Based Learning with the CCAF Model.* He reinforced the power of the Context-Challenge-Activity-Feedback (CCAF) model he pioneered. This approach creates authentic learning experiences rather than mere information presentation. He explained how CCAF enables individualization and creates engagement through active learning. This model remains one of his most enduring contributions to our practice.

- *Understanding the Importance of Individualization.* He presented individualization as perhaps the most crucial capability of elearning. He offered practical approaches to adapt learning for different learners, recognizing that one-size-fits-all approaches waste time and reduce effectiveness. The extensive table of individualization techniques shows how designers can implement this practically.

- *Practical Implementation Through SAM.* His Successive Approximations Model (SAM) provides a systematic yet flexible approach to developing learning experiences. The detailed explanation of both "Little SAM" and "Big SAM" offers practical guidance for implementations of various scales.

- *The Future of AI in Learning.* He thoughtfully addressed the emergence of artificial intelligence in learning design, showing both excitement about its possibilities and caution about potential misuse. His balanced perspective offers guidance for our practice moving forward.

When I say that Dr. Allen gave me a career, I'm not being facetious. For over 25 years, I've leveraged his software, his models and frameworks, his books, and his friendship to elevate myself, to understand the importance of what I do, and to ensure that the work I produce meets the standards he has established through his thought leadership, his work examples, and his unwavering commitment to excellence in the practice. His legacy is reflected in this seminal work you have just experienced, but it's also in the company and studios he founded, the award-winning learning products he's designed, and the generations of learning designers he has trained.

Now, as Dr. Allen has told me, "Go out and create, but make sure you don't waste a moment of the learner's time." With this work as your guide, you are one step closer to making his vision your reality.

Brandon Carson
Chief Learning Officer, Docebo
May 2025

THE BOOK OF ALLENISMS

Based on theory, research, and the extensive experience of the Allen Interactions studios, the following "Allenisms" are principles we at Allen Interactions have found important and valuable. We strive to adhere to them in our mission to create awesome elearning experiences. Complete at the time of writing *Rethinking eLearning,* this compendium continues to grow and will hopefully continue to do so for quite some time. It is offered here and online in hopes these principles will serve you as well as they have served us.

On Learning

Allenisms Online

On Instructional Design

On Process

On Outcomes

You Can't Learn Learners

Learning is a vicarious response to things we observe and experience in life, or an intentional process involving focus, concerted energy, and thought. In both cases, each learner must do the learning themselves.

We do sometimes learn serendipitously and sometimes through trauma or through what's called "critical incident" learning, but in general, people go through the process of learning through perceptional focus; linking new information, thoughts, and experiences to existing knowledge and skills; and practicing.

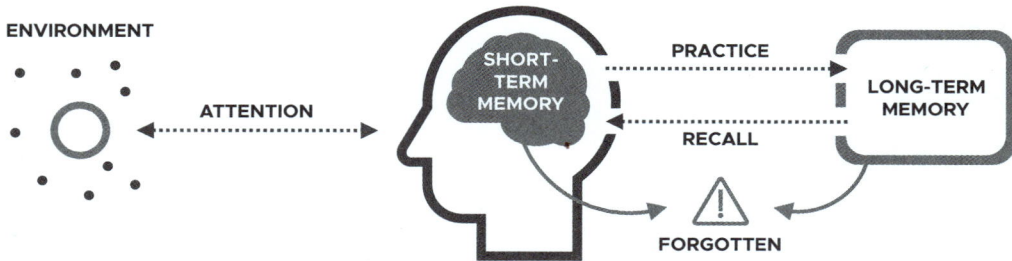

Effective instruction encourages, motivates, and guides learners. While this seems obvious, many teachers, trainers, and elearning developers seem to think their learners will be eager to learn just because they worked hard to develop and deliver a course. But learners have their own criteria. They focus on things of interest and put in a level effort they find appropriate.

Since intentional learning requires attention and effort, it makes sense to maximize learner interest and enthusiasm for the courses of instruction we offer. It's priority #1. We can take the negative route via threat of failing grades, losing a job, or being humiliated. Or we can use positive approaches, such as establishing relevancy to the learner's personal goals and making sure our delivery adapts to each individual's needs and skills.

Keep this in mind:

Motivated learners will find a way to learn, overcoming a poorly constructed or delivered course if need be.

Unmotivated learners will gain little, regardless of how well a course is put together.

So, with this understanding, how can we make learning happen? Or a better question: How can we get our learners to want to learn?

Answer: See the other Allenisms!

No Refunds for Time Wasted

When we have learners in our courses, they have essentially entrusted us to use their time beneficially. Whether a course is providing value or not, time is spent, and if it turns out to have delivered little value, our learners can't get a refund on their time to do better things with it.

The obligation to use learner time beneficially is an onerous one, especially if we haven't employed the means to adapt the learning to the individual's skills and needs. Good mentoring is ideal in this regard, such as all the mornings over the years my mother sat next to me on the piano bench every school day to be sure I properly practiced "every assignment three times" before heading off to school.

But when you have thousands of people to mentor, or hundreds, or even just ten needing training at the same time, mentoring is difficult, if not impossible. It's certainly convenient to put together classroom presentations and periodic assessments. Everyone gets the same treatment. Training begins on a scheduled date and similarly ends for everyone. Neat and tidy.

But how many hours of learner time are wasted because the instruction isn't sensing individual learner readiness and needs and adapting accordingly? There's more likelihood that, at some point throughout the course, *everyone* has wasted time rather than no one.

Non-individualized instruction is the most wasteful instructional paradigm there is. Which is why digital platforms can be so valuable. But only, of course, if they are created to continually sense learner performance and adapt to needs and opportunities accordingly.

THEORY ★ RESEARCH
ALLENISM
#3
★ EXPERIENCE ★

Train for Joy!

In working with physicians from the Mayo Clinic, we learned that while instigating changes in habits and thoughts is difficult, even harder is sustaining changed behavior. They introduced us to a powerful concept: Joy!

Even when people have managed to establish a new behavior pattern, powerful magnetic forces remain to pull them back to previous behaviors. The way to get the magnetic poles reversed and sustain new behavior is to make its performance a joyful, consistently rewarding experience.

While adopting new performance patterns isn't always a combative struggle akin to breaking bad or addictive behaviors, the notion that we can perform as desired doesn't mean we will always strive to. But if the performance is one that gives us joy, we are likely to push for the opportunities to experience that level of satisfaction whenever we can.

Joy is a level up, built on competency and confidence. It comes from a repeated pattern of excellence recognized by both ourselves and others.

It makes sense to think about ways to help our trainees experience the joy of great performance. We shouldn't feel our job is done until we've helped our trainees achieve performance joy.

Bobbie hated conducting meetings. She had attended several workshops on meeting management, including ways to keep groups focused and productive. But she continued avoiding the responsibility whenever she could. But then she attended a workshop (who knows what prompted her to do so) on stand-up comedy. She had always loved good jokes and discovered that after coaching and learning good timing she could get friends howling with laughter.

Bobbie risked telling a few jokes at the beginning of meetings she hosted and found that not only did people appreciate her sense of humor but that she also began looking forward to conducting meetings. Her joy was evident to everyone and sustained her successful performance in meeting after meeting. Best of all, people looked forward to attending her meetings.

Instructional Interactivity Makes You Think, Act, and Practice

Page turning is not instructional interactivity. Neither are scrolling, roll-over tags, or pop-up info boxes. Drag-and-drop doesn't automatically qualify.

In the Inuktitut language, there are 53 words for snow, which describe everything from wet snow that can be used to ice a sleigh's runners to crystalline powder snow that looks like salt. Interactivity, just like "snow," is not a single thing but a group of divergent things that have some similarities as well as important differences.

If only we had such a definitive vocabulary for interactivity, because interactivity is the capability that enables elearning to be extraordinarily effective, while also being the most generally practical means of training. Without it, however, elearning would be terribly inept.

What is *instructional* interactivity? Instructional interactivity is interaction that actively stimulates the learner's mind to do those things that improve ability and readiness to perform effectively.

More simply put:

> ## Instructional interactivity makes you think, act, and practice.

Perhaps there's no more concise way to sum up the responsibilities of instructional designers than to charge them with creating learning events that cause learners to think, act, and practice.

Serious Learning Games Yield Serious Learning Gains

Sometimes I hear people snicker or see them roll their eyes when we talk about making learning experiences fun. "This is corporate training. It's important and serious." So, what . . . are we supposed to make it arduous? Grim and grave? Would that qualify it as "serious"?

The Allenisms perspective swoops in from the opposite direction.

Why do we play games? Don't we in fact play games for the fun of playing, practicing, and learning—learning to play better and win? Making learning experiences ponderous, heavy-duty things burdens progress toward the learning outcomes we're seeking.

Video game designers are way ahead of us in areas where we tend to struggle. There are many takeaways from their work.

As Anita Breuer says, "Video games are not just a source of entertainment but also a fantastic way to learn."[24] She lists the following outcomes that entertainment game designers are achieving without even targeting learning:

Problem-Solving Skills: *Tackling challenges in games teaches us to think critically and find creative solutions . . .*

---

24   Anita Breuer, cofounder and CEO at Logiscool, the global franchise network for coding education of kids and teens, breuer.anita@logiscool.com.

Attention to Detail: *Games require attention to the smallest details . . .*

Perseverance: *Games teach us that failure is just a step toward success.*

Logical Thinking: *Structured thinking and planning strategies in games enhance our ability to . . . [do many things, such as] write efficient code.*

I'm personally thrilled when we find our elearning is so valuable and enjoyable that learners opt to go through programs repeatedly, often in this pattern:

1st time: To see how well they can do and learn what they can.

2nd time: To see if they can significantly improve their scores, perhaps reaching perfection.

3rd time: To see what happens if they can identify and make the worst choices.

If we set this as our goal, we will undoubtedly create more effective learning.

$e = m^2c$

Einstein's work has inspired countless scientific explorations and their resulting discoveries. Surprisingly to some, it's no less true in the field of learning and instruction! In fact, he was almost correct in postulating $e = mc^2$ except, of course, for a small error. It should have been $e = m^2c$.

Understanding that learning is a product of motivation and content:

e = edification (learning)

m = motivation

c = content (subject matter)

While proving successful in physics, the original equation $e = mc^2$ when applied to learning and instruction emphasizes the role of content by squaring the content component. Indeed, many designers have accepted the notion of content's supreme importance and do the same thing. They dive into content organization immediately, looking for logical hierarchies and the means of communicating content clearly and concisely.

While content is important, this Allenism suggests that motivation tops content expression as the critical component deserving the initial and primary attention for the simple reason that if learners are not engaged and motivated to learn the content, it doesn't matter how well organized or expressed it is; little, if any, learning is going to happen.

Conversely (and this is the critical notion), a highly motivated learner will learn even if the content is jumbled and not so easily assimilated.

Of course, we want both highly motivated learners and the benefit of well-structured and well-communicated content. But while content is almost never ignored in instructional design, motivation often is. We therefore make a slight adjustment to the Einstein theory of relativity and express our appreciation for his helping us reach this important understanding about instructional design:

$$e = m^2c$$

If Teaching Were Just Presenting, We Wouldn't Need Schools (Just Libraries)

Teaching is all about helping learners learn. It's helping them focus, extract and apply principles, correct misunderstandings, and practice, while selecting appropriate content and challenges, encouraging, motivating, providing tips and insights, and attending to the learner's feelings.

It's a complicated and heavy role sadly oversimplified by thinking of it as lecturing and providing assessments—"tell-and-test," as we call it. Good elearning takes on the role of teaching not just transmitting content, regardless of whether it's through text, graphics, animations, video, virtual reality (VR), or augmented reality (AR).

Although it's good at that. With worldwide access to libraries, online papers and videos, and artificial intelligence to do the legwork for us, access to content has never been faster or easier.

But that's not teaching.

Good teachers (instructors, if you prefer) know their audience. Ideally, they know their learners individually. And then they adapt, adapt, adapt. That's what good elearning does. It teaches by helping learners:

- Focus on what they need when they need it
- Extract principles from examples
- Apply principles to solve problems or meet challenges
- Correct misunderstandings
- Keep working
- Practice to mastery
- Feel good and confident about their newly acquired knowledge and skills

The Essential 3M's:
Meaningful, Memorable, Motivational

Successful instruction derives not from content presentation (as one might think from all the effort instructional designers put into wording content for scope, clarity, conciseness, accuracy, comprehensiveness, and logical sequencing), but rather from learning experiences that are Meaningful, Memorable, and Motivational. The 3M's.

Allenisms thinks of these characteristics as multiplicative, building on each other for maximum learning assistance. And in good mathematical form, if any characteristic isn't well developed—i.e., is a zero—then the other characteristics fail as well.

Learning Outcomes = Meaningful × Memorable × Motivational experiences

$$0 \quad = \quad 0 \quad \times \quad 100 \quad \times \quad 100$$

Meaningful   If a learner doesn't understand a learning event, whether it's the terminology, concepts, linkage between actions and outcomes, or any essential aspect that remains unclear, the learning experience fails.

$$0 \quad = \quad 0 \quad \times \quad 100 \quad \times \quad 100$$

Memorable   Even when a learner learns well with the support of elearning, if the newly acquired knowledge and skills are not retained, once again the learning experience fails. Forgotten skills are, well, null and void.

$$0 \quad = \quad 0 \quad \times \quad 100 \quad \times \quad 100$$

Motivational   If the learner was able to understand and is remembering what was learned but is not motivated to apply new skills and change behaviors for greater personal and/or organizational benefit, the learning experience fails.

While failure to provide support for any of the essential 3M's leads to instructional failure, higher scores of each M raise the impact overall.

Ask Why #1
Why Shouldn't We Do This?

When creating a training program, there are typically many, many questions to be answered.

What's the goal?

How do we define success?

How will we measure success?

Who do we need to train?

What training have we done in the past, if any, for these people on these skills?

What worked and didn't?

How detailed and up to date is the content?

Are there examples?

Are practice exercises defined?

What supportive media exist?

Are SMEs readily available?

Are representative learners available for feedback and run-throughs?

It's a very long list. While the answers to all these questions are important, sometimes projects die of exhaustion while this research delays the project start far longer than anticipated. There can be conflicting information. Information can take time to locate. Information can be incomplete when something is found. Content is out of date. And so on.

Projects aren't typically done in pristine academic contexts where perfection is a primary target and there isn't a critical rollout date. Sorting through myriad details can, indeed, take a lot of effort—effort that would seem justified. But what if there were a more practical and productive way to move forward? At least a somewhat easier and quicker way to get at the information most needed while also identifying what additional information is and isn't needed?

Well, there is. That's SAM—the Successive Approximation Model (see Chapter 32). After collecting and considering whatever information is readily available, SAM starts with asking one question. Not the typical question that engenders lengthy discussions, but one that gets to key considerations fast.

Instead of asking the typical question:

What should we do?

Ask:

Why shouldn't we do this?

What's "this"? you ask. It's an approach you suggest based on whatever information you know about the project and on your experience.

It would seem unprofessional to just throw out your first impression of who should be trained, on what, and through what means without a lot of preparation. Isn't that what a novice would do? Just dart out there.

Well, it's not exactly what I'm advocating. Two provisos are essential:

1. You should collect all the basic information you can, but if and only if you can get that information fairly easily and quickly. This will prevent throwing out ideas blindly and wasting more time than necessary on proposals that are immediately realized to be inappropriate.

2. As a professional training developer, you suggest an approach you've found successful in circumstances that look similar to what you're seeing. Novices are likely to suggest generalized legacy models that miss key opportunities in the specific situation at hand.

So, you put something on the table and then ask the key question, "Why shouldn't we do this?" You can count on the ensuing conversation to be revealing on many levels—revealing often in ways you wouldn't have exposed in lengthy up-front analysis.

Ask Why #2
Why Do You Think Your Answer Is Correct?

For a long time, too long, many elearning designers have presented content to learners and then quizzed them on what they were supposed to have learned. To ease building "interactive" questions and judging answers, those quizzes have often been constructed of multiple-choice questions in a framework such as the one diagrammed below.

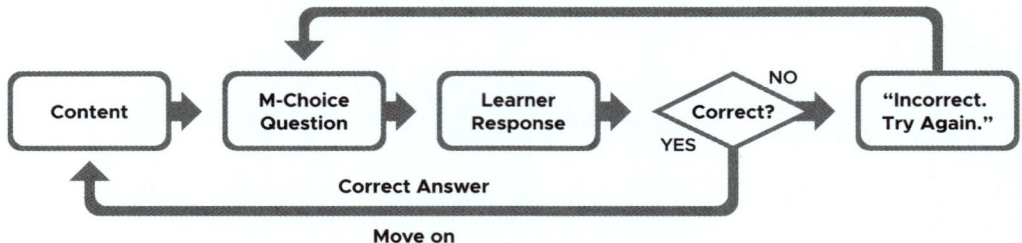

As fast and convenient as it is, this supposedly "interactive" paradigm is about as weak as you can get. Among other problems, it promotes guessing. Learners can just enter any key or click any answer to see if that happened to be the right answer. If not, they could mindlessly try another answer until they are finally able to go on. Little effort and little learning.

But there's a way to supercharge this framework. Instead of judging answers immediately, ask the follow-up question, "Why? Why did you choose this answer?"

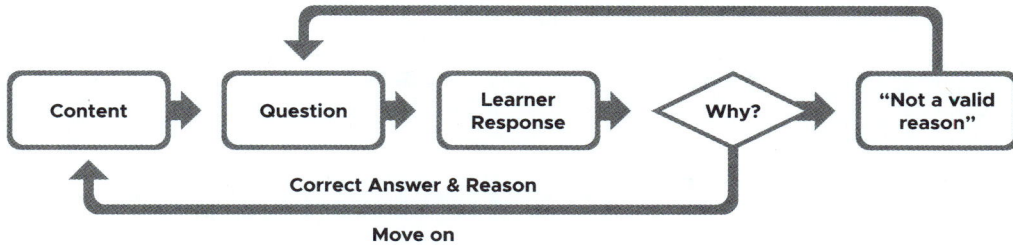

Ideally, you have the technology to allow learners to respond verbally so you won't be prompting them with the choices in a follow-up multiple-choice question. But even if you are restricted to doing so, the interaction created by simply tacking on a "Why?" question creates a much more powerful learning experience.

It also allows you to individualize the instruction in a meaningful way: If a learner selects a justification for a wrong answer or an incorrect justification for a correct answer, you have a great opportunity to present clarification that could be exactly what the learner needs.

If the correct answer was given, but incorrectly justified, you might return learners to consider whether they want to choose another answer or want only to modify their justification.

Similarly, if an incorrect answer was given, but the justification points are valid in themselves— but not applicable to this answer—you have another great opportunity for valuable feedback. And, of course, learners should return to select another answer. Some of these situations provide opportunities for additional interactions (thus the arrow on the right of the diagram).

No Justification for Multiple-Choice Questions

To be sure, this valuable model of asking "Why do you think your answer is correct?" is not restricted to nor a blanket justification for asking multiple-choice questions. It enhances the effectiveness of them, but asking for justification enhances task-based interactions as well. You can ask, "Why did you do this?" after individual actions. Or you can wait until a multistep task has been completed and then ask, "Do you think your actions were effective?" Or, "Do you think now you could achieve this goal better in another way?"

THEORY ★ RESEARCH ★
ALLENISM
#11
★ EXPERIENCE ★

Ask Why #3
Why Not Just Target Awareness?

Sometimes people want to minimize expense and/or effort in creating training by just targeting awareness. "We only need our people to be aware of the hazards of . . ." This is the time and place to ask, "Why? Why are you only targeting awareness?"

You may need to ask the "Why?" question repeatedly, as sometimes it's hard for people to admit they don't have the budget or training expertise they need. But eventually, with enough "Why?"s, you are likely to hear something like, "Because we need people to avoid mixing flammable waste materials that could cause sudden injuries."

Requests for awareness training are often based on the very poor assumption that if people have a certain awareness, they'll do what they need or should do.

"Why?" questions can helpfully expose how performance training is essential while just creating awareness doesn't promise desired behaviors. Additionally, showing people the consequences of what aware people might do helps learners discern key attributes of various situations. It can create a lasting impression that will prompt people to perform learned skills where and when needed. But, of course, they still need to learn those skills, not just be aware that they need to.

Expecting appropriate performance based on awareness is a risky, crossing-your-fingers proposition and potentially a much more costly route than developing a good training program focused not just on awareness but also on how to do the right thing at the right time.

Delay Feedback

In early development of elearning, one of the touted benefits was the ability to give immediate feedback. In B. F. Skinner's theory of operant conditioning, he noted that feedback closest to the desired behavior was most effective in training pigeons and rats. Immediate feedback was then extrapolated to contend that the same was best for instructing human beings.

Sometimes it is. Indeed, for physical skills, immediate feedback does seem to apply. You don't want learners repeating any incorrect movements.

Because elearning can give immediate feedback for every individual learner, it was postulated that elearning had unique value.

Good logic. But wrong.

At least partially. Allenisms are based not only on theory, nor even solely on research, but rather also on experience (which often leads to additional theory and research—the cyclic foundation of science). So, what have we found when implementing immediate feedback in elearning?

Humans aren't exactly pigeons or rats. They are a tad bit smarter. Usually. It's been said, "The purpose of life is finding the shortest path between two given points." We're lazy, I guess. That may or may not be the case, but it does seem to characterize learner behavior with immediate feedback in elearning.

With immediate feedback, we've observed how many learners game the system by responding to questions and challenges without thinking much at all. They just respond nonsensically, clicking or pressing whatever keys will bring up the immediate feedback in hopes it will reveal the right answer. When it does, learners can then just copy and submit answers to move on through the lesson quickly. Fast. Little effort. Learning perhaps nothing.

Earning Feedback

In some sense, we've found it wise to make learners earn feedback. We need to see some effort to respond to challenges thoughtfully. Put another way, we want to make that shortest path between two points be the one that exercises a little cognitive activity, even if the learner's first response isn't the one we're hoping for.

If we delay feedback when teaching multi-step tasks, we encourage learners to reflect on their actions and consider the efficacy of them. They might ask themselves, "Is this going to end up well?" Learners might decide to back up and make some changes or go forward a bit to see what happens. Both make for outstanding learning experiences.

As in another Allenism (#10), we often find it effective to ask learners why they think their response is correct, even when it is correct. With a correct response and a good justification of it, we've provided a good learning experience and readied the learner to move forward.

Encourage Mistakes

eLearning was born in the time of B. F. Skinner's work[25] on operant conditioning, the principles of which he introduced to education as "programmed instruction." Programmed instruction books were much like the popular Choose Your Own Adventure books by Ray Montgomery, with each answer to multiple-choice questions listing a page number. Learners would choose their answers to carefully structured and sequenced questions and then flip to the corresponding page to discover whether they were correct or incorrect.

If incorrect, an explanation of why the chosen answer was incorrect was provided. Learners were then returned to the question to select another answer. One fundamental design principle was to traverse content in small steps to minimize learner errors.

With programmed instruction, Sydney Pressey,[26] credited as the inventor of the first teaching machine, discovered that many learners used a low-effort, minimal thinking strategy. They would flip to the page corresponding to a randomly selected answer to see if it might be correct. If they found it wasn't, but an explanation revealed what the correct answer was, they would say to themselves, "Oh, sure, of course. I really knew that." And move on, exactly as we see learners doing today with elearning that provides immediate feedback (see Allenism #12: Delay Feedback).

---

25   https://www.bfskinner.org/product/the-technology-of-teaching-pdf/.
26   "Sydney L. Pressey," Wikipedia, https://en.wikipedia.org/wiki/Sidney_L._Pressey#The_%27teaching_machine%27.

Mistakes Are Wonderful Things

. . . for learning, that is. Rather than trying diligently to minimize mistakes, which reveal important information about learner thinking, the Allenism "Encourage Mistakes" takes a very different approach.

Much of learning is associating alternative actions with their consequences, both good actions with good consequences and bad actions with bad consequences. It's valuable to know not only the benefits of successful actions but also the problematic or even disastrous outcomes of other actions.

Design Implications

An important task in designing interactive learning is to identify the most common errors people make. Some errors are just accidents, of course, but many reflect faulty knowledge or lack of experience. People usually have a reason for what they do. If that reason leads to bad decisions and actions, it's important for training programs to identify and correct that reasoning.

Allowing learners to make mistakes and see the outcomes of mistakes is an effective way to help learners correct their misconceptions and remember what not to do as well as what to do.

THEORY ★ RESEARCH
ALLENISM
#14
★ EXPERIENCE ★

Tell-and-Test Isn't Teaching

If presenting information were adequate support for learning, we wouldn't have schools; we'd just have libraries and testing centers.

We can learn a lot, and do, on our own. But with good guidance and support, we can learn faster and more completely. Of course, the effectiveness of different types of learning assistance varies tremendously, from retarding the progress of those learners who could learn faster to helping those who are struggling and couldn't make it without special attention.

Teaching vs. Tell-and-Test: What's the Difference?

Some must think, *Not much*, because tell-and-test is so common. But Allenisms say there's a world of difference. Let's consider two contrasting components.

Active vs. Passive Learning

In active or, better yet, *inter*active learning, learners are applying their knowledge and developing new skills. Through practice, they're moving new knowledge to long-term memory, beyond the minimum necessary to pass a post-test. It takes practice to perfect skills for effectiveness, efficiency, and retention. Passively watching a presentation, lecture, or demonstration or just reading about how a task is performed works at a superficial level. Whatever learning takes place tends to evaporate quickly.

Testing to Adapt (Rather Than to Issue Grades)

While testing is a component of both tell-and-test and teaching processes, teaching uses frequent or even continuous testing, as in the case of highly adaptive elearning, to determine how best to assist learners from moment to moment. The expectation is that while learning time may vary, every learner will reach mastery. Rather than expecting a distribution of learning outcomes, perhaps represented by grading test scores from A to F, teaching watches learners perform and adjusts the difficulty of exercises to match learner readiness.

Tell-and-Test

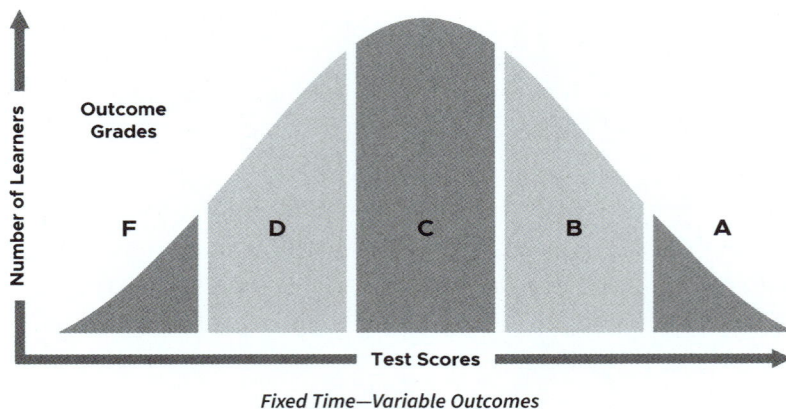

Fixed Time—Variable Outcomes

Adaptive Teaching

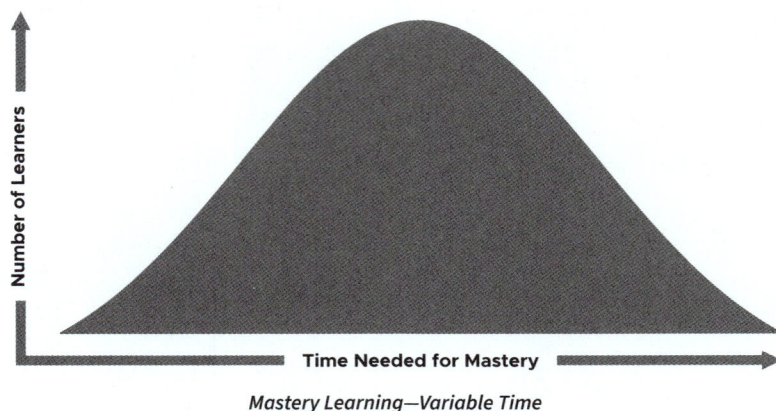

Mastery Learning—Variable Time

THEORY ★ RESEARCH
ALLENISM
#15
EXPERIENCE

Boring? It's Not the Content's Fault!

I've heard boring instruction justified by noting the content itself was boring. This argument doesn't win me over. When I hear it, I immediately think several things:

- Boring instruction is never effective instruction.

- If it appears the content is boring, that's usually because the designer doesn't understand how it empowers learners.

- It's not very often that people want to spend money and time teaching content that doesn't empower learners in some way.

Generally, it's interesting, if not exciting and rewarding, to become more capable, but even if some content fails on the empowerment scale, I submit learning never has to be boring.

But What If the Content Is Truly Boring?

Certainly, some content is more fascinating than other content. So, let's say that for whatever reason, we can't make the enabling power of the content interesting. Have we no choice but to produce boring instruction?

No, there's never justification for producing boring instruction.

One solution is to use "extrinsic games" (not to be confused with "extrinsic motivation" or "extrinsic feedback"), which are compatible with a wide range of content. The game rules and content are kept separate such that alternate content can be substituted without problem. *Jeopardy!*, for example, is a fascinating extrinsic game that is content agnostic. Although the familiar TV version asks contestants to recall factual information and structure a question about it, that constraint is not essential to the fun of playing. For instructional purposes, learners can just as well be asked to solve problems, describe the steps of a process in order, or arrange objects properly.

There are many extrinsic games that are suitable and make the learning experience fun. Intrinsic games, however, tend to provide more powerful learning experiences, since they are built around specific content. Business, engineering, or chemistry games are built around specific concepts and procedures and generate simulated outcomes that are often very memorable.

Non-Game Solutions

It's not necessary to use a game framework to enliven learning experiences. Humor, fascinating animations of concepts and procedures, interactive video, and challenge-based interactions can invigorate learning as long as they aren't used simply as adornments, which can become annoying and distracting. Don't plug in random things just because you can. Think carefully about what you would appreciate, enjoy, and benefit from rather than just piling things on.

Practice to Perfection (Corrective Feedback Paradigm)

In psychology, we call loss of a conditioned behavior *extinction.* Behaviors become extinct when they aren't practiced with enough regularity. Conversely, behaviors resist extinction through practice, especially practice distributed over increasing periods of time.

When we cram for a post-test, we don't have much time to practice and the practice we do is massed rather than distributed. This may suffice to get a good score on a test, but if we stop practicing after the test has been taken, we're likely to forget much of what we learned quickly.

Practice in eLearning

One of the many advantages of elearning is its patience. It doesn't get tired. It can support as much practice as learners request or need. And yet, it's pretty common to have little practice, sometimes judging a single correct answer as indication of adequate learning. And final tests or post-tests can come along quickly, perhaps immediately at the end of a microlearning module.

This model violates both the need for practice and having that practice distributed over time, as if elearning wouldn't have the patience to ensure adequate practice, the ability to distribute practice over time, and to delay a post-test some days or weeks after completion of the instructional program. *But it does!*

The Corrective Feedback Paradigm (CFP)

CFP is a powerful model that combines practice to mastery and practice distribution. It can be conducted easily without a digital platform and even more easily with one.

Imagine a set of flash cards, each with one task to perform. If using physical cards, the correct responses are typically on the back of the card. In elearning, software evaluates responses.

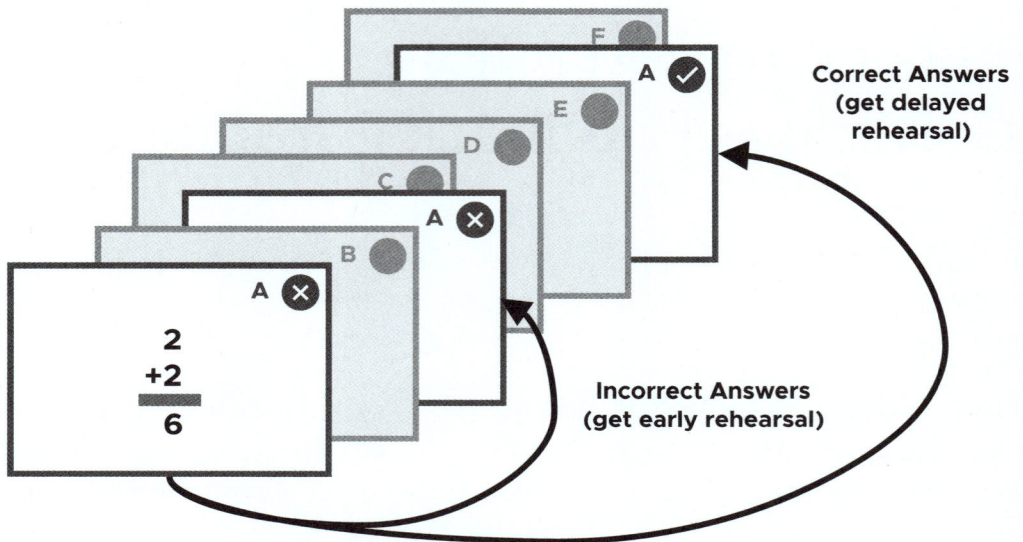

Correct Answers (get delayed rehearsal)

Incorrect Answers (get early rehearsal)

The rules are simple:

A. If the response is incorrect, the card is replaced in the deck one, two, or three cards behind the next one.

B. If the response is correct and this is not the third time answering it correctly without an intervening error, the card is placed deeper into the deck.

C. If the response is correct and this is the third time answering it correctly without an intervening error, the card is retired and removed from the deck.

Eventually, the deck is depleted, and the learner has practiced enough to be able to correctly answer repeatedly and over increasing spaces of time. Of course, the amount of time depends on the number of cards and the response time required for each card.

The deck can be used again after a day or two and then after more time, perhaps after a week or two and after a month or two, with the learning becoming increasingly resistant to extinction.

Engaging Learning

It's obviously important to engage learners and make learning experiences engaging. But what do we mean by "engaging"?

Engaging learning draws active learner focus and attention in a positive manner to stimulate cognitive activity. Distractions otherwise likely to interfere don't even register. Learners are completely involved and feeling they are where they need and want to be.

Signs of Learning Engagement

One of the best indicators of engaging learning is when learners volunteer to retake experiences because they thought they were so valuable and wanted to extract every morsel in them.

One of the best patterns we've seen and encourage is for learners go through learning experiences a second time to see if they can respond flawlessly. And then even go through a third time to see what happens when they make every mistake they can think of.

Another sign of engagement is when learners enthusiastically invite coworkers, friends, and even family to look at or experience the training themselves. This can happen with highly engaging learning, and it's a target designers should shoot for.

Making Engagement Happen

There are many ways to engage learners and keep them engaged. It's much harder to add engagement after an instructional program has been developed than to design for engagement at the beginning. Start by thinking about the learning experience. How do you want learners feeling? What do you want them thinking about and doing?

Here are a few concepts drawn from game design that help tremendously.

- **Goal-oriented tasks.** Start learners off by asking them to perform a goal-oriented multistep task. It's not only a way to find out what knowledge and skills learners already possess, but also much more engaging than confronting content presentations right off the bat.

  In response to their performance, you can either provide learners help to complete the task successfully, or congratulate them on their performance, pointing out how things they did led to their success. And then move them on to the next task.

- **Random obstacles.** As learners are practicing learned tasks, throw in some random obstacles of things that can disrupt task performance in real life. Having extra hoops to jump through can make the experience not only more realistic, but also more game-like, enhancing focus and engagement as well.

- **Scorekeeping.** Giving positive points for good responses and actions and subtracting points for faults can jump up concentration and thinking about possible consequences before taking actions. Scorekeeping is pretty easy to do and can enhance learning experiences tremendously.

- **Timing.** As learners progress in their abilities, you can take them to the next level by timing them and asking them to beat their best previous times. Timing is an easy mechanism to add to elearning and it enhances engagement significantly.

Don't forget the CCAF framework. It very naturally keeps learners engaged.

Flip Your Classroom!

As the adage goes, "To truly learn something, prepare to teach it."

This is the concept behind the flipped classroom. Many trainers have individually experimented with asking their learners to prepare presentations on selected topics and deliver them to hopefully questioning peers. Not only does preparing the presentation involve learning, but preparing to answer questions can get learners to learn more than is necessary for the presentation.

Flipping a classroom takes preparation and can be more difficult to implement than the simple concept sounds. For example, when a learner's presentation is poorly done, other learners will stop paying attention and perhaps become disruptive. If a learner's presentation has incorrect information, even though the teacher can correct it, learners can easily become confused. Rehearsing with students ahead of their presentations can take a lot of time, which can be hard to manage.

Benefiting from the Flipped Classroom

1. Select topics that have clear concepts to explore and that relate to other content being learned contemporaneously.

2. Provide guidance on ways to search for related content.

3. Give learners ways to get help and ask questions either outside of classroom hours and/or within them.

4. Consider having learners work in pairs.

Flipped eLearning

So, what can elearning glean from the successes of flipped classrooms and how might elearning address some of the challenges it has?

Various interactive models provide some of the advantages of flipping the classroom, even to the point of not needing the classroom.

1. Show topic presentations either through a video recording or a set of slides, possibly narrated. Ask learners to identify points that are and aren't valid and possibly identify contradicting evidence.

2. Guide learners in their presentation development by doing such things as:

    *   Providing a description of the audience the presentation should appeal to
    *   Having learners select a topic from a list or generate one that meets a set of criteria
    *   Providing links to resources that provide relevant information
    *   Submitting their presentation for subject matter expert review or online presentation to co-learners

3. Ask learners to create infographics to express key points of information found in data you or they provide, and then have them:

    *   Present those points for discussion via videoconferencing
    *   Exchange them via email for reactions

Bottom Line

The flipped classroom asks learners to explore new content outside the classroom and prepare it for presentation inside the classroom. The instructor, instead of preparing and presenting information as learners now do in the flipped process, becomes a moderator for discussion, questions the presenter and class, and interjects corrective information when needed.

When done successfully, the flipped classroom results in learners being more active, learning more fully, and becoming confident in conversation about the content they've researched themselves.

Postpone Post-Tests

Despite their popularity and purported value, post-tests often reveal little useful data.

I know—they're the staple of educational institutions: teach for a while and then give a test to measure what's been learned, issue grades or scores, and move on.

Apart from the very big issues of grades and scores (the result of fixed learning time and acceptance of variable outcomes) and the challenge of creating good tests, post-tests given at the conclusion of instruction periods aren't sensitive to anything but superficial learning. Give the same test a week or two later and prepare for dramatically different results.

Post-Test Enigma

For decades, researchers searched for learning outcomes that favored one instructional method over another. They logically expected some methods to produce more learning than others, but even with extreme instructional differences, study after study produced no significant differences in post-test scores.

Why?

Learners can quickly "cram" information into short-term memory. This happens in dormitory rooms everywhere near the end of school terms. Without rehearsal, "crammed" information doesn't readily make its way into long-term memory. Post-tests generally measure only short-term memory—not the outcome we're shooting for. Learners are often unable to do well on the same test only a short time later as short-term memory has a very short life.

Although one form of instruction may help learners internalize new learning, firmly anchoring it in long-term memory, another does not. And yet, the results of post-tests are likely to be indistinguishable and therefore quite misleading.

Two Lessons Learned

1. If we're training for future performance improvement, and it's important that what's learned sticks with learners, we need to be sure to provide sufficient practice, both during the training and spaced through time afterward. We need learning to be fully internalized and not just sitting in short-term memory where it can vaporize quickly.

2. Measures of learning and instructional effectiveness need to be delayed, not administered immediately upon the conclusion of training.

Gamification:
More Than Just Game Mechanics

In *Rethinking eLearning*, we're taking a strong look at affective influencers of learning that don't often enter into elearning design: considerations such as how people feel about themselves relative to the content and the use of their time while engaging it, as well as many other affective states.

Gamification is often defined as the application of game mechanics to elearning. And while certain mechanics, such as scoring, rewards, and "level-ups," are often employed, this is only part of what we've learned from video game designers.

Joy

Better than thinking of gamification as adding a clock, a progress or level meter, or scorecard (all of which might be good and appropriate), think first, *What would bring learners to feeling joyful?*

Build on motivators, such as control, making work easier, and gaining more respect. As Rick Raymer says, "For something to be perceived as rewarding, it must evoke positive emotions in a person."[27]

---

27 Rick Raymer, "Gamification: Using Game Mechanics to Enhance eLearning," *eLearn Magazine*, September 2011, https://elearnmag.acm.org/archive.cfm?aid=2031772.

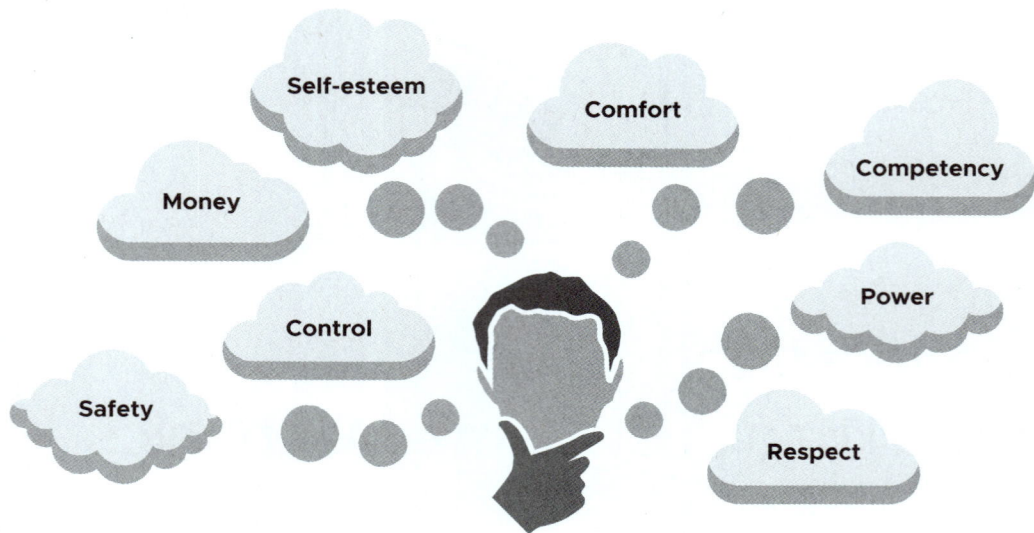

Note, however: This advice goes both ways. It's pretty easy to evoke *negative* emotions as well. For example, sometimes learners are so controlled or perplexed by non-intuitive interfaces, they feel like victims. Which naturally builds a desire to escape. Raymer offers this important observation, *"Giving your learner choices by designing nonlinear elearning can help engage your user."* We might want to think playground rather than classroom!

Learners are notoriously poor judges of when they're learning and when they're not. Brown and colleagues note, "When we're incompetent, we tend to overestimate our competence and see little reason to change."[28] The solution isn't to take all controls away from learners, forcing them through a preset sequence they might well see as irrelevant to their needs. Rather, these findings support letting learners experiment to see what they can and cannot do. Just knowing they have controls, such as what level of challenge they'd like to begin with, can help learners feel comfortable and engaged.

Unless used as part of a learner-understood risk element in a learning game, it doesn't pay to provide judgmental feedback that feels like punishment. Unjudged consequences (sales fall flat, the patient recovers quickly, you've lost your job) communicate better than "Good job!"

---

28   Peter C. Brown, Henry L. Roediger III, and Mark A. McDaniel, *Make It Stick* (Harvard University Press eBooks, 2014), 104, https://doi.org/10.4159/9780674419377.

or "Wrong!" or "No, try again." Reward learners for taking an active role in their learning and, when appropriate, suggest they might try several strategies.

Being treated with respect and having the freedom to play and experiment is one of those game-like motivators that appeals to us all.

7 Magic Motivation Keys

There are many ways to motivate learners. Some work well while others work less well. Some have undesired consequences. For example, paying bonuses for completing a training course: (A) suggests *We know training isn't fun, so we'll give you an incentive to push through it* and (B) sets expectations to be paid for future training as well.

Some training design components significantly improve the effectiveness of training by engaging and motivating learners in very positive ways. These are detailed in a variety of sources, including *Michael Allen's Guide to e-Learning, 2nd Edition* (Chapter 10), and in this book (see Chapter 25).

Very briefly, they are:

1. Establish relevancy	Make sure learners see how this learning will benefit them in ways that matter to them.
2. Put the learner at risk	Many games are fun primarily because players are at some sort of risk, such as having to start over or losing points if they make too many errors.
3. Create intrigue	Challenging learners to solve mysteries or use unique methods to solve a problem can engage them much better than asking them to memorize canned solutions.
4. Use an appealing context	While a pretty book cover doesn't make a great book, an ugly cover can fail to attract interest. Make your screens attractive.

5. Have learners perform multistep tasks	Real-world tasks seldom involve a single step. Having learners perform more realistic or "authentic" tasks with the possibility of going back to correct errors as learners identify them is much more interesting and engaging.
6. Provide intrinsic feedback	Instead of telling learners they were right or wrong, did well or not, just show them what happened. Linking outcomes to various actions, both good and bad, leads to deeper learning.
7. Delay judgment	With multistep tasks coupled with intrinsic feedback, delay judging learner actions, responses, or decisions in order to let learners decide whether they've done well or whether they want to try again.

The Serious eLearning Manifesto Is Serious Stuff

Some elearning, perhaps most elearning, confuses presentation of content with instruction. When we look at presentation-based elearning, it prompts the question, "Are you serious?"

Are you seriously thinking this presentation, no matter how beautifully formatted it is or how clear, concise, and complete, will teach someone? Borrowing from Allenism #7, "If Teaching Were Just Presenting, We Wouldn't Need Schools (Just Libraries)."

Disconcerted by the underuse, if not misuse, of elearning technology, four concerned (and frustrated) people—Julie Dirksen, Clark Quinn, Will Thalheimer, and myself—banded together to create a manifesto of values and principles we feel should guide elearning.

eLearning Manifesto

Serious eLearning Manifesto

| The Manifesto | Manifesto Premiere | Become a Signatory | Signatories | Trustees | The Instigators |

The Manifesto

typical elearning	SERIOUS eLEARNING
content focused	**Performance Focused**
efficient for authors	**Meaningful to Learners**
attendance-driven	**Engagement-Driven**
knowledge delivery	**Authentic Contexts**
fact testing	**Realistic Decisions**
one size fits all	**Individualized Challenges**
one-time events	**Spaced Practice**
didactic feedback	**Real-World Consequences**

The Principles

1. Do Not Assume That Learning Is the Solution
2. Do Not Assume That eLearning Is the Answer
3. Tie Learning to Performance Goals
4. Target Improved Performance
5. Provide Realistic Practice
6. Enlist Authentic Contexts
7. Provide Guidance and Feedback
8. Provide Realistic Consequences
9. Adapt to Learner Needs
10. Motivate Meaningful Involvement
11. Aim for Long-Term Impact
12. Use Interactivity to Prompt Deep Engagement
13. Provide Support for Post-Training Follow-Through
14. Diagnose Root Causes
15. Use Performance Support
16. Measure Effectiveness
17. Iterate in Design, Development, and Deployment
18. Support Performance Preparation
19. Support Learner Understanding with Conceptual Models
20. Use Rich Examples and Counterexamples
21. Enable Learners to Learn from Mistakes
22. Respect Learners

The following organizations, in their continuing efforts to promote quality instruction and valuable learning experiences, have provided their support to draw attention to the Manifesto.

Association for Talent Development
e-learning age
The eLearning Guild
International Society for Performance Improvement
Training
Australian Institute of Training and Development

SAM Says, "It's the Client's Money!"

The Successive Approximations Model for the design and development of elearning has been under refinement since we found so many problems with ADDIE over decades of use. When I was director of R&D for PLATO at Control Data Corporation, we had hundreds of designers and developers using ADDIE to create hundreds of courses.

We weren't amateurs with respect to ADDIE. In fact, I hired two of our leaders into our operations in Minneapolis from Florida State University, the birthplace of ADDIE. With their PhDs and research focused on the model, they were leading experts in the field. They did ADDIE officially right!

But the more we worked with ADDIE, the more we found weaknesses.[29] Among them are the bewilderment, if not exclusion, of those commissioning the project. They don't like the feelings of being out of control and unconnected. Client expertise in learning varies from none to advanced, but regardless of anyone's knowledge of learning, the complexity of building and delivering great learning experiences means a lot is going on. Clients (usually) need comfort and involvement, although some do just want a turnkey solution asap.

Every project is something of an experiment.

This is both a healthy and productive viewpoint. We want creativity. We don't want all our

---

29   As I enumerate and discuss in *Trends and Issues in Instructional Design and Technology*, Reiser, Carr-Chellman, and Dempsey, eds., 5th ed. (Routledge, 2025).

training to look alike, nor every module or exercise within a course to be identical in format and structure. We want optimization based on the attributes of the content and of the learner.

Since it's the client's money we're spending, we want clients to be involved at their defined level of comfort. This is something the pragmatic nature of the Successive Approximations Model (SAM) takes seriously. We don't want to burden clients with more involvement than they want, but conversely, we don't want them feeling shut out and wondering what they're going to get—not knowing until it's nearly finished and when changes are problematic.

How does SAM accomplish this? See Allenisms:

#24 Prototypes Are Indispensable
#27 Design Proofs Are Essential
#28 Iterate, Iterate, Iterate, Go!
#29 Defining Success Enables Success

Protypes Are Indispensable

Prototypes communicate:

1. **designs far more clearly and specifically than descriptive documents.** Words don't carry the same impact or clarity.

2. **faster.** As pictures "are worth a thousand words," prototypes convey not only better than those thousand words but also faster than those words could be read.

3. **interactivity.** To evaluate interactive learning experiences, it's important to see how the screen changes in response to learner actions. Verbal descriptions can cause readers to imagine very different things happening in very different ways from what is actually being proposed.

4. **spatial relationships.** The juxtaposition of display elements, labels, text, animations, and so on can clarify as well as confuse both content and user interface. It's an important design consideration that can only be assessed effectively via prototypes.

5. **more economically.** With proper tools, which sometimes are just paper and pencil, effective prototypes can be generated far faster than a detailed specification document attempting to communicate what even a rough prototype can convey.

Further, prototypes invite suggestions and revisions that optimize iterative design. We like to call them "disposable prototypes" to emphasize that prototypes are generated to evaluate alternatives. As a rule, we put only as much time and effort into each one as is necessary to communicate key design components. Trying to perfect prototypes with extensive effort makes it uncomfortable to set them aside to alternatives. Although advanced authoring tools and AI-generated code allow evolving a prototype into a final product, investing in prototype perfection before the alternative designs have been evaluated is an unnecessary and time-consuming expense.

In short, trying to design and develop great elearning without first generating disposable prototypes is certain to fall far short of what would have been accomplished faster, easier, less expensively, and better with them.

Storyboards Are a Waste of Time

One popular way of communicating and collaborating on instructional designs has been the use of storyboards, which visually communicate many design ideas more easily than verbal descriptions. They reduce the variety of expectations document reading engenders and form the basis for more productive discussion and evaluation.

Storyboards were popularized by Walt Disney, who showed how storyboards were used in the design and development of creative animated motion pictures. And for creating linear, noninteractive products, they continue to have great value. But there are major shortcomings for their use in creating interactive learning events and elearning.

Expressing Interactivity

Instructional interactivity is an essential component in elearning. It integrates learner input, conditional responses to that input, screen updates, animation, and timing. While storyboards can provide a crude semblance of interactive events, sometimes taking 30 to well over 100 boards to illustrate a single interaction with all its permutations, they become as arduous to produce as specification documents trying to do the same thing.

Sketching is a great tool for brainstorming and communicating design ideas. Sketches are not meant to be sufficient for funding approvals but identify and stimulate consideration of the many aspects of a design. From there, it's possible to skip over development of storyboards and move on to prototypes, which are considerably more valuable than storyboards due to their ability to demonstrate essential components of proposed interactivity.

Quickly built, disposable prototypes enact the essential active functions, which is not possible with sketches, specification documents, or storyboards. Timing and nuances of interactive software need to be experienced to judge the suitability of an instructional design. Functional prototypes allow stakeholders to experience just enough of the proposed interactions to generate common and accurate expectations of the final product.

See Allenisms:

#24 Prototypes Are Indispensable
#27 Design Proofs Are Essential

Specification Documents
Are a Huge Waste of Time

Specification documents written to describe a proposed training program can be anything from an overview of needs to be addressed to a comprehensive description of the instructional paradigms to be employed, the delivery platform, media integration, data collection, and much more.

Many training development teams have realized a fundamental problem with such documents. Reviewers, stakeholders, and decision-makers can imagine a wide variety of training programs when reading the same document. Their support and approval to proceed with development is given based on what they think will be produced, which is often not exactly what others are imagining.

When program development has been completed, the variance of expectations can become a nightmare. Pointing out in defense how the program conforms to the specifications doesn't often satisfy the variety of conflicting expectations. To prevent this misalignment from occurring, many organizations begin including more and more detail in their specification documents. But when the intent is to cover all aspects, specification documents can take months to write.

Even then, varied interpretations are all but unavoidable. Which means, simply, specification documents waste a lot of time and don't serve their purpose well.

See Allenisms: #24 Prototypes Are Indispensable
                   #27 Design Proofs Are Essential

Design Proofs Are Essential

Obviously, just as no training program is perfect, no organization can afford to develop training programs that don't work. There are so many factors that can cripple the effectiveness of a training program that might actually be superb otherwise. It's important to carefully assess both the proposed design and implementation before spending the full allowance of development time and budget to discover things that really need to be changed. Having to redo things doubles the cost when it could have been done correctly the first time.

This is not a case for "Just Do It!" There are too many variables to be confident that all components have been properly addressed. So, what's the alternative?

The Design Proof

The Design Proof is a test of all aspects of both the instructional design and the implementation/delivery methods proposed. It is a fully functional test, not a partial one. Two guidelines for developing the Design Proof are very important:

1. **Not all content** has been developed—only a sample. The remainder is awaiting the evaluation of the Design Proof.

2. A **fully produced sample** of all content, including media, is developed. At least one instance of every component and every type of interaction must be included.

The purpose of the Design Proof is to make sure, confidently sure, that the direction we're taking is a good one. To be sure, we want to test a representative slice of the design to discover any problems that might be embedded. Because of all the possible but not always obvious problems, it's hard to comprehensively list all the things to be checked. The lists provided in the books *Leaving ADDIE for SAM* and its *Field Guide* are very helpful tools.

We're looking for such varied things as:

- Is the user interface intuitive?
- Do media display properly and in a timely fashion?
- Is text written clearly and at the right level for comprehension?
- Are the proposed development tools capable of implementing the design?
- Does the LMS track progress as intended?
- Does the application adapt properly to all supported devices?

Skipping over the Design Proof in haste is almost always the most expensive route. But to keep the process moving, you don't want to put too much finished work into it as anything in the Design Proof could be redone if it isn't acceptable in evaluation. Only samples of each component are necessary. And they are necessary.

The Objectives × Treatments Matrix is a primary tool for determining what needs to be in the Design Proof. See Allenism #30, The Objectives × Treatments Matrix Speeds Design & Reduces Cost.

ALLENISM #28

THEORY ★ RESEARCH
★ EXPERIENCE ★

Iterate, Iterate, Iterate, Go!

One, two, three, go! Iterating instructional designs has many benefits, including producing superior designs, generating them faster, and buying stakeholder support. You can't really afford not to iterate.

But, as with most good things, you can iterate too much as well.

Let's look closer.

Producing Superior Designs

No design ever reaches perfection. It's neither realistic nor affordable to set perfection as the expected outcome. But neither should we expect the first design idea to be the best we can generate. Allenisms recommend three iterations as follows:

Iteration 1. After collecting whatever relevant background information is readily available, the principal instructional designer or design team puts forth sketches of Design One for key stakeholders to consider.

Iteration 2. Key stakeholders, together with the design team, respond to the question, "Why shouldn't we do this?" Under this Allenism Rule, the creation of a second design must be entirely fresh, neither incorporating the desirable characteristics of Design One nor the faults identified in it.

Iteration 3. Finally, we ask, "Why shouldn't we go with Design Two?" Again, an attempt is made to address faults in the proposed design and to come up with something fresh. But if it feels it would be a mistake not to incorporate something really powerful from either Design One or Design Two, the process allows pulling it into Design Three.

Go! Iterations could continue, but at this point there would likely be diminishing returns. Sometimes it's apparent that a fourth iteration would be beneficial and it does prove to have been wise to check it out, but it's generally best to resist the temptation.

Producing Superior Designs Faster

Getting something to the Design Proof is efficient and usually a better use of time than creating more designs. In fact, building out Design Three and rolling it out to a validation group often returns insights even several Additional Design iterations would have missed. You can decide at that point whether making modifications would be worthwhile.

But a primary advantage of "Iterate, Iterate, Iterate, Go!" is that it goes quickly. The constraints stimulate creativity and productivity. And the overall process keeps everyone involved.

Defining Success Enables Success

Lewis Carroll wrote: "If you don't know where you're going, any road will get you there." Robert Mager pointed out in *Preparing Instructional Objectives*, "If you don't know where you're going, it's hard to find the best path to take."

For training development projects, this suggests:

If you haven't defined success, how will you know if you've achieved it?

Defining success at the outset not only lets us know when we've gotten there at the end of the project but also tells us:

- What's most important to focus on as we design
- What we will need to be able to measure when it's put in use
- What measured impact will meet the criterion or criteria for success

In many cases, defining success turns out to be harder than one would suspect. For example, while increasing sales by 10% seems a simple enough criterion, other factors may be simultaneously affecting sales. The sales training might be having a positive effect even while sales dropped 3%.

It's appropriate to view every training development project as an experiment. Ideally, we would find a way to control all the variables that could affect the measured success criteria, but there are evaluation techniques that help objectively appraise the effects of multiple variables when necessary.

One probably should say it, because measuring impact can be such a valuable guide to training effectiveness: Even if quantitative measurement isn't in the cards, defining success and getting all stakeholders to agree to it is a critical step not to be bypassed.

The Objectives × Treatments Matrix Speeds Design & Reduces Cost

What Do We Want?

We want a quality training program that results in the targeted performance outcomes. We want trainees fully and energetically engaged. We want learning experiences to be Meaningful, Memorable, and Motivational (see Allenism #8). We want the experiences to be fun.

When Do We Want It?

Yesterday! We never have as much time as it feels a project deserves, and certainly we never have an open budget. So, we need maximum efficiency.

SAM Is Here to Help

SAM, the Successive Approximations Model, keeps its eye on both quality and efficiency. And one of the places this stands out most strongly is in the use of the Objectives × Treatments Matrix.

The Matrix lists the instructional objectives to be covered in a course or segment of a course. Objectives are identified by number as in the pro forma matrix illustrated on the next page.

Objectives	Treatments			
	A	B	C	D
1	✓			
2		✓		
3		✓		
4			✓	
5		✓		
6	✓			✓

A treatment can be any instructional approach, such as role-playing or problem-solving. When the first objective is analyzed and an appropriate instructional treatment designed, that treatment becomes the first column in the matrix, or Treatment A. The Treatment remains available for consideration of reuse for other Objectives. Check marks in the example above indicate Treatment A will be used for both Objectives 1 and 6.

When the next instructional objective is analyzed, Treatment A is considered. If it can be reused appropriately, then a check mark indicates so, but if it needs another treatment, then a second treatment column is added for Treatment B along with an appropriately placed check mark.

Sometimes an objective requires more than one treatment, and the matrix conveniently documents this as shown in the example for Objective 6.

Speed and Efficiency

Perhaps the most important utility of the matrix is identifying when treatments can be used appropriately multiple times, saving development costs, speeding development, and keeping the user interface consistent for learners.

Another advantage comes from realizing that often a small adjustment to a treatment before it has been developed can make it have broader applicability. We want always to be looking for such synergies. Use of this Matrix makes this almost second nature.

ALLENISM

THEORY ★ RESEARCH
#31
★ EXPERIENCE ★

Design Backwards

It's eminently logical to begin with the basics when designing a training program. Basic terms. Basic principles. Let's lay a foundation and build the learner's journey up from there.

I can easily list many reasons why it makes sense to start from the basics and build toward the targeted skill set. However, I think this is not only the least effective design path but also the slowest and most costly. Let's talk about the alternative.

What's the Last Thing You Want Learners Doing in Your Course?

My answer: Demonstrating their proficiency. Whatever your answer was, wouldn't you agree that demonstrating proficiency is the best outcome? It tells you the learner is ready to apply their new skills on the job.

How Can Learners Demonstrate Their Proficiency?

Well, it wouldn't usually be through correctly selecting the right answers on multiple-choice questions, would it? Unless the course is designed specifically to help learners take multiple-choice question tests, that abstraction absolutely does not allow learners to demonstrate proficiency.

What we need is a Context, Challenge, and user interface that supports learner activities that correspond as authentically as possible to the actual behaviors they would need to meet the Challenge or solve the problem it represents. We need something of a simulation of the world as it is and how the world would respond to the various things learners might do.

In designing them, it's important to identify the most probable mistakes a learner is likely to make and then enable the learner to make that mistake as readily as doing the things that effectively meet the challenge.

So, This Sounds Difficult to Design and Build. How Can It Save Time and Costs?

The answer is designing *and building* the final learning experiences first. Those final experiences are the most valuable components of your course (or module). They are the most valuable to get right not only from the learning perspective but also for enabling efficient courseware development.

Once those final experiences have been created, components can be extracted and reused for enabling lessons. Consider them "part task" training modules in which components of the ultimate skills are developed. Reusing the components that make the final learning experiences authentic and effective and backing toward the most elementary components will make the entire course more effective.

With this process of working back from the end to the beginning, your energy and creativity as a designer and/or developer will also assure you didn't tire out or run out of time before you encountered your most important and complex challenges. It will help keep focus on the targeted outcomes. And it will yield the most sophisticated interactive components for those entry experiences, making the course fun and engaging from the outset.

Sketch with Paper and Pencil

It's amazing how we see new insights, ideas, and problems when we transfer imagined design ideas to physical representation. But we don't want to wait until an elearning program has been fully implemented to have these insights, ideas, and problem recognitions. We want to have a good, solid design before development begins; otherwise, rework costs and delays become problematic.

Sketching is an invaluable way to get these thoughts out for evaluation very early in the design and development process. As Bill Buxton teaches us in his book *Sketching User Experiences: Getting the Design Right and the Right Design*, paper and pencil sketches help us both visualize our thoughts and solicit those of others.[30]

If we use graphic design tools (or even a pen), sharing our ideas in a more refined fashion says, "I hope you'll like my design." People will feel you mostly just want their approval.

If hastily sketched, perhaps even with pencil on a napkin(!), we communicate that we are early in our thinking, still cogitating, and very much open to revisions. "Feel free to modify my sketches."

So, as we begin to put together ideas, whether during the Savvy Start or in other design work, start sketching. This delays ownership and premature acceptance of ideas that may still have space for refinement or even replacement with a whole new approach.

Avoid problematic redesign and redevelopment work downstream while speeding up the process from the start. All at reduced cost!

---

30. Bill Buxton. *Sketching User Experiences: Getting the Design Right and the Right Design* (Morgan Kaufmann, 2007).

Breadth Before Depth

While there are many advantages to an iterative process, there are some critical guidelines. If any of these guidelines are ignored, the potential advantages of the process are lost, and problems arise. Many problems. Major problems. Allenisms calls one of those critical guidelines "Breadth Before Depth" or "Depth First Design" protocol.

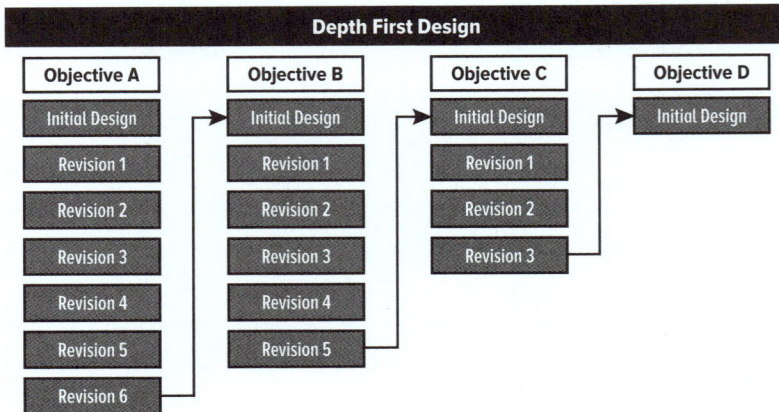

Depth First Design

Objective A	Objective B	Objective C	Objective D
Initial Design	Initial Design	Initial Design	Initial Design
Revision 1	Revision 1	Revision 1	
Revision 2	Revision 2	Revision 2	
Revision 3	Revision 3	Revision 3	
Revision 4	Revision 4		
Revision 5	Revision 5		
Revision 6			

This Allenism refers to the sequence of design focus, suggesting that designers try not to finalize designs on topics before moving on to the next. Designs can always be improved regardless of how much time is spent on them. And it's very tempting to try "just one more" iteration before thinking the design is good enough.

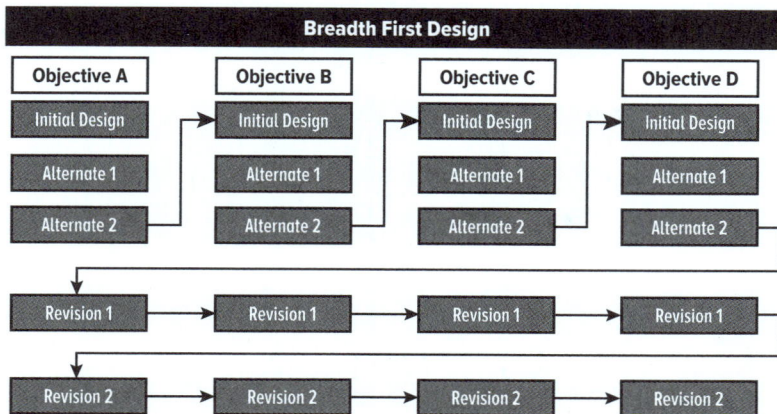

Breadth First Design

Objective A	Objective B	Objective C	Objective D
Initial Design	Initial Design	Initial Design	Initial Design
Alternate 1	Alternate 1	Alternate 1	Alternate 1
Alternate 2	Alternate 2	Alternate 2	Alternate 2
Revision 1	Revision 1	Revision 1	Revision 1
Revision 2	Revision 2	Revision 2	Revision 2

The problem is that too much time, energy, and money can be spent on the first few topics or modules. It leaves too little for the remainder of the subject matter, which is then rushed to completion. With Breadth Before Depth or Breadth First Design, we plan and expect to return to all our original designs at least once, if not more times, after we've developed something for all the content.

The benefits of limiting time or the number of iterations before shifting attention to the next content segment include:

- Allowing you to devise a UI that works for all learning events. You won't usually have the level of familiarity you need to do this before you actually do some exploratory design work on all of the content.

- Providing the insight you need to backstitch ideas and devise preparatory content.

- Creating reusable interaction designs.

- Being consistent with language, graphic style, and other elements throughout the course.

- Delivering the best course you could possibly build within the time and budget allotted.

Align Goals (or Plan to Fail)

It's proper to have many goals when setting out to develop a training program. Many important and valuable things can be achieved, but success is better assured by having clearcut goals. The trick to success with multiple goals is to be sure you aren't pursuing conflicting goals.

Why would goals conflict? Business goals and learning goals sometimes conflict because they measure the successful use of time and resources differently.

Business/Organizational Goals

In the general operations of an organization, budgetary management is essential. A wary eye is kept on costs, striving always to minimize them. Investments are seen differently, perhaps most concisely described by the adage, "It takes money to make money." The expense is evaluated from the perspective of an anticipated Return on Investment (ROI).

When viewed as an investment, training is charged with and evaluated by its ROI. Quality is essential to meet the goal.

Transferable Learning Goals

The primary goal of training is to transfer what's learned and practiced to improved performance of value-producing tasks. Various measures of effectiveness and efficiency of performance inform success. This aligns nicely with the business/organizational goals.

The Conflict: Cost vs. Investment

This rosy alignment is characteristic of enlightened organizations and their leadership, but too often the picture is quite different. When training is viewed as a cost and measured as such, there is pressure to cut corners, use available but unskilled personnel to develop it, and evaluate production and implementation based on speed of delivery, number of learners rushed through, post-test scores, and smile sheet evaluations.

These measures can indicate success without having achieved the goal of improving on-the-job performance. When it does so, management looks at the *cost* of training with greater determination to reduce it. This is a cycle of failure.

Alignment

Unless goals are aligned, it's a plan to fail. The key to alignment is defining success at the outset. Doing so naturally nudges training out of the cost category and into the investment category. It's not as simple as that, but it's a good first step. (See Allenism #29, Defining Success Enables Success.)

Success Is Doing the Right Thing at the Right Time

In other words, knowing how to do something correctly doesn't create successful outcomes unless that task is actually performed correctly and done at the right time.

Nearly all, if in fact not all, successes come from doing the right things at the right times. Prerequisite, of course, is *being able* to do the right things and *knowing when* to do them. Training programs need to train for the ability to perform tasks well, to know when an action is appropriate, and to determine the right thing to do.

When + What + Performing

The purpose of training is always to achieve some measure of success. Even if it's just knowledge training, the intent of the training is to enable the more knowledgeable person to do something he or she couldn't otherwise do. But armed only with knowledge of how something should be done leaves a gap that training must bridge.

This is why game and simulation-based training is so valuable. Clearly, in perhaps all games, winning occurs only to the player who properly does the right thing at the right time. To become a successful person, just as to become a winning player, we must practice:

1. Perceiving **when an action** is needed
2. Identifying **what action** to take
3. **Performing** the correct action effectively

Success is not enabled by learning to do only one or two of these things. Training for success must have learners practicing all three to a point of mastery and performance confidence.

When It's Time to Perform, It's Too Late to Practice

Practice is underrated. "Once and done" doesn't work.

There's a tendency to make a couple of common errors when designing elearning and perhaps all forms of training:

1. When we receive a correct response from a learner, we think the learner has learned what we were teaching.
2. When a learner does well on a post-test, we think the learner is ready to perform.

Essential Benefits of Practice

Far from an optional nicety, practice provides:

Retention. In general, the more we practice, the longer we retain what we've learned. Forgetting most if not all of what we've learned after doing well on a post-test is typical unless the tested abilities are performed repeatedly, beginning very soon after the post-test.

Deeper Learning. More practice allows us to build more associations with the context of performing and awareness of what effects slight variations in performance might have on outcomes.

Confidence. We don't like to fail, so we shy away from situations in which we lack confidence. Conversely, if we have repeatedly done a task successfully, our confidence helps us assert our abilities and continue to perfect them.

Costs of Too Little Practice

When practicing is left until it's time to perform, the following can result:

Lost Opportunities. Just as attempting to fly a plane without having practiced with an instructor could have disastrous outcomes, ineffective interaction with a sales prospect, being unprepared to answer customer questions, and other disqualifying behaviors can cause not only an initial failure but also preclude even a second try. Further, since dissatisfactions tend to be shared more widely than satisfactory experiences, even unidentified opportunities can be lost due to word spreading about dissatisfactions.

Forgotten Learning. An obvious penalty of too little practice is learning that doesn't stick. Lack of practice often terminates the chain of learning from perception, short-term memory, to long-term memory such that learning quickly evaporates. While echoes of past learning may persist and aid relearning, lack of sufficient practice invalidates invested time, energy, and associated costs to the point where training had little or no value. (And that's expensive training.)

Valuable Mistakes. It's valuable not only to practice effective performance but also to experience outcomes of mistakes before heading into the field. Associating specific behaviors with positive outcomes and other specific behaviors with negative outcomes provides strong, flexible guidance. It avoids at least some devastating outcomes when circumstances in the field require improvised tactics.

When it's time to perform, it's definitely too late to practice!

The Purpose of Training Is Behavior Change

Is imparting knowledge really the purpose of education and training?

If learners are not able to do anything with newly acquired knowledge, of what use was the time and effort to learn it?

We too easily make the assumption that knowledge enables new capabilities. And sometimes it does, of course. But knowing how to do something or how it should be done does not always enable performance. I can read about how to write well, give good speeches, cook, or lead. But there's so much more to learn via practice before that knowledge enables successful behaviors.

Target Desired Performance

While my junior high Latin teacher repeatedly justified our learning the language because it would make learning French, German, and Spanish easier, that path unquestionably delayed learning languages most of us would have found far more useful.

Instead of taking roundabout paths to achieve performance behaviors we want, it makes much more sense to directly target useful behaviors, imparting supporting knowledge along the way. Because the real purpose of knowledge is to enable behaviors, not just answer questions on post-tests.

THEORY ★ RESEARCH
ALLENISM
#38
★ EXPERIENCE

The Most Unaffordable Training

The most wasteful and unaffordable training isn't what you might expect. It isn't necessarily face-to-face training with travel and classroom expenses. It isn't necessarily time-consuming personal mentorship. Nor is it necessarily high-production-quality video, AR, VR, or elearning.

Based on unrecouped production expenses, time away from the job, missed business opportunities, production/service errors, and employee attrition, the most unaffordable training is training that doesn't work.

Highly effective training isn't easy to create. And while quality isn't a simple matter of spending more, high-impact training development isn't inexpensive. It takes more talent and expertise to create an inexpensive effective learning program. Will Thalheimer, in his excellent book *The CEO's Guide to Training, eLearning & Work,* notes, "Every year new people flood into the learning field without a background in learning. They work hard to get up to speed, but they can't possibly learn everything they need to know—at least not fast enough."

He goes on to note many graduate programs produce instructional designers who know theory but not how to use it as a practical guide. As we promote in Allenisms, successful instructional programs that more than pay for themselves derive from a combination of theory, research, and experience.

Throughout this book, we are reviewing what is and isn't important in training. Intuition is often wrong. Even research must own up to many instances of being wrong. But the more we understand about how people learn, remember, and forget and the more experience we have from which to derive robust principles, the more frugal we can be without sacrificing the all-important outcomes of knowledge and skill development.

To do otherwise is, well, unaffordable.

ACKNOWLEDGMENTS

First and foremost, my appreciation to **Matt Holt**. Matt talked me into writing my first book. I wasn't at all confident in my ability to accomplish the task, especially given the responsibilities I had in managing and building my company. When he and I talked at a conference about the prospects, I was recalling my wife's very recent admonitions that I took on too much. I needed to learn the power of the word "No."

So, I told Matt, after I got home and discussed the opportunity to write and publish a book, I'd call him up and tell him, "No." But here my appreciation extends also to my wife, **Mary Ann Allen**, who almost immediately said, "Well, yes! What a great opportunity. You should do it, definitely." And in the months following, she made extraordinary efforts of support to give me time to think and write.

The first book was an unimaginable success, both in the market and professionally. It blew me away and also helped me get my thoughts and perspectives together. From the amazing outpouring of feedback, it seems it's been helpful to others in our challenging field. I'm so very rewarded by that.

So now, I'm doing this book again with Matt. It's a true privilege to do so. Thanks, Matt and Mary Ann. It couldn't have happened without you.

Christopher Allen, our son, has grown up as a savvy bystander to the world of elearning. He's become a true expert and leader in his own right. Now as president of Allen Interactions Inc., he has kept our commitment to quality and to learners first and foremost. By taking the business reins, he's given me the time to write and rewrite and rewrite. He's been a great sounding board to my ever-changing perspectives and even came up with the concept of creating the online bank of examples that support this book.

Steve Lee is our mastermind of operations at Allen Interactions, and that's in addition to his broad technical expertise and instructional design prowess. With an uncanny memory, he can recall past projects that exemplify the application of every sound instructional principle one can think of. So, of course, I turned to him with a request for fitting examples of our own work to include in the book and website, which he provided in minutes.

Jennifer Jesse is an amazing Graphic Designer and eLearning Developer. Many of our elearning projects and publications have achieved their appeal from her work. Along with her extensive technical prowess, Jen creates artistic as well as beautifully organized assets that have been vital to keeping all the book's parts and pieces together, all done with many laughs and inexhaustible energy. Many of the illustrations herein are her creations.

Special appreciation goes to my longterm friend and dedicated employee, **Rich Person**, who coined the concept of Allenisms after culling over fifty principles by searching through our books, papers, blogs, and presentations. Many of them have become shorthand communications within our studios and even among our clients.

Bill Mills led the task of soliciting examples of great elearning from a cadre of vendors and institutions. He teamed with **Michael Rickman**, a humble and yet extraordinary technical and creative talent, and also with marketing geniuses **David Milne** and **Steve Milne** of Digital 1 to create the supporting website and its "Treasure Trove of Awesome eLearning." Example contributors rolled up their sleeves, got permissions to share, and provided examples of their work for all of us to learn from, reaffirming that we creators of elearning are enthusiastic supporters of each other and quality instruction everywhere. This project couldn't have happened without their enthusiastic energy, extra hours, and superior talent.

The BenBella team are pros! I was given invaluable and patient support from the talented **Katie Dickman, Michael Fedison, Jessika Rieck, Aaron Edmiston, Brigid Pearson,** and **Morgan Carr**. Be assured, whatever errors you may find in this book are not theirs!

EXAMPLE CONTRIBUTORS

I'm deeply appreciative of the contributors of elearning examples presented herein. Principles are important to understand. But that understanding deepens considerably when principles are seen in application and even more, of course, when personally applied.

All the contributors care deeply about their learners and about helping all of us in the business of creating instructional programs. With the number of people rotating in and out of the field, we constantly have many people working to catch up to our advancing insights and experiences. We welcome newcomers, of course, and don't want them to have to make all the mistakes made before them. eLearning leaders, such as the ones contributing their examples here, work to advance the entire field. We eagerly share and help each other.

Those contributing to this edition of *Rethinking eLearning* and the perpetually updating Treasure Trove of Awesome eLearning at www .rethinkingelearning.com are:

Treasure Trove

EXAMPLES

Garima Gupta	Artha Learning
Diane Elkins	Artisan Learning
Clark Aldrich	Clark Aldrich Designs
Karl Kapp	Commonwealth University's Inst. for Interactive Tech.
Pooja Jaisingh	Dr. Pooja Jaisingh
Richard Vass	ELB Learning
Phil Cowcill	PJ Rules
Donald Becker	University of Houston

And, of course, I proudly call out and appreciate the amazing work done by the great men and women of the Allen Interactions studios and our many independent contractors.

My sincere thanks to you all.

VALUED RESOURCES

Christopher Allen, "Every Word Counts," *TD Magazine* 78(5) (2024): 26–31.

Albert Bandura, "Self-Efficacy: Toward a Unifying Theory of Behavioral Change," *Psychological Review* 84(2) (1977): 191–215, https://doi.org /10.1037/0033-295X.84.2.191.

Markus Bernhardt, Michael Allen, and Steve Lee, "Navigating the Realities of AI in Learning and Talent Development: A Guide for Leaders," TrainingMag.com, March 18, 2025, https://trainingmag.com/navigating-the-realities-of-ai-in -learning-and-talent-development-a-guide-for-leaders.

Elaine Biech, *The Art and Science of Training* (ASTD, 2016).

Peter C. Brown, Henry L. Roediger, and Mark A. McDaniel, *Make It Stick: The Science of Successful Learning* (Cambridge, MA: Belknap Press, of Harvard University Press, 2014).

Pedro De Bruyckere, Paul A. Kirschner, and Casper D. Hulshof, *Urban Myths about Learning and Education* (Academic Press, 2015).

Bill Buxton, *Sketching User Experiences: Getting the Design Right and the Right Design* (Morgan Kaufmann, 2007).

Yu-kai Chou, *Actionable Gamification: Beyond Points, Badges, and Leaderboards* (Sheridan, WY: Octalysis Media, 2015), http://ci.nii.ac.jp/ncid/BB18977357.

Julie Dirksen, *Talk to the Elephant: Design Learning for Behavior Change* (New Riders Publishing, 2023).

Niels Floor, *This Is Learning Experience Design: What It Is, How It Works, and Why It Matters* (New Riders, 2023).

James Paul Gee, *What Video Games Have to Teach Us About Learning and Literacy,* 2nd ed. (Macmillan, 2007).

Isabela Granic, Adam Lobel, and Rutger C. M. E. Engels, "The Benefits of Playing Video Games," *American Psychologist* 69 (1) (January 2014): 66–78, https://www.apa.org/pubs/journals/releases/amp-a0034857.pdf.

Linda Harasim, *Learning Theory and Online Technologies* (Routledge, 2012).

Larry Israelite, *More Lies About Learning: Leading Executives Separate Truth from Fiction* (Association for Talent Development, 2015).

Ray Jimenez, *Transforming Learning Design with AI. ChatGPT* (Lulu.com, 2023).

Karl M. Kapp, *Action-First Learning: Instructional Design Techniques to Engage and Inspire* (American Society for Training and Development, 2025).

Michelle Lentz, *Partner with AI for Instructional Design* (Alexandria, VA: ATD, 2025), https://www.td.org/product/td-at-work-guide--partner-with-ai-for-instructional-design/252502.

Robert F. Mager, *Preparing Instructional Objectives* (West Yorkshire, UK: Pitman Learning, 1975).

Cathy Moore, *Map It: The Hands-On Guide to Strategic Training Design* (Montesa Press, 2017).

Clark N. Quinn, *Learning Science for Instructional Designers: From Cognition to Application* (Association for Talent Development, 2021).

Robert A. Reiser, Alison A. Carr-Chellman, and John V. Dempsey, *Trends and Issues in Instructional Design and* Technology, 5th ed. (Routledge, 2025).

Allison Rossett, *First Things Fast: A Handbook for Performance Analysis* (Pfeiffer, 2009).

Manik Sahu, "Breaking Down the Essence of Video Games: The AROG Framework," *Game Developer*, July 21, 2023, https://www.gamedeveloper.com/blogs/breaking-down-the-essence-of-video-games-the-arog-framework.

Will Thalheimer, *The CEO's Guide to Training, eLearning & Work: Empowering Learning for a Competitive Advantage* (Work-Learning Press, 2024).

INDEX

IMAGE CREDITS

Sourced from Adobe Stock, augmented by Allen Interactions: Designer's Notebook icon, Buyer's Checklist icon, My Story Icon, and Video Game icon, as well as pages xvii, 2, 12, 13, 14, 16, 19, 20, 23, 25, 26, 29, 34, 42, 57, 63, 64, 72, 88, 102, 112, 114, 119, 126, 156, 158, 161, 163, 171, 177, 180, 198, 199, 202, 204, 238, 243, 244, 271, and 276

Created with Midjourney and modified using Photoshop AI: pages 17, 18, 21, 35, and 90

Created with ChatGPT: pages 79 and 81

Public Domain: page 109

Examples courtesy of:

Artha Learning: pages 33 and 70–71

Artisan Learning: pages 103, 179, 186, and 280

Clark Aldrich Designs: pages 40, 43, and 52

Commonwealth University's Institute for Interactive Technologies: pages 51 and 221

Dr. Pooja Jaisingh: page 197

ELB Learning: pages 47, 50, 188, and 193

Phil Cowcill, PJ Rules: page 68

Don Becker, University of Houston: page 203

Unless listed above, remaining graphics created by Jennifer Jesse / Allen Interactions.

ABOUT THE AUTHOR

Often referred to as the Godfather of eLearning, Dr. Michael Allen has had a long and lauded career in elearning. From his work with IBM on their Coursewriter III system in the 1960s, to leading R&D of Control Data's international groundbreaking PLATO system, designing and developing its LMS, to leading the creation of Authorware—one of the most successful and game-changing authoring tools ever—Michael has been recognized with the most prestigious career awards including those from ATD (career contributions award), Ellis Island (humanitarian award), and the e-Learning Guild (Guild Master).

Dr. Allen holds a PhD in educational psychology from The Ohio State University. He has authored or edited nine previous books including the industry's go-to book, *Michael Allen's Guide to e-Learning* (2 eds.), and the bestseller *Leaving ADDIE for SAM*. He is currently chairman and CEO of Allen Interactions and Allen Learning Technologies.

Recently, Michael has gathered the most relevant methods, processes, best practices, lessons learned, learning models, and other helpful concepts to create a library of "Allenisms" to help those who follow his works quickly identify and incorporate the magic Allen Interactions has created in elearning for over 30 years.

ABOUT ALLEN INTERACTIONS

Since 1993 Allen Interactions has been innovating training and creating interactive, engaging programs that produce incomparable benefits. Combining technology, creativity, and proven learning science, Allen Interactions consistently makes the most of every training budget, creates experience-based elearning that delivers targeted performance improvement, and delights learners.

alleninteractions

Allen Interactions Inc.